TRUE RESILIENCE

BUILDING A LIFE OF STRENGTH, COURAGE, AND MEANING

D0754085

PRAISE FOR TRUE RESILIENCE

"This superb book provides a blueprint to live a rewarding life of meaning and success."

—Rose Gantner, PhD
Workplace Wellness: Performance with a Purpose

"*True Resilience* will help countless people greatly improve their well-being."

—David A. Sharar, PhD
Managing Director, Chestnut Global Partners

"Whether you're a professional helping people deal with life's stresses or just exploring your own life path, this book will make a difference."

—John E. Riedel
President, Riedel and Associates Consultants, Inc.

"*True Resilience* represents Gail Wagnild's rich and deep lifelong exploration into how to bounce back when adversity pushes us to our limits."

—Margaret Moore, MBA (aka Coach Meg)
Founder and CEO, Wellcoaches Corporation

"Get inspired and find out what interpretation of resilience applies to you to improve your quality of life."

—Ronald van Meggelen
Owner and CEO, Qvive Consultancy

"Gail Wagnild's *True Resilience* is a treasure. You will be pulled in by her clarity, warmth, and wisdom, as if this book was written just for you."

—Dr. Constance Staley
Professor of Communication
University of Colorado at Colorado Springs

"Path-blazing… Twenty-five years of research delivers a work of pure honesty and discovery. "

—Elisabeth A. Doehring
President and Founder
North American Center for Worksite Wellness™

"*True Resilience* can help anyone confidently stare down the barriers they face everyday and build avenues to destinations that were falsely labeled unreachable"

—Rahul Dubey
Executive Director, Business Development
America's Health Insurance Plans

TRUE RESILIENCE

BUILDING A LIFE OF STRENGTH, COURAGE, AND MEANING

AN INTERACTIVE GUIDE

GAIL WAGNILD, PHD

CAPE
HOUSE
CAPE HOUSE BOOKS
ALLENDALE, NEW JERSEY

TRUE RESILIENCE
Building a Life of Strength, Courage, and Meaning

Copyright © 2014 Gail Wagnild

ISBN 978-1-939129-06-2

Cape House Books™
P.O. Box 200
Allendale, NJ 07401-0200
www.CapeHouseBooks.com

Cover and book design by Bill Ash

Some names and identifying details have been changed to protect the privacy of individuals.

Cataloging in Publication Data

Wagnild, Gail
True Resilience: Building a Life of Strength, Courage, and Meaning

p   cm

ISBN 978-1-939129-06-2

1. Resilience—Adaptability 2. Decision-Making—Problem Solving 3. Personal Transformation—self-help 4. Self Awareness

I. Title II. Author III. Monograph

Includes bibliographical references and index.

Every effort has been made in preparing this book to provide accurate and up-to-date information. The author has no responsibility for the persistence or accuracy of URLs for external or third party websites referred to in this publication, and does not guarantee that any content on such websites will remain accurate or appropriate.

BF 504.3 W2014   158.1 W1521

For my parents,

Dorothy and Clarence Wagnild

CONTENTS

PREFACE

PAIN, GRIEF, AND loss transform us. One moment we're going about our ordinary lives. In the next, everything changes.

Many years ago when I was an assistant professor, I received a telephone call that was the first in a series of painful, heartbreaking events. My mom told me my dad was dying and they were coming to Seattle to stay with me so he could receive experimental treatments that doctors hoped would prolong his life and ease his suffering. They did neither.

His suffering intensified. All we could do was helplessly stand by with broken hearts as he went through bone-breaking pain, nausea, severe weakness, and frailty.

In the midst of the turmoil I learned I was pregnant with my first child, which was an extraordinary joy. That news was followed by sadness and loss, though, when my husband abandoned us six months later.

One morning as I taught fifty students, I suddenly went into labor—two months too soon. I drove myself to the hospital and had an emergency Cesarean section. My premature baby weighed less than four pounds. I spent every moment in the neonatal intensive care unit. Taking advantage of my absence, a ring of thieves moving through the hospital stole my driver's license, all my cash, and every credit card in my wallet. They racked up thousands of dollars of charges, leaving me with no way to purchase anything.

To add insult to injury, a policeman pulled me over shortly after I was discharged from the hospital. Asking me to step out of the car, he cited me for no driver's license, no proof of insurance, out-of-state license plates, and speeding. I practically had to take out a bank loan to pay for the ticket.

At work I was going through the arduous review process for promotion and tenure, navigating my way through a painful divorce, providing around-the-clock care for my baby, and of course, trying to hold myself together as my dad's death grew nearer.

I'd already begun my research on resilience and, the way my life was going, I had a ticket to a front-row seat on the topic. I knew pain and grief firsthand and I felt anything *but* resilient. The irony was not lost on me.

Happily, I was interviewing people at that time who'd overcome much more than I and many were calm, reflective, and optimistic. They accepted their lives. They persevered. They had found a way through loss, pain, and grief. They knew contentment. Even more remarkable, they expressed joy, and most were leading meaningful lives.

Pain and grief had transformed them into people who could feel empathy for others' pain and accept circumstances they couldn't change. As I listened to their stories, I felt hope that I could make it through my difficult journey and perhaps become stronger and more resilient as well. They led the way for me, as they do throughout this book.

I imagine many of you reading this book have overcome similar adversity, and perhaps a lot worse. Maybe you've had an illness or injury and worked hard to get better. Most of us have lost someone close to us through death, divorce, or separation and have had to adapt to the loss and keep going. Have you ever been fired from a job or failed to complete a college degree or achieve a major life goal? Have you ever declared bankruptcy? If so, you know grief, pain, and the agony of defeat firsthand and how much effort it takes to pick up the pieces and put your life back together. And we both know it's possible to get back on your feet and keep trying.

I suspect I'm not alone in my desire to be a more resilient person— someone who bounces back and grows stronger from difficulties; someone who is courageous and full of passion and purpose; someone who dives into life with enthusiasm. It seems like a lot to ask. Yet each of us has the potential to be very resilient.

All around us people are living resiliently. They frequently go unrecognized and are seldom celebrated. We tend to think of resilience in connection with heroism and deeds done by soldiers, firefighters, prisoners of war, and other extraordinary men and women. In truth, most stories of resilience are about ordinary people who live quietly and with courageous optimism, determination, and faith. They "fly under the radar" of everyone but those closest to them.

Over the past twenty-five years, I have interviewed and surveyed thousands of people and learned a lot about how to build and strengthen resilience. Along with Heather Young, then a graduate student, I conducted research and developed the Resilience Scale™—a strengths-based questionnaire that measures a person's capacity for resilience, and the first to actually measure resilience in adults. (Note: If you are interested in measuring your own resilience, the Resilience Scale is available online at www.resiliencescale.com or in Appendix A of this book.)

I learned directly from resilient people, which is an approach that makes sense. It's always good, I have found, to learn from those who are "living proof" rather than to postulate theories or decide that something must be so and then seek validation. From working with resilient people, I have concluded we can all choose to live resiliently no matter what life may throw at us. (Note: Appendix B includes a description of several studies on resilience.)

How does this book differ from others about resilience? Most others would have you believe that resilience is a destination reachable by taking tactical steps. I write about resilience as an overall life strategy. This book provides a blueprint for resilience that takes the long view on achieving and sustaining your own personal resilience.

You will learn many things from reading this book. You will learn about genuine resilience. You will learn how to recognize your own resilience, how to build and support it, and, finally, how to apply it every day of your life in your community, workplace, and relationships. This knowledge will create fundamental and lasting changes in how you view the world and your place in it—at any age.

Armed with this knowledge you will be better prepared to live a healthy, productive, rewarding life true to your potential.

—Gail Wagnild, RN, PhD
Founder, the Resilience Center
Worden, Montana

INTRODUCTION

"He knows not his own strength who hath not met adversity."

—William Samuel Johnson

I F THERE'S ONE thing those of us who are now past midlife have learned, it's that life is full of surprises. But in the midst of uncertainty, losses, and failures, we've managed to keep trying. Maybe we've even become stronger.

Most of us have experienced difficulties in life. Over time we develop determination and flexibility. Each time we overcome some adversity, we're better prepared to deal with it the next time. Considering life's almost daily onslaught of demands, great and small, the ability to regain balance is extraordinary.

But how is it accomplished? Where do we find the will and desire to keep fighting? For me, it's a combination of religious beliefs, support and encouragement from others, and a sense of direction. For you, the mix may be different. But the fact remains that we get to choose what direction to take at every fork in the road. We can choose to live resiliently.

What exactly is resilience? Most people would say it means, "to bounce back from adversity." While this is true, resilience is much more than merely bouncing back, or returning to a baseline after difficulty. When I first began to study resilience in the 1980s, the word was used more often in engineering and physics than human behavior. Now it's become a popular way to define emotional agility, resourcefulness, and tenacity to keep going despite hardship.

Over almost thirty years of research into the subject, I've come to understand resilience is best defined as "the capacity each of us has for growth and positive adaptation in spite of the constant barrage of stress we all feel on a daily basis." Our world is a stressful place, and the ability to respond favorably to distress is essential if we are to have productive, meaningful, and satisfying lives.

At college in the 1970s, I was taught that as we age, we can expect inevitable decline leading to withdrawal from life as we prepare for death. This decline could include desperation, despair, dementia, disability, delirium, disease, defeat, decrepitude, dizziness, dependency, despondency, discouragement, disillusionment, and so on. I found this thought to be really depressing. As a result, I began to call this pervasive, widely accepted, and negative content "The Dreaded D's of Aging."

While the Dreaded D's were true for some, they did not describe many of the people I knew. It was because of the people who did not experience decline that I decided to study positive adaptation. I wanted to understand how people, despite the vicissitudes of life, get up, keep going, find a way through pain, and actually thrive.

In the early 1980s, there were many people across the United States and Europe working in this area of "healthy aging," which was then considered a contradiction in terms. So I taught and studied healthy aging at the University of Washington in Seattle, which put me on the path to learning all about the characteristic I'd later call resilience.

Through interviews and surveys, which now number in the thousands, I learned firsthand from resilient people what constitutes the very core of resilience. I heard many stories that helped me put together a unique and genuine definition. Here's one example:

Mary was forty-six years old when her husband of twenty-four years came home one night and said, "I'm leaving you. I've found the love of my life." He was starting over while she felt like her life was coming to an end. One month later, she was diagnosed with breast cancer. Alone and terrified, she couldn't sleep or eat. She wondered if she could go on. She told me more than once that she was sure he would come to his senses and walk through the door and back into her life and be there by her side as she fought to regain her health. He did, but not in the way she had pictured. One evening she came home to find his fully packed bags by the door. He was waiting for her in the kitchen, his house key on the table. He kissed her on the cheek and said, "I will always care about you but I just don't love you like I once did. I'm sorry." She said she lay awake at night and sobbed, "It can't get worse." But it did. Chemotherapy left her weak and sick. Her hair fell out. She despaired. She was certain that her life was over and that at any moment her heart would shudder to a stop.

If you have ever been hurt, and almost everyone has, then you know that at some point there's a choice to be made; whether you will give up, lie down and die, or get up and keep trying. We can't always choose or control what happens in life, but we can choose how we're going to deal with it. Viktor Frankl, who survived imprisonment at the Auschwitz concentration camp during World War II, said of his ordeal, "When we are no longer able to change a situation, we are challenged to change ourselves."

We get to choose our response to adversity. We can choose to respond with resilience, or not. In fact, most people choose to keep going and get on with their lives, even when no clear path presents itself. Sometimes it takes weeks, months, or even longer, but over time we learn to cope and move on. Seemingly out of nowhere, we wake up one day and we're better.

In time we even learn how to smile and laugh again. In the process we find out more about what we're capable of and, like Mary, eventually we look back and say, "If I could get through that dark night, I can get through anything." Mary did emerge from her ordeal with new insights and strengths. She returned to teaching high school English, reignited her passion for photography, and fulfilled her lifelong dream of becoming a licensed pilot:

I learned from Phil who was sixty-nine when I met him. Four years earlier, he learned he had heart disease and diabetes. His wife helped him get back on the path to good health and just when it seemed that their lives were returning to normal, she died suddenly one evening as they cooked supper together. He told me he had been peeling potatoes and she had reached into the refrigerator and was gently chiding him for eating the last pudding. The ordinariness of the evening ending in the shocking and tragic death of his dear wife almost killed him. He went into an emotional tailspin and ended up in the hospital with chest pains. The next morning he learned that his teenage grandson had been killed in a car accident. In a matter of twenty-four hours, it seemed that life was no longer worth living. Even so, when I met him he was doing better. He said that at times his life had been unbearable and he couldn't even get out of bed some days. But his grandchildren, friends, fellow workers, and people in his church needed him and he chose to keep trying. He later became a Wal-Mart greeter who gives out shopping carts. Who would guess what a courageous and extraordinary man Phil is?

There are many stories of resilience but they all have several things in common. Resilient people do bounce back, but they also have the capacity to learn and grow from their experiences and become even stronger. Adversity comes in all sizes and shapes, and each encounter with it has the potential to move us in a direction that will strengthen our resilience. Each time we overcome an obstacle, we add yet another tool in our coping repertoire that will help us in the future. That's why many resilient people say, "I have gone through worse than this, and I can get through this, too."

DARK NIGHTS

Most (and probably all) of us have experienced dark nights and adversity. I have known profound depression and despair that have left me feeling empty and hopeless. Sometimes this period of grief and loss lasted weeks and, unfortunately, there were times it went on much longer. I felt alone. Although my faith in God told me otherwise, I often felt adrift.

We all know feelings of complete defeat—when we lose someone we love, fail repeatedly, lose our confidence. Sometimes we do seem to give in and quit trying for a while. When we're injured or sick, we wonder where we'll get the will, strength, and desire to build up our health again and become aware of our mortality. These scenarios can leave us despondent and desperate at the same time. When we lose sight of the good and the meaningful, we find we can't muster up a reason to get out of bed in the morning.

At some time, every one of you will walk down some dark and twisty path. When you're on it, and you can't see where you're going for sure, and when you're scared and lonely, you're probably thinking, *I can't stand this much longer. I want to numb the pain. I don't even want to keep* living. I want to get to the end of this path and feel normal or at least a little better so I can get on with my life, however pointless it seems right now. Sometimes you may even think that ending your life is a good solution.

Believe it or not, the seeds of resilience reside in this pain. Turmoil and trauma are necessary for resilience to begin growing and take root. While one would never seek out this despair, experiencing it, going with it, and accepting it as part of the fabric of your life actually will help you grow even stronger. It's impossible to define resilience in the absence of adversity. Arthur Golden wrote in *Memoirs of a Geisha*: "Adversity is like a strong wind. It tears away from us all but the things that cannot be torn, so that we see ourselves as we really are."

How often have you been defeated or confronted with roadblocks? Every day people slip, are thrown, and fall into a crevasse of misery. But every day, people, with support, also find their way out, and they re-enter their lives much, much stronger. If you don't believe such triumph is possible, ask anyone who has gone through a dark night of the soul.

POST-TRAUMATIC GROWTH

When confronted with adversity, we suffer first. Our suffering may include tears, aimless wandering, and an inability to think, let alone focus. We may not eat, or we may eat too much; we may sleep poorly, drink too much, quit exercising, isolate ourselves, or wear out our friends with our problems. We may feel physical pain or deep anguish and wonder if we'll ever feel better again. We may even experience guilt for whatever part we played in our current situation.

Although there may be a period of much suffering, for many there is also post-traumatic growth, defined as significant and positive changes resulting from the pain and suffering of major life disruptions. Suffering can be transformative and lead to greater emotional strength, wisdom, insight, and spirituality.

Think about your own life. Have you had difficult experiences that threatened to crush you but instead you survived and even thrived? What made the difference? People who thrive tend to have a number of common abilities. They recognize and remind themselves of what is meaningful in their lives, don't give up, and have a "can do" spirit. They don't sink helplessly into a bottomless pit of despair, and they remain true to themselves and their values. During adversity we make choices that will either help us move through the pain and grow stronger, or wind us up even more tightly in the pain.

You probably know people who are struggling with multiple problems, such as unemployment, depleted bank accounts, overwork, broken relationships, addictions, illness, job demands, and disability. I know I do. In time, though, most come through it all with greater wisdom and stamina.

> Amy Palmiero-Winters, a divorced mother of two small children, was the first amputee to qualify for the U.S. national track and field team. After losing her foot and ankle in a motorcycle accident, she was told she would not run a marathon again. She refused to quit and went on to win many marathons, triathlons, and some of the world's most extreme races. She says that she has no regrets and wouldn't wish for her leg back. She said if she could "... rub the magic genie lamp and take it all away and have my leg back, I wouldn't. Because my life is much better the way it is." Amy Palmiero-Winters tackled her problems directly and didn't flinch. She was determined to succeed and did not quit.[1]

To live resiliently is to respond and adapt positively to adversity, to learn and grow stronger from life's experiences, and to have good judgment and make decisions that lead to a fulfilling life. Choices that promote adaptation, growth, and sound and healthy decision-making are those that lead to quicker recoveries from adversity and its aftermath as well as increased resilience.

> John T. Downey and Richard G. Fecteau were two CIA officers in their early twenties who survived the shoot-down of their [flight] mission over China in 1952. They were captured and spent the next twenty years in Chinese prisons, much of it in solitary confinement, before being released. They saw each other for the first time two years after they were captured during a secret military tribunal. Fecteau's first words to his emaciated friend dressed in new prison rags made him smile. He said, "Who's your tailor?" After receiving their lengthy prison terms Fecteau whispered to Downey, "My wife is going to die childless," which made Downey laugh out loud, angering the guards.

Their story is one of suffering, endurance, and extraordinary adversity. How did they manage? What did they do? Despite psychological cruelty, a diet of maggoty rice and vegetables, draughty cells and loneliness, they chose a response that included learning survival strategies such as physical exercise, humor, sticking to a routine, learning Chinese, and "daydreaming." They devised a communication system using distinctive coughs. After their release in the early 1970s, Fecteau returned to his alma mater as an assistant athletic director at Boston University and Downey married, graduated from Harvard Law School, and ultimately became a judge.[2]

These two remarkable men experienced the relentless grind of prison life, with no release date in sight, and yet they didn't give up hope. They took care of themselves even when they didn't know if they'd live to see the next day. Their purpose was to survive, but they actually learned to thrive. They made choices that led to a resilient life.

There's almost no chance you or I will experience what these men did, but we are going to face challenges of one kind or another. We will feel overwhelmed. We're going to make mistakes, and, from time to time, we're going to fail. At times we'll experience extremely difficult events such as deaths, serious illnesses, destroyed relationships, job loss, and natural disasters that are completely out of our control. Can you adapt positively? Can anyone? Yes.

Once I started studying resilience, it seemed that everywhere I looked there were stories of remarkable resilience among ordinary people. I began to realize that anyone who has experienced stress and faced it head-on is resilient. Whoever manages to keep going despite the odds is resilient.

You and I have the same choice as John Downey and Richard Fecteau: to get up and keep going, to learn something, to grow even stronger. and make decisions grounded in a healthy and robust resilience. The more you and I can do this, the more capable we become. Every day is an opportunity to exercise this ability.

Jean-Dominique Bauby was a French journalist and editor of Elle magazine, living a fast-paced life in the world of fashion. In 1995 he suffered a stroke that left him totally paralyzed and speechless; a rare condition called "locked-in-syndrome." His mind was fully functioning and he could only blink his left eyelid. Blinking his eye was his only means of communication. He learned to write by spelling each word in the sentence by blinking once when the correct letter was read that matched the letter in the word he was thinking. Driven to write, he explained, "I had to rely on myself if I wanted to prove my IQ was still higher than a turnip's." He wrote a 144-page book entitled "The Diving Bell and the Butterfly" in this way. His book is full of humor and devoid of self-pity. He chose to accept his situation and turn it into something good rather than live as a vegetable. He said, "My diving bell becomes less oppressive, and my mind takes flight like a butterfly. There is so much to do. You can wander off in space or in time, set out for Tierra del Fuego or for King Midas's Court.3

I think you'd agree the need for resilience is indisputable. But what would you say if I told you to "be optimistic," "laugh more," or "don't quit." You might say something like, "Easier said than done." Especially when you find yourself in a very demanding and stressful situation, it isn't easy to be resilient.

But I have good news. You and I can build an extensive coping repertoire that promotes good decision-making and an abundance of sound judgment. We can choose to respond with resilience. Resilience is not something we're born with like brown eyes or skin color. With practice and repetition, we can learn to be more resilient at home, in the workplace, and in our communities. It's an approach to life we can practice every day.

FOUR WAYS WE RESPOND TO ADVERSITY

"Between stimulus and response there is a space. In that space is our power to choose our response. In our response lies our growth and our freedom."

—Viktor Frankl

Every day you have the opportunity to choose your response to events and circumstances. Maybe you've had a quarrel with a friend. Maybe your computer got a virus, or someone scraped a key along the length of your new car. Perhaps something traumatic occurred, such as losing your job, getting cheated out of a lot of money, discovering your spouse wants a divorce, or losing a loved one to death. Each event presents a challenge and an opportunity to choose your response.

My conversations with many people about how they did, or did not, respond resiliently have taught me that, in general, people tend to respond to adversity in one of four ways: give up, lose ground, get by, or learn and grow. As you read the stories below, think about events in your life and how you have chosen to respond. Also, realize that if you can recognize and strengthen your core of resilience, it's easier to choose a response that leads to growth and positive adaptation.

ONE: GIVE UP

Some people are so overwhelmed and disrupted by difficult events that they're unable to keep going. They blame people or things outside themselves and take little or no responsibility for their situation. They become so depressed, discouraged, or physically ill that they no longer can participate in life. Many become addicted to drugs and alcohol, are unable to function at work, live with severe depression, and some even commit suicide. They literally give up.

Carlos and his wife had been married for twenty-six years and their three children had grown up and left home. You can imagine Carlos's reaction one morning as he and his wife Sandy were getting ready for work; she turned to him and said, "I want a divorce." He looked at her and said, "Do you have a brain tumor?" He was confused and shocked. Her unhappiness was news to him. Once he finally realized how final her decision was, he fell apart. He began to think that he was nothing but a loser in life. Within a short time, he started to drink more alcohol, eat more junk food, and quit going to the fitness center. His children pleaded with him to take care of himself and so rather than deal with them, he began to avoid contact with them altogether. He went to work every day, as usual, but didn't care whether he won or lost his legal cases. His boss tried to get him to see a counselor but he refused. He quit trying. He said to me, "What's the point? I don't care anymore. If I died tomorrow, no one would miss me. In fact, they would benefit from the life insurance." His boss finally fired him and he began to think of ways to end his life.

TWO: LOSE GROUND

From the outside, some people respond to adversity as if nothing has happened. But they are unhappy and defeated, even ready to explode, on the inside. Maybe no one else realizes that they aren't sleeping or are drinking too much, that they find little joy in life and just can't see the point of living. But despair is eating away at them, and it's just a matter of time before they, too, give up on life.

Since Sarah graduated from high school eighteen years ago, she had been working for the same hospital and promoted to managerial positions, but unexpectedly, her supervisor fired her because the organization was restructuring and they were forced to make cutbacks. On the day Sarah lost her job, she said she drove like a crazy person. "I was so mad, I took it out on other drivers. I screamed at them and honked my horn every time someone got in my way." For the first two weeks she complained to anyone within earshot. Her family and friends listened patiently and then said, "You need to find another job. What's your plan?" But Sarah couldn't quit going over and over the day she was fired, and all of the years she had given to the hospital. She was bitter and resentful of everyone who still had a job. Within three weeks, she did start looking for another job for about thirty minutes a day. She watched television the rest of the time and waited for the telephone to ring. She went to three interviews, but when she didn't get any of the jobs, she told herself that she would try harder tomorrow. Soon the effort to spend thirty minutes a day looking for work became too much and she quit altogether. Most of her friends and family thought that she was moving ahead and putting her life together but she was really discouraged, angry, and defeated.

THREE: GET BY

Still others bounce back after a setback and go on living just as they did before. It's not that they weren't affected, but they have learned nothing and are no stronger for the experience. These people may be weakened by adversity but don't know it yet and may be just one short step from being unable to bounce back at all.

Fran and her sister Ellen lived three miles from each other for 73 years and their families did everything together. They celebrated every birthday, holiday, and anniversary together, and were inseparable. After their husbands died, they became even closer. Then Ellen became ill. For almost two years, Fran took care of Ellen until her final hospitalization and death. Fran said, "I cried, it seems, for months. It's so painful when you lose your best friend." But she started to feel better and picked up the threads of her life and kept going. She spent time with her grandchildren, volunteered at her church, and exercised at the Y. From the outside, she looked as if everything was normal and said philosophically, "Life goes on." But to herself she admitted that she felt frail and empty without her sister and was just treading water until her turn to get sick and die. She said, "I know I need to go on and keep living but I feel empty. I've gone through so much and I just don't have a lot of energy any more. Is there anything left in this life to do?"

FOUR: LEARN AND GROW

Those who experience problems and learn and grow from them are responding to adversity with resilience. They are tenacious and resourceful. They don't blame others. They, too, may suffer for a time but then they look straight into the face of adversity and choose their response. They draw from prior experiences in working through problems.

Resilient people survive and endure setbacks. They make good decisions. They become stronger in the aftermath of trauma.

Martin was only thirty-four years old when he was diagnosed with lymphoma. He had been married for five years and had a three-year-old son. He was a diesel mechanic and loved his work. The diagnosis came at a terrible time as he and his wife had just learned that she was pregnant with their second child. His first response was fear that he wouldn't be around for his young family and for a short while he was in shock. But within a few weeks, he came to terms with his diagnosis, his family rallied around him, and he began the fight for his life. He changed his diet, worked out a schedule at work to accommodate his treatment regimen, and moved forward one step at a time. A year later he was able to look back and know how precious his life and family were to him and this helped him realign his priorities. He chose to work less and spend more time with his family, and his faith in God was strengthened. He realized that his illness was a gift.

THE RESILIENCE CORE: THE FIVE ESSENTIAL ELEMENTS OF RESILIENCE

From the thousands of people I've interviewed and surveyed, I have gleaned five essential elements of resilience. I call these five essential elements the Resilience Core. The strength of your resilience core will determine in large part whether you can respond to adversity in a positive way.

ELEMENT ONE: PURPOSE

The first core element is having a sense of purpose. Having a good reason to get up every morning is the very heart of resilience, because that reason will give you a sure foundation upon which to build a rich and rewarding life. Life without purpose is futile and aimless. Purpose provides your driving force. Whenever you experience inevitable difficulties, your purpose pulls you forward or pushes you from behind. It reminds you that your life is worth living and that you absolutely must keep going.

But what is a purpose, and how do you get one? Your purpose is the reason or reasons that you exist, the "why" of your life. Despite popular self-help books that emphasize "finding your purpose," a person's purpose is rarely lost or hidden. Your purpose isn't necessarily something you have set out to become or achieve. Your purpose could lead you to some notable accomplishment, but often it isn't only just what you've decided in your head to do. Finding your purpose often consists of looking around and becoming aware of what you have been *called* to do. It's that which others depend on you to deliver. Typically, your purpose finds you, not the other way around.

The opposite of living with purpose is living aimlessly. If you've ever felt a lack of direction and can't seem to get going or keep going, you're living aimlessly. Do you ever feel adrift? Like you're wandering here and there and dabbling in one thing and then another? You may try one job and then a second job in a futile effort to find your way. It's like when Alice asked the Cat for directions in *Alice's Adventures in Wonderland*. Their conversation went like this:

"Would you tell me, please, which way I ought to go from here?"

"That depends a good deal on where you want to get to," said the Cat.

"I don't much care where——," said Alice.

"Then it doesn't matter which way you go," said the Cat.

"——so long as I get SOMEWHERE," Alice added as an explanation.

"Oh, you're sure to do that," said the Cat, "if you only walk long enough." [4]

ELEMENT TWO: PERSEVERANCE

Perseverance, also called persistence, is a core element of resilience. Having perseverance means you don't give up easily on anything. Even though you may experience difficulties and discouragement, as we all do, you still feel a strong determination to keep going. You've no doubt experienced failure or rejection. Both can create a formidable roadblock in life. Grief and loss also can immobilize you and prevent you from attaining your goals.

But resilient people bounce back when knocked down. They use their failures to move them forward, which takes perseverance. It may be tempting to give up or set your feet to walking on the easy path. But fighting the good fight takes a great deal of courage and emotional stamina, and resilient people clearly demonstrate this ability.

Less resilient people can be easily discouraged and give up as soon as they encounter a barrier. At times I have sometimes felt like quitting before I even started and I know firsthand that even the slightest rejection, when it comes at just the wrong time, can cause a person to quit trying.

If the perseverance element of your resilience core is strong, though—and it can always be strengthened—you'll be more likely to finish what you set out to do.

ELEMENT THREE: EQUANIMITY

Resilient people have equanimity, a balanced view of their lives. Do you know anyone, maybe even yourself, who dwells on disappointments, tends to become weighed down with regrets, or turns everything bad that happens into a catastrophe? Theirs is a skewed view of life. With equanimity comes balance and harmony. Resilient people learn to avoid extreme responses and, as we say in Montana, "sit loose in the saddle." Simply put, they're flexible.

Life is not all good. Nor is it all bad. Resilient people accept life as it comes and remain open to many possibilities. That's one of the reasons they're described as optimistic: even when a situation looks grim, they're on the lookout for opportunities. They look for the pluses, not just minuses, present in all situations. Resilient people also have learned to draw on their own (and others') experiences and wisdom, and to use both to guide their responses.

Finally, equanimity also manifests itself in humor. Resilient individuals can laugh at themselves.

Being out of balance can lead to extreme responses to difficult events. Do you know anyone who says things like, "This is the worst day of my life," or "I'll never get over this. My life is ruined!" This is called catastrophizing. When your resilience is low, you're more likely to respond to a crisis or difficulty in such a way. People living out of balance are easily overwhelmed and frustrated. Their glass is always half empty.

ELEMENT FOUR: SELF-RELIANCE

Self-reliance is belief in yourself and sure and certain understanding you can do what needs to be done. You can figure it out. You can make it happen. At times you will need help, support, and encouragement, especially when you encounter particularly difficult circumstances, but ultimately you can work it out. Resilient people have a clear and realistic picture of both their capabilities and their limitations. It comes from experience and the "practice, practice, practice" that leads to confidence.

Resilient people are resourceful. They're able to come up with common-sense solutions. Others are drawn to them because they think in terms of solutions, not problems. They don't run from responsibility.

You and I are going to encounter challenges. Sometimes we'll meet them successfully. Other times, we'll fail. Self-reliant individuals have learned from such experiences and have developed many problem-solving skills. Furthermore, they use, adapt, strengthen, and refine these skills throughout life, which, in turn, increases their self-reliance.

When your self-confidence flags, it's easy to get rattled. People with low self-reliance may be the ones who run around in circles, screaming, in an emergency. Or they may be paralyzed and unable to function at all. Their behavior could be the result of a lack of preparation and practice. When your self-reliance is low, you may be more apt to worry about the uncertainties in life: What if this happens? What if that happens? You can see self-reliance is an integral part of resilience because this trait leads to people who insist, "I'm going to find my way, whatever it takes. I will either find a way or make one."

ELEMENT FINE: AUTHENTICITY

Resilient people are happy with who they've become, warts and all. They're true to themselves. We call this being authentic. We all live in the world with other people, but resilient individuals learn to live with themselves. They become their own best friend. This is what "coming home to yourself" means. In the end, each of us will face some of life's challenges alone. If we're content with ourselves, the encounter is that much easier. Coming home is a journey that begins with getting to know yourself well. Along the way, you become comfortable in your own skin.

Self-acceptance doesn't deny the importance of shared experiences. Nor does it diminish significant and close relationships with others. But it does mean you're able to accept yourself just as you are. When you live an authentic life, you're not realizing anyone's dream but your own.

When you don't respect yourself, it's difficult to live resiliently. Are you highly critical of yourself? Do you ever have trouble recognizing how unique you are? Do you want to be like everyone else, craving approval and worrying what others think of you? When you lack authenticity, your resilience will be low. Less resilient people are never content with themselves and who they have become. This lack of contentment may lead to pursuing dreams that aren't their own and ultimately to disappointments and regrets.

On the other hand, resilient people know they're in a class of their own and do not feel pressure to conform. Most of us are ordinary people going about ordinary lives, but each of us is unique and has much to contribute to the world around us. Many people fail to recognize this truth and are filled with despair. Resilient individuals do recognize their own worth, though, and can go it alone even when the majority opinion is against them.

Resilience doesn't happen overnight, of course, and it does take effort. That's what this book is about—teaching you how to recognize how resilient you are right now and how to take steps to build your resilience core.

THE FOUR PILLARS OF RESILIENCE

You will need a strong and agile resilience core in order to live resiliently. In addition to understanding the five elements of the resilience core, there are four ways you can strengthen and support your core. I call these the Resilience Pillars. While they're not essential to living resiliently, it's very difficult to have a strong resilience core without them.

PILLAR ONE: TAKING CARE OF YOUR HEALTH

Taking care of your health increases your energy and stamina and gives you the ability to keep going even when you're tired and discouraged. This stamina supports your capacity to respond with resilience to adversity. When you have good health, you'll have more enthusiasm for life and feel good about yourself. Taking care of yourself includes eating nutritiously, exercising, getting enough rest, staying away from tobacco products, and avoiding excessive alcohol use.

PILLAR TWO: GIVING AND SEEKING SUPPORT FROM OTHERS

Giving and seeking support from friends and family, even when doing so is difficult, will enhance your ability to live your most meaningful life. It will help you pursue your dreams, be yourself, and keep going in the hard times. You can be resilient without social support, but life won't be nearly as fulfilling and purposeful, and could often feel lonely and even empty. Giving back to others may be as important as receiving support. It, too, strengthens resilience.

PILLAR THREE: BALANCING REST, RESPONSIBILITY, AND RECREATION

Living a balanced life means that no one single aspect of your life, such as work responsibilities, will dominate every waking moment. Resilience is almost impossible when one area of your life consistently outweighs others. If the pursuit of recreation becomes most important to you, for instance, it's clear that responsibility to family or work will take a backseat and detract from a well-lived life.

PILLAR FOUR: ENGAGING FULLY IN LIFE

Engaging in life means that you'll stay involved in the world around you and not withdraw or isolate yourself. When you're engaged, you remain curious and open to opportunities. You stay in the mainstream of life. It's difficult to be resilient when you withdraw from life around you and shut down. There are many fictional examples of this (and far too many real ones). Dr. Seuss's character the Grinch withdrew, and so did Charles Dickens's character Ebenezer Scrooge. Only when each character re-engaged in life was he able to regain fulfillment and meaning.

Being fully engaged can be likened to running a marathon. Imagine you're running your first marathon and hoping to cross the finish line. What will support your reaching this difficult goal? Certainly good nutrition, rest, and hydration will give you energy and stamina to keep going. A cheering section of loyal friends might make the difference between quitting and going on. Maybe you're running with a partner and his or her encouragement and support will help you cross the finish line. Likely, your support will help your running partner finish, too. When training for this race, you have to balance work, responsibilities, rest, and recreation in order to be prepared. And finally, by the time you get to the last mile, you most certainly will be far outside your comfort zone! But that's not the time to withdraw and quit. It's the time to stay fully engaged.

Now think about how the four pillars work to support and strengthen your resilience in all areas of your life. If you have recently divorced, lost your job, or become a caregiver or a new parent, think about how important it is to be resilient and how the four pillars strengthen, support, and hold up your resilience. If you are working toward finishing a college degree, a license, or certification in a specialized area, you can readily see how important the four pillars are in strengthening your sense of purpose, perseverance, equanimity, self-reliance, and authenticity.

NOTES

1. Vicki Michaelis, "Running down a dream: Leg amputee makes U.S. track team," USA Today, Apr. 27, 2010, http://usatoday30.usatoday.com/sports/olympics/summer/track/2010-04-25-amputee-runner_N.htm (accessed June 2013).

2. "Two CIA Prisoners in China, 1952-73: Extraordinary Fidelity," Central Intelligence Agency Library, https://www.cia.gov/library/center-for-the-study-of-intelligence/csi-publications/csi-studies/studies/vol50no4/two-cia-prisoners-in-china-1952201373.html (accessed Aug. 2010).

3. Jean-Dominique Bauby, The Diving Bell and the Butterfly (New York: Alfred A. Knopf, 1997), 5, 17.

4. Lewis Carroll, Alice's Adventures in Wonderland (Dover Thrift Editions, 1993), 41.

FIVE ESSENTIAL QUALITIES OF RESILIENT PEOPLE

CHAPTER 1: PURPOSE

"Life without a purpose is a languid, drifting thing; every day we ought to review our purpose, saying to ourselves, 'This day let me make a sound beginning, for what we have hitherto done is naught!'"

—Thomas Kempis

IN THIS CHAPTER you will learn how a purposeful life will help you be more resilient as well as:

- Three ways your purpose finds you
- Six roadblocks preventing you from living a meaningful life
- Three steps to a meaningful life
- Five key points on the power of purpose

《 《 》 》

"WHY AM I on this earth? What was I born to do? Does my life have a purpose?" People have always asked these questions. Understanding your purpose in life is the very heart of resilience. Your purpose pushes you from behind when you're weary or doubtful and it pulls you forward when you need inspiration. When your life has meaning, when you live "on purpose," you will be more content and focused, which translates into the ability to reach important goals.

Knowing what is truly meaningful to you will expand and enrich your life. Living purposefully leads to a great feeling of satisfaction and accomplishment because you'll be making a difference in your corner of the world and getting somewhere. Sometimes your commitment will mean taking a more difficult course, but the complications will be worth it.

Knowing what gives life purpose is like "hitching your wagon to a star." When you know where you're headed:

- You won't lose your way because you have a built-in compass that helps you stay focused.

- You won't use up lots of energy spinning your wheels as you try one thing after another, searching for direction.

- You will be more content because you'll be doing what you are especially and perfectly suited to do.

- You will view setbacks as detours rather than roadblocks because you'll know where you're headed, even if your route changes.

But what if you don't understand your purpose and don't have a lot of meaning in your life? At times everyone can feel as if life is a "languid, drifting thing," as Thomas Kempis wrote. At other times we know we're headed in the wrong direction. So how do we grow to understand our purpose and gain some meaning? Purpose and meaning can come from your career, everyday activities and hobbies, raising a family, being a friend, and volunteering. But sometimes our work seems to be at odds with our purpose.

WILL A PURPOSEFUL LIFE HELP YOU BE MORE RESILIENT?

Life can be very stressful and often is filled with difficulties and losses. Over time we will all lose something, whether it's a job, confidence, love, money, or health. If you're like the rest of us, you'd like to be able to find meaning and purpose through the challenges because without a reason to keep going, it's easy to feel despair and futility. In the end, we all want to believe our lives have been significant.

WHY IT'S IMPORTANT TO LIVE A MEANINGFUL LIFE

There are compelling reasons for understanding what gives meaning to your life. You're more likely to survive adversity, take better care of yourself, overcome depression, live long, and cope better with illness if you do get sick. People who have a clearer understanding of what is meaningful to them cope better with adversity.

Viktor Frankl, an Austrian psychiatrist, survived several concentration camps during World War II and lost almost his entire family in the Holocaust. In his book, *Man's Search for Meaning,* he described camp life as unbearable and brutal. He wrote that those with a sense of purpose were more likely to survive the camps and adapt to life once they were liberated. He quoted Nietzsche who wrote, "He who has a why to live can bear with almost any how." According to Frankl, prisoners perished soon after losing the will to live. Cigarettes were precious in the camps and prisoners sometimes would take only one puff and save the rest for later. Frankl came to realize that prisoners would smoke a cigarette all at once only when every last bit of purpose and meaning had been wrenched from them. Predictably, they died soon thereafter.[1]

Frankl learned that purpose is found in many places. He realized it's important to hold onto hope for the future, whether it be distant or whatever's around the next corner. He also wrote that meaning includes "suffering and dying, privation and death." [2]

"Everyone has his own specific vocation or mission in life," he said. "Everyone must carry out a concrete assignment that demands fulfillment. Therein he cannot be replaced, nor can his life be repeated, thus, everyone's task is unique as his specific opportunity." [3]

Dan Buettner, author of *Blue Zones: Lessons for Living Longer from the People Who've Lived the Longest,* studied people worldwide and identified life purpose as a critical factor in a life well lived. Those whose work was valued were most content, regardless of age or type of work. He also found that people with purposeful lives also appeared to live longer. Indeed those with a reason for waking up in the morning may have a buffer against stress, which may lead to less disease in general.[4]

Robert Butler also studied sense of purpose and longevity. He followed people between the ages of sixty-five and ninety-two for eleven years and discovered that those who had a clear purpose in life lived seven years longer, on average, than those who didn't.[5]

In my research I've learned that people who feel purpose, have interest in the world around them, and maintain goals throughout their lives also benefit in other areas. They are much more likely to take care of themselves, manage their stress well, and feel an overall sense of satisfaction. In a study of 776 adults, I found that a high sense of purpose was specifically associated with good nutrition and exercise, good stress management, self-responsibility for health, and seeking support from others. In a separate study of more than eight hundred adults, I learned that a greater sense of purpose also means less depression and more satisfaction with life.[6]

People with a sense of purpose also cope better with health problems. Results of a Rush University Medical Center longitudinal study, published in 2012, back up this assertion. Researchers at the Chicago center found that people with a strong sense of purpose, even when there are changes in the brain associated with the normal aging process, are able to function mentally at a much higher level than others who no longer have goals and meaning in their lives.

A sense of purpose also may slow down or prevent Alzheimer's disease. The Rush University research team studied 951 men and women with an average age of 80.4 years. At the onset of the study, none showed any signs of developing Alzheimer's disease. The researchers measured participants' sense of purpose with statements such as, "I have a sense of direction and purpose in life." They learned that the men and women with the lowest sense of purpose were twice as likely to develop Alzheimer's as those with a sense of purpose at the beginning of the study.[7]

STAGES IN LIFE

What is meaningful to you may, at different stages in your life, shift. This evolution is normal. What is purposeful to someone in her twenties will likely change significantly by the time she is in her eighties. While life can seem meaningless and you can feel adrift at any age, it's important to know that, regardless of your stage in life, your life can have meaning.

In your twenties

I know a young man starting his second year of college who needs to declare a major soon. He is being pressured by his mother, his girlfriend, and two professors to pursue pre-med because of his high grades in biology and chemistry. "Medicine seems like a good idea," he said, "but the thought of working in hospitals and being around sick people all the time leaves me cold. I'm not sure what I want to do, so this is probably as good a place to start as any. But there are so many things I want to do. I feel so pressured."

If you are very young and just starting out, understand you're at a stage in life that can be very difficult. As you choose a career, complete education and training, and try to settle on and prioritize the many goals you probably have, it's easy to begin pursuing goals that others think you should have. Some of these possible goals come from well-meaning friends and family, while others emerge from societal expectations of so-called "successful people," namely, money, possessions, power, and recognition. But is it right to base your life strategy on externally driven goals?

In your thirties and forties

A high school teacher wrote, "I have just finished earning a master's degree in English. It took me five years and all my savings. I know I'm considered successful, and my career is promising. But sometimes I wake up in the middle of the night, unable to fall back to sleep. I feel that something is missing. I feel empty. It's not that there is anything wrong; it's just that things are not 'right.' I'm not depressed, really, but my life lacks color. You could say I have the blahs. I've worked so hard to get here. Have I arrived? Is this it?"

Even for those who are in established careers, finding meaning and purpose can be challenging, especially in a busy life encumbered by the demands of excelling at a job, perhaps raising children, pursuing other interests, and staying in touch with friends and family. The pressure leads to a vague uneasiness and perhaps sleepless nights thinking, *Is this my life?* If you've been pursuing goals that aren't a good fit for you and your values, you may begin to feel serious discomfort as you drift further away than ever from living a satisfying and meaningful life.

In your fifties, sixties, and beyond

A man in his mid-fifties wrote, "I was ten years away from retirement when my company downsized and I lost my job of twenty-five years. My dreams have gone up in smoke. I've been a loyal employee and have given my all to the organization. My wife and I have been scrimping and saving and planning for retirement, and now this. We're going to have to postpone our plans for now, and maybe forever. I gave them the best part of my life, and they are tossing me out on my ear. Where do I go from here? I hardly know where to start."

When people reach middle age and beyond, their goals are re-prioritized. For people who plan to retire, the idea of leaving a meaningful career and job behind can be troubling. If you've lost your job, you may have no idea what to do next. As people age, they become more aware of how much actual time is left in their lives—a realization that can lead to despair over undone things or a sense of urgency to get moving. It's not unusual to wake up thirty years later and realize your life isn't fulfilling and you're stressed and unhealthy. Indeed the realization can lead to profound depression.

Fortunately, many people today find meaning in their work and life well into their seventies, eighties, and beyond. One look at the United States Senate, House of Representatives, and Supreme Court shows that productivity and meaningful work do not end when you're sixty-five years old. At this writing, forty-five of one hundred senators and 125 of 435 representatives are at least sixty-five years old. Four of the nine Supreme Court Justices are older than seventy.

Older adults also are well represented in business, the arts, education, science, and all other vocations. Warren Buffett, an American business leader and philanthropist, is eighty-two. Woody Allen, top comedian and movie director, is seventy-seven. Picasso painted until he was ninety-one. The list is long of those whose purpose continued to call them well into their nineties and even into the tenth decade of life. As nineteenth-century author George Eliot said, "It is never too late to be what you might have been."

HOW DO YOU FIND YOUR PURPOSE?

In all stages of life it's useful to consider the many and varied ways that purpose "calls" us. As we age and mature, some of these callings remain constant. If music always has been one of your passions, for instance, it probably will continue to be so your entire life. But other aspects of your life may change. Being an active parent in the school system may be very purposeful to you when your children are young, but once they are on their own, the meaning you may have derived from this activity likely will change.

People of all ages and walks of life say, "I can't seem to find my purpose." Maybe you feel like that sometimes, too. There are thousands of books and articles on "finding my purpose." A recent Google search on the topic listed 243 million hits. If you've ever wondered about your purpose, you're not alone.

Here is the astounding truth: you will **never** find your purpose. Even if you turn over every stone in the universe, you will never find it. Why? Because your purpose is not hidden. No wonder so many people are frustrated and exhausted as they search everywhere but the right place. Purpose and meaning reside within you. They always have, and they always will.

"But if purpose always resides within me," you ask, "why don't I know what it is? How do I find out what gives meaning to my life?" First, you must find out if your life is on course. The following exercise can help.

FIVE QUESTIONS TO SEE IF YOUR LIFE IS ON COURSE

Take stock of your life and look where you're currently headed. Are you moving in the right direction? Check the boxes below after each question if it applies to you. Your answers may help you start thinking about whether your life is on course.

1. I have meaningful goals in my life. ❑

2. I have exciting dreams for my life that I'm not afraid ❑
    to follow.

3. I'm satisfied with how my life is turning out. ❑

4. My goals are a good fit for the real me. ❑

5. I rarely lose sight of my goals. ❑

Checking most of the boxes above may indicate that your life is purposeful and rewarding and on course.

If you're concerned that your life is drifting, can you think of what might lead to a more focused and satisfying life for you? This point is where most people get stuck. They're aware they want something different because they're feeling discouraged, or even depressed, but they can't get from "My life is pointless" to "I have purpose in my life." Let's see how you might make this transition.

THREE WAYS YOUR PURPOSE FINDS YOU

ONE: PASSION

> *"Hide not your talents. They for use were made. What's a sundial in the shade?"*

> —Benjamin Franklin

"If only I could find what I'm supposed to do, if only I could find my passion, I'd be happy." Who hasn't uttered those words? Many people live a life that seems devoid of purpose or one that someone else has mapped out for them. Of course, neither ever feels quite right. One of the greatest regrets of many people as they near death is that they pursued a dream someone else had for them rather than their own.

Everyone is born with gifts, abilities, and talents that no one else on Earth possesses. Each human being is unique. Some people recognize and develop their talents early, while others lose sight of them and pursue goals that don't fit their gifts and skills at all.

In his 2005 Stanford commencement address Steve Jobs made a powerful argument for recognizing and nurturing your unique abilities and not settling for anything less. He said, "Your work is going to fill a large part of your life, and the only way to be truly satisfied is to do what you believe is great work. And the only way to do great work is to love what you do. If you haven't found it yet, keep looking. Don't settle. As with all matters of the heart, you'll know when you find it. And, like any great relationship, it just gets better and better as the years roll on. So keep looking until you find it. Don't settle." [8]

How do you find the work for which you're well suited? There are clues. J.K. Rowling became a literary sensation in 1999 with her Harry Potter book series, which have become some of the fastest selling books in history. Despite a series of difficult life events, including her mother's death, divorce, and the need to support herself and her daughter on welfare, Rowling persisted with her writing because she recognized it as her passion. After nine years spent writing her first book and numerous rejections by publishers, she finally succeeded in getting her books published and is now one of the most successful writers ever.[9]

Clues to your passion

If you like to do something, that's a strong indicator you're hardwired from birth to do it. When you like to do something, you want to do it more and more until you excel. No one has to motivate you. You're motivated from the inside.

The first step in understanding what you're meant to do is to know your strengths and abilities. Go through the list below and check your preference for each activity.

Remember: In order for this to work, you need to be completely honest with yourself. Do not check something you wish you liked to do. Answer with what you know you love to do, even if it's been a long time since you did it. If you don't love to do it, don't check it.

Activity	I wouldn't do this	I would love to do this!
1. Fix mechanical problems.	❑	❑
2. Sew, knit, make quilts, or do other needlework.	❑	❑
3. Play, listen to, and/or write music.	❑	❑
4. Understand what makes others tick.	❑	❑
5. Write.	❑	❑
6. Work or play with animals.	❑	❑
7. Do things requiring competition.	❑	❑
8. Attend religious services.	❑	❑
9. Learn new languages.	❑	❑
10. Go shopping.	❑	❑
11. Do exactly what I'm doing right now.	❑	❑
12. Talk about strategy and the big picture at work.	❑	❑
13. Travel frequently for work.	❑	❑
14. Teach others.	❑	❑
15. Be an actor.	❑	❑
16. Make people laugh around me.	❑	❑
17. Create beautiful and/or comfortable surroundings.	❑	❑
18. Inspire and motivate people.	❑	❑

Activity	I wouldn't do this	I would love to do this!
19. Sell things to others.	❏	❏
20. Help people sort out their life.	❏	❏
21. Design and grow flower or vegetable gardens.	❏	❏
22. Perform for others, such as public speaking or acting.	❏	❏
23. Help people negotiate and reach an agreement.	❏	❏
24. Create order out of chaos.	❏	❏
25. Invent things.	❏	❏
26. Help others to be comfortable and secure.	❏	❏
27. Lead others.	❏	❏
28. Design computer software.	❏	❏
29. Create art (e.g., paint, sculpt, throw pottery).	❏	❏
30. Protect others.	❏	❏
31. Manage and invest money.	❏	❏
32. Raise and sell livestock.	❏	❏
33. Help people who are ill.	❏	❏
34. Do the same work every day.	❏	❏
35. Do the job I'm doing right now.	❏	❏

Activity	I wouldn't do this	I would love to do this!
36. Do work that requires reading and studying.	❑	❑
37. Build things.	❑	❑
38. Camp, fish, hunt.	❑	❑
39. Work with kids.	❑	❑
40. Cook and bake.	❑	❑
41. Do things that some consider dangerous.	❑	❑
42. Do athletic things like bicycle, run, and ski.	❑	❑
43. Travel to different countries.	❑	❑
44. Follow and analyze politics.	❑	❑
45. Meet new people and initiate conversation.	❑	❑
46. Play games like card, board, or video games.	❑	❑
47. Connect people to each other.	❑	❑
48. Work by myself.	❑	❑
49. Make money.	❑	❑
50. Be the boss.	❑	❑
51. Enforce rules and laws.	❑	❑
52. Do research.	❑	❑
53. Work with numbers and equations.	❑	❑

Activity	I wouldn't do this	I would love to do this!
54. Create useful and practical things.	❏	❏
55. Run a business.	❏	❏
56. Volunteer.	❏	❏
57. Sing in the choir.	❏	❏
58. Go to parties, luncheons, and other gatherings.	❏	❏
59. Work in teams.	❏	❏
60. Spend time in quiet contemplation.	❏	❏

Take note of the items you marked "I would love to do this!" Of those items select the five most important. Write this list on a piece of paper. Compare it to the life that you are living right now. Are you on the right track, or are you far from doing what you are designed to do in this life?

Take note of those items you listed in the "I wouldn't do this" column. This list shows you activities that you almost never want to do, things that are boring or even poisonous to you. If you are doing these activities, especially as part of your work, you need to sit up and take notice. Maybe you've chosen the wrong career or moved into the wrong job.

Maybe it's necessary right now to do things that you don't love. For instance, you may be in school or working toward a promotion. But if these unloved activities are part of your daily routine, and especially if they will be for the foreseeable long-term future, you may want to think about making a change.

Look at the two columns again. Does anything surprise you? Look at the first column. Did you have to do any of these activities in the past week? Look at the second column. Did you get to do any of those activities in the past week? If you answered "yes" to the former and "no" to the latter, pay attention.

Here's another exercise that works very well. If you would like to know a little more about yourself and what you were born to do, give these questions a try:

1. What activities do you excel at? (Try to list two or three. Think of the times someone has said: "You're really good at that!")

2. What do you enjoy doing so much that you lose track of time?

3. What bores you to tears?

4. What topics can you talk about with authority and enthusiasm?

5. What do you do that comes easily to you? In fact, it comes so easily that you wonder why other people can't do it as well.

If nothing came to you or you aren't sure of your answers, do the same exercise but this time think back to an earlier time in your life. Think back to when you were twenty or maybe even ten years old. Another way to remember what you liked to do when you were younger is to look at old photographs of yourself and people you knew. Sometimes the images bring back strong memories of what you liked to do, such as play in the school orchestra, compete in speech and drama activities, play on an athletic team, build things, go backpacking, draw and paint, or do mechanical repairs. Try to get in touch with what makes you happy.

Tama Matsuoka Wong dreamed of having a garden of her own after spending more than twenty-five years in Hong Kong and New York. Her mother had instilled in her a love for the feel of dirt. "Dirt is good!" she said. Initially her carefully planned garden failed because she ran out of time to care for it. But then something happened. Her friends pointed out that the "weeds" growing in her garden were delicacies in Japan. She took her plants to a New York restaurant chef de cuisine who taught her how to prepare them. In 2011 they sold a cookbook called *Foraged Flavor*, giving Wong the confidence she needed to leave her law practice and find a distributor. She now provides her edibles to more than one hundred restaurants.[10]

TWO: OPPORTUNITIES

"For all sad words of tongue and pen, the saddest are these, 'It might have been.'"

—John Greenleaf Whittier

Did you know that your purpose also finds you through opportunities? Doors are opened to you. Others seem to remain closed. It's good to be aware of opportunities that are presented to you so that you can embrace them, just as it's good to be aware of doors that remain closed so that you don't waste your time and energy trying to pry them open.

Alexander Graham Bell said, "When one door closes, another opens; but we often look so long and regretfully upon the closed door that we do not see the one which has opened for us."

You can plan for the future, but jobs, careers, and relationships aren't completely under your control. Sometimes there are circumstances over which you have no influence. Much as you may try, something stops you from continuing in a certain direction.

For instance, you may want to be a Navy Seal more than anything in the world. Or a test pilot, or an astronaut, archaeologist, or engineer. But if you aren't selected, or if you haven't the necessary physical, mental, or emotional skills for the job, no amount of desire will make it happen.

You also may fail to reach for a dream because you're reluctant, afraid, or unsure of yourself. An excellent example of someone who overcame her fear in order to succeed is Susan Boyle of Scotland, known for her astounding 2009 performance on a reality TV program called *Britain's Got Talent*. She appeared on stage as a modest middle-aged woman with a dream of singing like Elaine Paige. The judges and audience openly scoffed and laughed at her as she walked onstage because she didn't look like a world-class singer. But when she opened her mouth, they realized how wrong they were. Her performance was electrifying and she became an instant Internet sensation. Indeed Amazon reported her first album enjoyed the highest number of pre-sales in its history. Since that fateful first performance, Paige has called Boyle a role model for everyone who has a dream. Can you imagine the terror she experienced at appearing in public in such a hostile venue? She was able to overcome her fear with her confidence in her immense talent, which she finally revealed at age forty-seven.[11]

Opportunity often is defined as recognizing the favorable juncture of circumstances. It is said that passion plus reality equals opportunity. How do you recognize opportunity in your own life? You do it by keeping your eyes open and your senses alert. Do you know how to open yourself up to new adventures and experiences that might at first glance seem scary, as Susan Boyle did? Sometimes you need to take a chance, even a huge chance, and see what happens. Stay open to new ideas and ways of doing things.

Opportunities have a way of revealing themselves. They come in many sizes and shapes and arrive at different times in our life. Back in 2009, 57-year old Todd Bol, in a tribute to his mother, built a small dollhouse-sized red wooden box and painted to look like an old-fashioned school house. He placed it in his front yard in Hudson, Wisconsin, stocked it with about two dozen books, and put up a sign inviting neighbors to take one book and then return one book. Before long the box was drawing dozens of people who both looked through the books and stopped to have conversations. As his little library grew in popularity, Todd thought that he might expand it and joined up with Rick Brooks, an outreach manager at the University of Wisconsin-Madison. They decided to promote little libraries on a larger scale. They put together fully constructed models. Then they sold kits so people could build their own. There are now 10,000 to 12,000 *Little Free Libraries* around the world. They serve to share books and build communities.[12]

Sara Blakely has had to overcome several phobias—fear of heights, fear of flying, and stage fright—to market her wildly popular invention "Spanx." She didn't plan to invent anything but always had a knack for making a buck. As is true of many ideas for start-ups, Spanx was a solution to a problem. When Blakley had to wear panty hose on her job, she found them hot, uncomfortable, and unfashionable. She wanted the slimming effect without the feet. "I've got to figure out how to make this," she said. "I need an undergarment that doesn't exist." At twenty-seven, she used her entire savings of $5,000, and for two years planned the launch of her product while still working a "nine to five" job. She was rejected many times but kept trying. When she finally shipped samples to Oprah Winfrey, who named Spanx her favorite product, orders poured in. Blakely made $4 million in her first year and

$10 million in the next one. Her $5,000 investment has turned into a $1 billion enterprise. But it's not about the money for her. She says it's fun to make and fun to spend, but it's also fun to give away. Sara Blakely is a resilient woman who combined passion and opportunity to achieve her success.[13]

THREE: PERSONALITY

"In the world to come, I shall not be asked, 'Why were you not Moses?'
I shall be asked, 'Why were you not Zusya?'"

—Rabbi Zusya

Personality science explains that each of us is distinctly unique. Our personality affects how we experience and interpret events in our life, and it directs us to pursue satisfaction in a variety of ways. Our personality will reflect what motivates us and what we define as success. When we understand our personality style and recognize how it influences our behavior, we can look at how to achieve a meaningful life from a fresh and fascinating perspective.

Although it's called "personality science," it isn't really a science. It isn't possible to categorize someone exactly into a specific personality type. Most of us can find characteristics that fit us from all the personality types. Frequently, though, one type will dominate and we will recognize ourselves right away. Understanding your personality is one more clue to figuring out what suits you and what doesn't. It's also a way to gain insight into why you're drawn to certain lifestyles and vocations and not others. When you're working out of character, or against your unique personality, you will experience tension, anxiety, frustration, discouragement, and even depression.

"Personality" comprises the thoughts, feelings, and behaviors that make you unlike anyone else. Your personality will remain fairly consistent throughout your life. When you understand more about your personality, you will recognize patterns in how you act in a variety of situations. You express your unique personality through your behavior in the world. And knowing your personality will help you choose best "fits" for your life.

For instance, Sheryl Sandberg, chief operating officer of Facebook, was ranked as one of the "50 Most Powerful Women in Business" by *Fortune Magazine*. She foregoes an office and sits in an open workspace with everyone else, reflecting self-confidence and the knowledge that she's working with her personality rather than against it. Sandberg is an inspirational leader passionate about her vision. She is polished, personable, extroverted, and a good fit for her role at Facebook.[14]

Larry Page, co-founder and CEO of Google, Inc., is passionate about innovation, too. According to Susan Cain, author of *Quiet*, he also is quiet and reserved but will succeed because he's in a position where capability is more valued than charisma. Page listens well and has a natural ability to implement other people's creative ideas.[15]

If you're interested in whether you are a good fit for your work and in other areas in your life, there are multiple surveys you can take to find out your personality type. The most widely used is the Myers-Briggs Type Indicator® (MBTI®) that describes sixteen basic personality types. No one type is better than another, but each reflects a person's preference for an overall combination. Remember that the MBTI and other personality tests don't measure aptitude. They simply measure a person's preferred way of thinking and feeling.[16]

Two well-known aspects of personality are introversion and extroversion. People classified by the MTBI as extroverted are energized by action: they are inclined to act, then reflect, and then act again. When inactive, their motivation diminishes. In contrast, more introverted people diminish their energy reserves through action. Their preferred way is to reflect, then act, and reflect again. To build up energy, introverts need quiet time for thinking, time that is removed from activity. The extroverted person directs energy outward and the introverted person directs it inward.

Again, personality tests do not measure ability. People who prefer "thinking" versus "feeling" don't think better than those who score high on feeling. The test reveals how different personality types prefer finding their way to solutions.

Taking a personality test or inventory will give you an intriguing glimpse into what makes you who you are. Ideally, you want to take advantage of the strengths of your personality and your preferences for thinking, feeling, and behaving. If you combine this understanding with your passion, you'll be guided toward a more meaningful life.

Julia Child, popular TV chef and author, combined her passion, opportunity, and unique personality to achieve success in her forty-year career. She set out to make sophisticated French cuisine available to every housewife in America, which led to a two-volume cookbook called *Mastering the Art of French Cooking.* She also became a TV icon with *The French Chef,* her popular cooking show. As a young girl, Child was athletic, adventurous, and considered a prankster. She was fired from her first job for insubordination. Her hearty humor and forthright personality found its niche, however, when her TV show was syndicated to ninety-six stations in the United States. Not everyone was a fan of her exuberant and sometimes flamboyant behavior in the kitchen. One viewer wrote, "You are quite a revolting chef, the way you snap bones and play with raw meats." Child worked right up to her death at age ninety-two, saying, "In this line of work you keep right on 'til you're through. Retired people are boring." Child recognized opportunities and took them, and was a natural entertainer with her playful attitude and ability to connect with people.[17]

What can you do? Take a personality test and find out what you like to do. The classic test is the MBTI, but if you have access to the Internet, type in "personality test" and you will see many others available online. You're likely to enjoy learning more about yourself. Your personality type plays a strong role in arriving at a place where your purpose and meaning in life are part of your daily existence.

SIX ROADBLOCKS PREVENTING YOU FROM LIVING A MEANINGFUL LIFE

I've identified six things that can interfere with living a life filled with meaning and purpose. The following list will acquaint you with some of the obstacles that may be keeping you from choosing to live a significant life.

ONE: YOU HAVE NO BLUEPRINT FOR ACTION

You don't know how to get from here to there—from what you are doing now to what you want to do. You may have ideas about what is meaningful in your life, but no plan. Without a blueprint for action, you don't know where to start.

TWO: YOU ARE IN A RUT

You're in a rut in your work, your relationships, or in other ways. You keep slipping back into this rut. Remember that a rut can be comfortable. You may have become complacent while waiting for the right opportunity. Years may pass and you may begin to feel discouraged, frustrated, and even desperate. But at least it's comfortable. Inevitably, though, you ask yourself, *Is this all there is?*

THREE: YOU ARE SCARED TO TAKE THE LEAP

You may catch a glimpse of an opportunity, but you are afraid to do anything about it. Maybe you'll look foolish or fail. You may need to change your work, leave familiar relationships behind, and even relocate to a different part of the country. It takes courage to consider something new in your life, even if your current life is miserable.

FOUR: YOU LACK CONFIDENCE

You're unsure of your ability to do something different even if you're quite sure it's what you want to do. You may lack confidence. Others may discourage you from taking a chance. Maybe you're afraid to open yourself up to criticism or even derision. You already can hear the voices saying, "You want to do *what* with your life?" While it's important to listen to others, especially people you trust, you know yourself better than anyone else in the end.

FIVE: YOU DON'T KNOW HOW TO SWITCH GEARS

You're unwilling to quit pursuing the goals you're pursuing now even though you're not going where your heart wants to go. Your current job, for instance, may be leading toward a higher salary, more recognition and prestige, and greater benefits. You may be gaining momentum, albeit in the wrong direction. What does your heart say? You may need to slow down and switch gears, but maybe you don't know how.

SIX: YOU HAVE BLINDERS ON

Maybe you're stressed, anxious, and depressed. Because you're working all the time, you're missing the cues that you're not living the life you really want. You're wearing blinders.

THREE STEPS TO OVERCOME ROADBLOCKS

STEP ONE

If you can imagine something, you can achieve it. Whatever you dream, you can become. Close your eyes, get comfortable, and imagine that tomorrow morning you wake up in exactly the life you want. Your envisioned life is perfect for you. Take your abilities and unique personality type into consideration as well as the ways in which others need you. Write down what you see in your mind's eye or tell someone else about your vision. One rule: what you envision must be realistic.

STEP TWO

Think about the last year or even the last week. Did you ever have an absolutely incredible day when your life felt meaningful and headed in the right direction? When you were focused and meeting important goals? If you can't remember any, then start keeping count today. Think about the best day you've had in a long time. What was your best day like? What did you do on this day? What do you remember? Why was it great? How many days did you have like that? Would you like more of these days? Again, write the details that occur to you so you can see this excellent day clearly from the moment you awakened to the moment you fell asleep.

STEP THREE

Put together the answers from steps one and two into a statement that takes into account your abilities, strengths, personality, opportunities, dreams, and the ways in which others need you. For instance, you might write:

"For me, a life of purpose and significance is one in which I am a parent, church member, husband, volunteer firefighter, gardener, engineer, and inventor."

"For me, a life of purpose and significance is one in which I am a grandparent, bail bondsman, volunteer at the hospital, seamstress, and wife."

"For me, a life of purpose and significance is one in which I am a nursing student, daughter, violinist, long-distance runner, and volunteer at the local homeless shelter."

"For me, a life of purpose and significance is one in which I am a salesman, husband, horse trainer, and amateur historian."

Keep this statement in front of you and look at it daily. Maybe you could put it on the refrigerator with a magnet, or affix a note to your computer monitor or bathroom mirror, or on a frequently used door. Maybe you could use your statement as a screen saver. Maybe you could display pictures of yourself doing the activities on your list to provide a quick visual reminder of what is truly meaningful in your life.

You will face adversity of one kind or another today and tomorrow and for the rest of your life. Practice keeping your statement of purpose and significance in front of you as you go through each day and you'll be amazed at how it puts everything else into perspective. Your statement always keeps your priorities straight and will help you put your goals in the right order. What gives your life meaning will shift as you age: purpose is a lifelong process. What's important is that you never ignore or deny who you are or the many important ways you are needed every day. Never fail to share your gifts and talents with the world.

If you finally decide you need to make changes in work and personal relationships, or in your career, or even where you live, you'll need courage to take the next step. Clarifying what gives meaning to your life will help you stay on course. You will be very thankful that you did.

FIVE KEY POINTS ON THE POWER OF PURPOSE

1. Excelling at anything requires a great deal of practice. If you want a competitive edge, it's worth your time and effort to choose something you love that comes naturally to you.

2. Think about when you were ten or twelve years old. What did you want to be when you grew up? The actual vocation may not have been exactly on the mark (think astronaut or brain surgeon), but the underlying ideas and feelings probably were dead-on. Does being an astronaut suggest adventure? Does being a surgeon suggest helping others? These desires probably are still strong within you.

3. What do you like to do in your spare time? Do you think about riding your bicycle? Target shooting? Sewing a quilt? Volunteering at a homeless shelter? Buying new tools for fixing your car? Studying a foreign language? Designing a garden? These, too, are clues to what will bring meaning and even excitement to your life.

4. Look around. Is anyone leading a life that you find appealing and you would like for yourself? Do you know someone who travels frequently? Is that exciting to you? What about someone who works outdoors, tries a case in front of a jury, or works from home? Do you find yourself thinking you'd like to do any of those things, too? Your daydreams in this regard are another clue as to how you might want to work.

5. Do you have a big picture view of your life? In other words, are you busily engaged in many activities with lots of motion and

energy but little direction? It's easy to deny the lack of meaning in your life by never lifting your gaze to the horizon. Take the long view and ask yourself if you're living consistently with what is truly meaningful to you.

We all want to believe we can live a life of significance and that when we reach the end of our lives, we'll have realized our potential to the best of our ability. But this ultimate goal requires an understanding of our gifts, personality, passion, and opportunities. It's not enough to know what you are meant to do. You must also do it.

NOTES

1. Viktor E. Frankl, *Man's Search for Meaning* (New York: Washington Square Press, 1984), 26.

2. Frankl, 103-104.

3. Frankl, 131.

4. Dan Buettner, *The Blue Zones: Lessons for Living Longer from the People Who've Lived the Longest* (Washington, DC: National Geographic Society, 2008), 245.

5. Robert Butler, *The Longevity Prescription: The 8 Proven Keys to a Long, Healthy Life* (New York: Penguin Group, 2010).

6. Gail Wagnild, *The Resilience Scale User's Guide for the US English Version of the Resilience Scale and the 14-Item Resilience Scale (RS-14)* (Worden, MT: The Resilience Center, 2009).

7. Patricia Boyle, et al., "Effect of purpose in life on the relation between Alzheimer disease pathologic changes on cognitive function in advanced age," *Archives in General Psychiatry*, vol. 69 (2012): 499-505.

8. Steve Jobs, Stanford University 2005 Commencement Address, *Stanford News*, http://news.stanford.edu/news/2005/june15/jobs-061505.html (accessed July 1, 2013).

9. "J.K. Rowling Biography," *A&E Networks*, http://www.biography.com/people/jk-rowling-40998 (accessed Oct. 2013).

10. Frances Lam, "Tama Matsuoka Wong, High-End Forager," *Bon Appétit*, Mar. 28, 2013, http://www.bonappetit.com/people/article/tama-matsuoka-wong-high-end-forager-interviewed-by-francis-lam (accessed Oct. 7, 2013).

11. Susan Boyle, *The Woman I Was Born to Be: My Story* (New York: Atria Books, 2010).

12. "The History of Little Free Library," *LittleFreeLibrary.org*™, http://littlefreelibrary.org/ourhistory (accessed Oct. 8, 2013).

13. Clare O'Connor, "How Sara Blakely of Spanx Turned $5,000 into $1 Billion," *Forbes*, Mar. 14, 2012, http://www.forbes.com/global/2012/0326/billionaires-12-feature-united-states-spanx-sara-blakely-american-booty.html (accessed Oct. 8, 2013).

14. Miguel Helft, "Mark Zuckerberg's Most Valuable Friend," *The New York Times*, Oct. 2, 2010, http://www.nytimes.com/2010/10/03/business/03face.html?_r=2&pagewanted=print (accessed Oct. 6, 2013).

15. Susan Cain, "Introverted Leaders: Three Reasons Larry Page Will Succeed as Google CEO (As Long As He Avoids One Fatal Misstep)," http://www.thepowerofintroverts.com/2011/01/23/introverted-leaders-

three-reasons-larry-page-will-succeed-as-google-ceo-as-long-as-he-avoids-one-fatal-misstep/ (accessed Oct. 8, 2013).

16. "MBTI® Basics," *The Myers & Briggs Foundation*, http://www.myersbriggs.org/my-mbti-personality-type/mbti-basics (accessed July 1, 2013).

17. "Julia Child," *A&E Networks*, http://www.biography.com/people/julia-child-9246767 (accessed Oct. 8, 2013).

CHAPTER 2: PERSEVERANCE

"Nothing in the world can take the place of persistence. Talent will not; nothing in the world is more common than unsuccessful men with talent. Genius will not; unrewarded genius is a proverb. Education will not; the world is full of educated derelicts. Persistence and determination alone are omnipotent."

—Calvin Coolidge

IN THIS CHAPTER you will learn how perseverance is essential to resilience as well as:

- Three steps to more perseverance
- Brief biographies that will inspire you
- Nine common roadblocks to success
- Five key points about perseverance

« « » »

FRAN WAS EXCITED about finally figuring out what she wanted to do with her life. She believed with all her heart that achieving her dream would lead to a life that was rich, rewarding, and meaningful. She envisioned her newfound purpose would revolve around caring for her family, starting a floral design business, and pursuing better health. She was over the moon with excitement.

To achieve her dream, she knew she would need to quit smoking, lose weight, and start exercising. She even had a name picked out for her business, Fabulous Flowers by Fran, and she created a collage of images for her new life. They included pictures of a healthy, slim woman and a Paris flower shop with a green striped awning and vibrantly colored blooms in the window displays. Fran also had a Winston Churchill quote taped to her bathroom mirror: "Success is going from failure to failure without losing enthusiasm."

Then the bank turned down her request for a business loan, her husband lost his job, and Fran had to keep working as an administrative assistant at a large hospital. Discouraged, she let go of her dreams in complete defeat. She took down the pictures because they make her depressed and said, "I guess it's just not meant to be." What happened?

Brendon is twenty-eight years old. Last year he finished a graduate degree in psychology but decided not to work as a therapist. He thought about trying something else. He considered pursuing a degree in music since he played with a band, and his fellow musicians thought it might be fun to go on tour. They're not very good, but they're not going to let that stop them! He needed to make more money than an entry-level psychologist so he decided to work for a while in the Bakken Oil Fields in North Dakota. After six months, he grew bored with the work and wasn't sure what to do next.

To be a psychologist, Brendon would need a doctoral degree. To be a really good guitarist, he'd have to put in at least four hours of practice time daily and that sounded tedious. His friends encouraged him to look into a business career and he started to mull that idea.

If you are like Fran or Brendon, you probably have given up on a goal or two in your life, believing that you didn't have enough gumption to carry you through to the end. It's normal to feel discouraged, defeated, done in. It's normal to want to quit, thinking you can't possibly succeed. Everyone has experienced rejection, loss, fear of failure, and disappointment, and will continue to do so for the duration of their life.

In his popular book *Adversity Quotient*, Paul G. Stoltz described how three categories of people respond to adversity. He labeled them quitters (they give up), campers (they reach a certain level and go no further), and climbers (they continue to learn, grow, strive, and improve). Stoltz conducted a poll in which he asked one hundred fifty thousand leaders to identify the percentage of employees who were quitters (5-20 percent), campers (65-90 percent), and climbers (5-15 percent). Many other writers would agree: there are more who quit short of success than those who persist and succeed.[1]

Some have referred to the ability to learn, grow, strive, and improve as "grit," which is defined as persistence and passion for long-term goals. In her fascinating research on grit, Angela Duckworth found this quality accounted for educational attainment and fewer career changes among more than two thousand surveyed adults. It predicted grade point average among Ivy League undergraduates as well as retention in more than two thousand cadets at the U.S. Military Academy at West Point. Grit was a more reliable predictor of success than intelligence. Researchers have concluded that the achievement of difficult goals requires not only talent but sustained and focused application of talent over time. According to Duckworth, successful people don't abandon a goal because they see something more interesting to do. Those who flit from one goal to another are dilettantes. Successful people don't give up because of obstacles, either. Instead, they are tenacious.[2]

Duckworth made three points about grit. First, she said it takes about ten years, or ten thousand hours, of dedicated practice to become proficient at a discipline like music, psychology, business, teaching, sales, or medicine, and so perseverance is essential to getting good at anything.

Second, sustained and focused effort is imperative when it comes to perfecting a skill. School or business success cannot be achieved by pulling "all-nighters" and cramming preparation into a short intense period. For many people, sustained effort means working at something for four hours at a time every day.

Third, the drive to get better and better must be ever present. It's what propels people beyond what they already do well into areas where they aren't proficient. If I only play piano passages I've already mastered, for instance, I don't improve. Drive requires a willingness to fail.

Elizabeth Colerick, a nationally recognized researcher in the field of gerontology, wrote that stamina, or staying power, is contingent upon "a triumphant, positive outlook." Those who view their situation as overwhelming and potentially defeating have lower levels of perseverance. In contrast, those who cope and maintain a positive outlook during times of change, challenge, upheaval, and stress are able to keep heading toward their dreams.[3]

Resilient people rarely give up. They know that if they want to succeed, no amount of luck, intelligence, money, connections, or talent will substitute for persistence. Nothing predicts success as well as determination. It takes time and effort to achieve success. Even though everyone understands the importance of persistence, it's very difficult to keep going when you're tired and sick, you've been rejected, or you're afraid, discouraged, or full of doubt.

Have you ever struggled to lose weight or start an exercise program? What about earn a college degree while you're working and raising a family? Work two jobs in order to care for your children? Keep moving forward in the aftermath of divorce? Have you ever worked at recovering after illness, surgery, or an injury? What about finding and keeping a job while caring for an ill family member? Or maybe you've tried to get back on your feet after bankruptcy. During these times, quitting is rarely, if ever, the best option.

If you have experienced any of the above, then you know how much persistence and effort it takes to keep going when all you want to do is quit.

WILL PERSEVERANCE HELP YOU BE MORE RESILIENT?

Without a doubt, the ability to keep going and never give up is essential to resilience. If you're going to bounce back following adversity and grow even stronger, you'll have to persevere. If you're going to learn from your mistakes, you'll have to take chances and risk failing. All who have achieved things in life did so through dogged determination.

Irving Stone, who has written biographies of great men, including Michelangelo, Sigmund Freud, Vincent van Gogh, and Charles Darwin, observed this about the qualities they share: "I write about people who sometime in their life have a vision or dream of something that should be accomplished and they go to work. They are beaten over the head, knocked down, vilified, and for years they get nowhere. But every time they're knocked down they stand up. You cannot destroy these people. And at the end of their lives they've accomplished some modest part of what they set out to do." 4

Of course, that kind of deep resilience is easier discussed than accomplished. How do you keep going when there are lots of reasons to quit and few reasons to continue? Author Patsy Clairmont tells a story of her seven-year-old son who went off to school one day and returned a few minutes later saying he'd quit school because it was too long, hard, and boring. "You have just summed up life," she said. "Now get on the bus." 5

A good deal of the time all of us have to just "get on the bus" and keep going. Many athletes are great examples of perseverance. At age twenty-seven, Michael Phelps was the most decorated Olympian of all time with twenty-two medals. But his record was made possible by years of dedication, discipline, and sacrifice. His coach said that from the age of eleven, he didn't take one day off from practice. Not one. Not for Christmas, his birthday, or any other reason. When asked why he was so driven, Phelps said: 1) I didn't want to lose. 2) I wanted to do something no one has ever done.6

Wilma Rudolph, the world's fastest woman and winner of three Olympic gold medals, was crippled from polio as a child. Her doctor told her she'd never walk again. "I ran and ran and ran every day," she said, "and I acquired this sense of determination, this sense of spirit that I would never, never give up, no matter what else happened." She said that if you're going to achieve anything in life, you must realize that sometimes you'll lose but you have to pick yourself up and go on.7

When he was on his way to breaking Babe Ruth's career home run record, Hank Aaron regularly received death threats and hate mail. When he finished the 1973 season one home run short of the record, he said his only fear was not living to play the next season. "My motto was always to keep swinging," he said. "Whether I was in a slump or feeling badly or having trouble off the field, the only thing to do was keep swinging."

Maybe you're thinking, *That may work for Phelps, Rudolph, and Aaron, but what about us mere mortals? They chose to do what they did. What about when things happen that we don't choose? How do any of us "keep swinging" when the odds are against us and we feel tired, discouraged, and defeated?*

We've all been there. Whether we're trying to quit smoking, jump-start a stalled career, recover from illness, prepare for a test, or pick up the pieces after a failed relationship, we've all experienced exhaustion. So what is the key to perseverance? What is the answer?

On January 4, 2011, my mother, then ninety-one years old, began to lose sensation in and control over her right arm and left leg. Her speech became garbled. We all thought "stroke," rushed her to the emergency room, and watched her deteriorate rapidly. By day four she couldn't do anything: she was paralyzed and there was still no diagnosis. She hadn't had a stroke. She was a mystery. We were heartbroken and had been told to prepare for her imminent death.

The news was difficult to take. You see, ten days earlier she'd helped prepare Christmas Day dinner for twenty-five people and she'd played cards until 2:00 a.m. on New Year's Eve. Determined to care for her away from the chaos of a hospital, we took her home. Despite all medical prognoses, she didn't die. She had hospice care for several weeks and then "graduated." She was no longer eligible for end-of-life care because she was no longer dying. She began moving her toes, her fingers, and finally her legs and arms.

Within two weeks my mother was walking and caring for herself. By summer that year she was on her beloved farm mowing her own grass, tending her garden, and driving her car. She is the picture of resilience. She never, ever gave up despite everyone telling her she was about to die.

"I never thought I was dying," she said. "I just intended to get well again." She refused to quit and epitomized grit with her clear goals, daily practice, and willingness to push past failure every hour.

There are thousands of examples of people who have persevered through difficulties. Some are famous; others are ordinary people around the world whose stories appear in local newspapers or go unobserved in their communities. We often are inspired when we see how people keep going with grit and determination.

WHAT SEPARATES THOSE WITH PERSEVERANCE FROM THOSE WHO GIVE UP?

It's tempting to make excuses about not being able to reach a goal by saying you weren't born smart enough. In fact, your IQ can't predict future success. It's only part of the story. It's natural to look at extraordinary people such as pro athletes, gifted entertainers, or tech whizzes and say to yourself, *They are so lucky to have won the DNA lottery*. But even Albert Einstein said, "It's not that I'm so smart; I just stay with problems longer."

If you want to succeed, you can't quit every time you fail. If you do, you'll never get anywhere. Consider these people who succeeded against the odds. Abraham Lincoln did not have an easy life and yet was one of the greatest presidents the United States has ever known. His mother died when he was nine years old and by his own admission he was not very educated but could "read, write, and cipher." Three of his four children died in childhood. He said, "Always bear in mind that your own resolution to succeed is more important than any other." [8]

Theodor Geisel aka Dr. Seuss, the beloved author of children's books, was rejected by twenty-seven publishers for his first book, *To Think That I Saw It on Mulberry Street*. He later stated that after so many rejections, he almost burned the manuscript. Over his lifetime he wrote more than sixty books and sold more than 222 million copies. He said, "Think left and think right and think low and think high. Oh, the thinks you can think up if only you try!" [9]

Winston Churchill did not do well in school and failed the exam for the Royal Military College three times. He resigned his military post following the disastrous Battle of Gallipoli, believing he was to blame for proposing the expedition. At the age of sixty-two Churchill became prime minister of England. He famously said, "Never give in—never, never, never, never, in nothing great or small, large or petty, never give in except to convictions of honor and good sense." [10]

Colonel Harland Sanders was a very successful businessman and entrepreneur. He worked very hard to achieve success, traveling around the country from restaurant to restaurant and making deals to be paid a nickel for every chicken each restaurant sold. He said, "I made a resolve then that I was going to amount to something if I could. And no hours, nor amount of labor, nor amount of money would deter me from giving the best that there was in me. And I have done that ever since, and I win by it. I know." [11]

Nor is success a matter of good luck, as some would believe. Millions of people give up quickly and prematurely when confronted with obstacles and then point to successful people and say, "They got a lucky break and luck isn't on my side." Successful people work hard. Luck has nothing to do with it. Lucille Ball, one of the most popular entertainers in the United States, was the first woman to run a major television studio. She was shy, told she had no talent, and suffered from rheumatoid arthritis. But she had great tenacity. "Luck? I don't know anything about luck," she said. "I've never banked on it, and I'm afraid of people who do. Luck to me is something else: hard work—and realizing what is opportunity and what isn't."

The quick guide below will help you identify your strengths as a person with perseverance, as well as the common characteristics of those who give up.

"I'm not quitting!"	**"I give up!"**
Goal-driven	Aimless
Patient	Wants immediate results
Focused	Easily distracted
Expects to succeed	Expects to fail
Adaptable	Rigid and unyielding
Learns from failures, keeps goal in mind, but changes strategy	Applies same strategy over and over even when it fails
Gives all-out effort	Goes halfway
Remembers successes	Remembers failures
Continues the struggle even when no one believes in him/her	Gives up because no one believes in him/her
Finds a way over, around, or through a roadblock	Takes foot off gas pedal and coasts to a full stop

KNOWING WHEN TO FOLD 'EM

Think you've tried hard enough? There is a point, of course, when you have to be realistic. Let's say you've always dreamed of being an astronaut and every year you're denied admission to an astronaut program. Or maybe you want to be an attorney but, try as you might, you can't pass the bar exam. You may need to rethink how you want to reach your goals. While it's true there are many people who quit just short of success, it's important to know when to change direction.

Several studies now show that doing so leads to better health, including lower cortisol and better sleep, as well as subjective well-being. These findings were true for older adults who were able to reengage new and meaningful goals as well as for young adults and parents of children with cancer.[12-13]

In one study ninety adolescents were followed for a year: their ability to manage unattainable goals was assessed at the beginning of the year and then six and twelve months later. Their concentrations of C-reactive protein (CRP), an inflammatory molecule, also were measured. The more difficult it was for an adolescent to disengage from unattainable goals, the greater the concentration of CRP at the beginning of the study and over the six- and twelve-month follow-up period. Excessive inflammation contributes to a variety of medical conditions and outcomes. This study shows persistence that is unrealistic actually may be detrimental to good health and well-being.[14]

The point is, when goals are clearly unattainable, it's healthy to adjust them and go after alternative ones. Such a decision is yours to make. The important thing is that you make this decision based on realistic information and trustworthy advice and not merely due to impatience or frustration at your sometimes slow progress.

HOW MUCH PERSEVERANCE DO YOU HAVE?

Do you see yourself as a person with determination? The brief checklist below will help you assess your level of perseverance. Make a check mark if the statement fits you.

1. If I don't succeed right away I usually say enough is enough and quit. ❑

2. Sometimes I just seem to run out of steam. ❑

3. I "dig my heels in" when I'm up against it. ❑

4. If I were to keep score, I tend to give up more often than I stick with it. ❑

5. When the pressure starts to build, I usually say, "This just isn't worth it." ❑

6. I've been told that I'm a "real trouper" and have "true grit." ❑

7. Once I start something, I will not stop until it's finished. ❑

8. Rejection is my undoing; it takes a long time to get back up. ❑

9. I am patient. No matter how long it's going to take, I'm going to do it. ❑

10. I've noticed in my life that I tend to give up just short of succeeding. ❑

11. I am willing to go through a lot of pain to reach my goal. I know this for a fact. ❑

Do you see a pattern in how you approach obstacles and goals in your life? Do you tend to work until you succeed or quit short of success?

THREE STEPS TO PERSEVERANCE

How do you strengthen your perseverance? There are three steps. First, you must have a dream and a desire to achieve it. You have to want something very much. Second, you have to be determined to keep going toward your goal despite discouragement and disappointment. Third, you have to be self-disciplined. There are many obstacles that will trip you up and it's good to be prepared for them as much as possible.

ONE: DREAMS

We must have a reason to keep going. Those who have a goal that is important to them will feel pulled, pushed, and compelled to achieve it and will do whatever they can to succeed.

Sean Swarner, who twice survived cancer, is an inspiring example of perseverance. At age thirteen, he was diagnosed with cancer and not expected to live three months. Instead he miraculously got better. Two years later, he was clear of cancer. Then he was diagnosed with an entirely new cancer and given two weeks to live. Fifteen years later, with only partial use of his lungs due to his earlier illness, he climbed Mount Everest. Swarner has since climbed the highest peaks in Africa, Europe, South America, Antarctica, Australia, and North America. He said:

> *Frankly I don't know why I'm alive. But I'm incredibly grateful for the third life I have been given and I'm committed to shouting from the rooftops of the world that there is hope and miracles up and down the sides of every mountain. Somehow I found the inner will to get up and out of that hospital bed.*[15]

Michael Dell dreamed of owning his own business. At age twelve, he was washing dishes at a Chinese restaurant to pay for his stamp collection. He bought an Apple computer at fifteen, just to tear it apart and understand how it worked. By the time he was twenty, he used his $1,000 savings account to start building computers in his dorm room. In his first year of business, he had $6 million in sales. Eight years after he founded Dell, he was the youngest CEO of a Fortune 500 company and, sixteen years later, Michael Dell was a billionaire. When Dell Computers ran into some problems, its founder decided to take his business private again. Recently, true to his dreams, he bought his own company back in one of the biggest buyouts in recent history. He said, "Whether you've found your calling, or if you're still searching, passion should be the fire that drives your life's work." [16]

When you don't have any identifiable goals in your life, it's tempting to do either or both of the following. You might allow others to determine and define your goals for you. Have you ever gone along with someone else's plan for you for a while? If their idea of what you should do wasn't consistent with your own values and goals, it probably led to disappointment and frustration. You probably quit.

Do you ever look around and see others enthusiastically pursuing their goals and think to yourself, *That looks fun*. And then you take off toward those new goals with little thought as to whether they are congruent with what's purposeful to you. That plan won't last long, either.

You can learn all the tricks of strengthening your perseverance, but if you don't have a good reason to persist, you're wasting your time.

So the very first and most important step is to identify your purpose or your dream. You may have many, but start with one. Try to imagine what success looks, feels, sounds, and smells like. Make it real. If you can see your goal in such specificity, you'll find it much easier to head in its direction and not stop until you get there. Ask yourself how much you want to achieve your dream. Are you willing to put in the ten thousand hours to realize your dream for yourself?

TWO: DETERMINATION

What is a "mindset"? It's a belief about your intelligence, personality, and abilities. Some people believe these traits can't be changed and that if you're born with a lot of talent and intelligence, you should be able to achieve a lot. Right?

In her groundbreaking work on achievement and success, Stanford University psychologist Carol Dweck explained that brains and talent alone do not lead to success, as some people believe. According to her book, *Mindset: The New Psychology of Success*, you also need a "growth mindset," a belief that you can develop your talents and abilities through determination, dedication, and drive.[17]

It helps to have talent and abilities but they won't carry you through your life without some work. Think of some of the most accomplished people you've read about or met—Michael Jordan, Pablo Picasso, Johann Sebastian Bach. If they hadn't studied and practiced, they wouldn't have accomplished much, or anything, despite their great talent. Once you harness the power of a success mindset, there's nothing you can't do. Edna Ferber created such a formidable character in Selina Peake De Jong, the protagonist of *So Big*, her 1924 novel. "Life has no weapons," the author said, "against a woman like that." [18]

But how do you develop and strengthen your success mindset? Focus on your successes instead of your failures. Think of what you can do and not on what you think you can't do. What success have you already achieved? Is there any reason to think you can't be successful again?

You can choose your response to any situation. If you have failed at something, for instance, you can choose to label yourself a failure or you can choose to say you failed *this time* and keep trying until you succeed. Failures are for learning, not stopping.

Sonia Sotomayor is the first Latina Supreme Court justice in U.S. history. Raised in poverty, she is an inspiration to anyone facing disease, discrimination, drugs, alcoholism, divorce, and her 3 ½-pack-a-day cigarette habit. When she was eight years old she developed diabetes, which taught her discipline and self-reliance. When she was nine her father died of alcoholism. She had to learn English. At times her challenges must have seemed insurmountable. But at a young age she dreamed of becoming a judge after watching an episode of *Perry Mason* on TV. She describes herself as stubborn and determined. When she got into fights on the playground to defend her brother, she always refused to concede defeat.

When her book *My Beloved World* was published, Sotomayor said, "I wanted my readers to be able to say, 'She's just like me, and if she can do it, I can do something, too.'" [19]

When you're discouraged and confused about what to do next, think about people with a lot of perseverance and ask yourself, *What would they do in this situation?* Think of someone you admire and imagine his or her response to the obstacle blocking you from your goal.

You can frame failures as opportunities from which to learn and grow or as threats that stop you dead in your tracks. When you're frightened and anxious, reframing can be difficult, but with practice you will begin to do it easily.

Visualize success. This process gets your brain to thinking you've already done something even if you haven't. It speeds up progress toward success. As Stephen Covey wrote in his book *The 7 Habits of Highly Effective People*, "Begin with the end in mind." [20]

THREE: DISCIPLINE

The dictionary defines self-discipline as "correction or regulation of oneself for the sake of improvement." It is an ability each of us has to motivate ourselves and stay on track. Research shows that self-discipline is like a muscle: it gets stronger the more you use it.

Self-discipline is an essential skill for reaching your goals because it provides the ingredient of self-control to follow through on your plans. When you experience setbacks, it's tempting to quit, but as your self-discipline grows, you're less likely to change your mind and give up.

Self-discipline is a combination of thoughts and actions. Due to the neuroplasticity of our brains, over time and with practice, we can change and restructure how we think and even feel about things. As you strengthen this valuable ability, you'll find it easier to overcome procrastination and resist distractions. Even if the road to your dreams is difficult, keep going because it will get easier and the knowledge that you can do it will grow.

An exceedingly common reason for failure to follow through is a lack of self-discipline. You may want to reach a goal but just aren't willing to force yourself to get there. Reaching a goal takes hard work. It's that simple. It'll get easier but it takes practice and willpower. Psychologist Phillippa Lally of University College London and her colleagues concluded from their research that it takes, on average, sixty-six days to develop a habit so that it becomes automatic, or done without thinking. The time period varies, of course, depending on the changes you're making.[21]

For instance, if you've ever wanted to lose weight, you know that you have to control your desire and habits when it comes to reaching for high-calorie snacks, second helpings, and other temptations that will sabotage your reaching your goal. You also probably have learned that if you want to make exercise a regular part of your life, you'll need to choose something you genuinely enjoy doing at a time that is realistic for you so you can more easily incorporate the practice into your life.

If you need to study for a licensing exam, meet the requirements for a college degree, or complete the steps to earn a certificate, you'll need self-discipline after the initial rush of enthusiasm has diminished.

Self-discipline helps you fulfill the promises you make to yourself and others.

Some simple actions you can take right now that will strengthen your self-discipline include:

- Exercising at least five days a week instead of sitting in front of the television
- Setting your alarm to get up in the morning
- Choosing a healthy snack over one that is too sugary and fattening
- Selecting a consistent time and place to study, read, or meditate and following through

A key to self-discipline is to think thoughts and choose actions that lead you toward your dreams and not away from them. For this reason, it's essential that you keep your dream in front of you to remind you how important it is and tell yourself you can achieve it.

You must also learn to control your desire for immediate gratification and instead focus on a greater future success, even if this means work and effort. You cannot lose weight, for instance, if you find yourself giving into a late night bowl of ice cream night after night. You will never achieve physical fitness if every time you need to exercise, you choose to sleep in or allow a television program or video game to distract you.

Diana Nyad's mantra for 2013 was "You don't like it. It's not doing well. Find a way." For thirty-five years this long-distance swimmer, journalist, and broadcaster has dreamed of swimming the shark-infested waters between Cuba and Florida without a shark cage. Having already earned a reputation as the greatest long-distance swimmer in the world in the 1970s, her dream of swimming from Cuba to Florida would not die. After four failed attempts and three decades, she succeeded on August 31, 2013.

The feat required tremendous self-discipline. For forty-nine hours Nyad endured strong winds and rough water. She sang lullabies to relax. In preparation, the sixty-four-year-old made hundreds of long and grueling training swims. In her previous attempts, she endured paralyzing jellyfish stings and an asthma attack and survived dangerous lightning and 45 mph winds. Yet she persevered.

How did Nyad find the will to keep going? She pictured herself walking onto the beach after her marathon swim. The dream kept her pushing Cuba back and pulling Florida toward her. She committed herself to reach for the stars, even if she failed. Pumping her fist when she finally walked ashore, she said, "We should never, ever give up." 22

NINE COMMON ROADBLOCKS TO SUCCESS

Your ability to persevere will require dedication and discipline to overcome obstacles that will always be in front of you. It's good to know ahead of time what they are. Forewarned is forearmed. Remaining committed to your dreams means knowing what's likely to drive you off course. Here are some of the most common roadblocks to achieving your goals in life:

COMPARING YOURSELF TO OTHERS

Dream your own dreams and pursue your own goals. If you don't have a goal you can too easily find yourself pursuing someone else's goal and even comparing your progress to theirs—an exercise sure to leave you frustrated, discouraged, and defeated. What's more, you're going to quit because you don't have someone else's skills, likes, or dislikes. For instance, you see that an acquaintance or friend is pursuing a college degree and you do likewise, although you don't know what to study. As with many misguided decisions, this one could be costly in terms of time and money.

LISTENING TO SABOTEURS

Be aware of those who might be threatened by your potential successes and undermine you lest you get ahead of them somehow. They will ridicule you and throw up roadblocks, hoping you will quit or fail. Has this ever happened to you? Maybe a coworker or even a friend is jealous of your accomplishments. It may not be that they want you to fail as much as they're afraid you'll succeed and leave them behind. Whatever the explanation, be aware of those who might put obstacles in your way.

BLAMING OTHERS FOR DERAILING YOUR EFFORTS

When you feel like quitting or you fail at something, one of the hardest things to do is point a finger at yourself and take responsibility. It's easier to say it was because of someone else that you failed. But blaming others will never teach you anything about yourself and where you need to work harder.

WAITING FOR CONDITIONS TO BE PERFECT

Conditions will never be perfect. Heading toward a goal will always require juggling parts of your life and making sacrifices. It may always seem that you don't have enough time, support, resources, money, help, and so forth. The list is endless. If you wait for the perfect alignment of the stars or whatever sign you expect, you'll never start. If your goals are important enough to you, you'll need to look at your current circumstances and say, "I will need to carve out a space in my life for this goal. That may mean letting go of something else because my resources are finite." The process is one of discerning what is most meaningful to you and prioritizing your goals.

FEELING OVERWHELMED BY THE JOB AHEAD OF YOU

Reaching the top of an immensely high mountain will always seem daunting and impossible. That's when you have to remind yourself that you can't do it all at once and that you have to take the journey one step at a time. Every journey truly does start with a first step. Every day we're surrounded by stories about people who've lost everything but their lives. As they stand in the midst of ruin and wreckage, they proclaim they're going to start over and, brick by brick, rebuild their lives. Such a response is common. Remember Scarlett O'Hara in the last line of *Gone with the Wind* when she said, "After all, tomorrow is another day."

BEING HAUNTED BY YOUR PRIOR FAILURES

It's easy to be burdened with the memory of your failures. Each time you fail it may reinforce the belief that you are a failure. A vicious cycle is created by such thinking. Before you quit trying because everything you do seems futile, the cycle has to be interrupted. Success will lead to more success. Everyone fails and everyone fails a lot. It's failure that helps us learn and grow stronger. If you aren't willing to make a mistake, then you'll have no opportunities to grow. It's OK to fail. Even better, it's good to fail. Failing doesn't make you a failure. But fearing failure can make you timid and cautious, two qualities that won't get you anywhere.

WORRYING ABOUT THINGS THAT MIGHT HAPPEN

Before taking a risk, it's easy to start dwelling on things that could go wrong. If you let such thoughts run unchecked, you'll quickly talk yourself out of heading toward a goal. Giving up is difficult to do when you're calculating your risk. You want to figure out how much time and money you can afford to lose before you call it quits. You have to strike a balance, however, between being stopped by the risks and going overboard and disregarding potential pitfalls.

LETTING THINGS DISTRACT YOU

You may really want to start moving toward an important goal. But every time you start, something else seems more important. You head toward the goal in fits and starts, ultimately gasping and sputtering your way to a standstill because your initial momentum is lost.

ALLOWING YOUR FEELINGS TO DICTATE YOUR ACTIONS

When you start something new, it's normal to feel fear, impatience, discouragement, frustration, and a whole host of other negative emotions. These feelings become a problem only when they start to occupy most of your time and direct your actions. It won't take much to talk you out of your goals if you're consumed with fear of failure. Gen. George Patton said, "Never take counsel of your fears."

WHEN YOU NEED INSPIRATION

Dreams, determination, dedication, and effort are required for success. When your spirits are flagging, however, find predictable sources of inspiration to help you get back up and move forward. Biographies and autobiographies of people with great determination are excellent for giving you a shot in the arm when you're discouraged. Novels, essays, poetry, and children's stories can give you a much needed boost, too. Compile your own library of music that reliably energizes you and movies that inspire and fill you with hope.

BRIEF BIOGRAPHIES OF INSPIRATION

Stephen Hawking, a brilliant theoretical physicist, has suffered from amyotrophic lateral sclerosis (ALS) for almost fifty years. In all that time neither his purpose nor perseverance has wavered. He has said, "It is no good getting furious if you get stuck. What I do is keep thinking about the problem but work on something else. Sometimes it is years before I see the way forward. In the case of information loss and black holes, it was twenty-nine years."

Superman star Christopher Reeve lived nine years as a quadriplegic after a horse riding accident left him paralyzed. His courage and determination are well known. He said, "Don't give up. Don't lose hope. Don't sell out." After his accident he continued to live with purpose and perseverance, wrote, directed, and acted in movies, and never gave up his goal of regaining the ability to move again.

Leo Tolstoy, author of *War and Peace* and *Anna Karenina*, flunked out of college and was described as both unable and unwilling to learn. Many now consider him the world's greatest novelist.

After the *Kansas City Star* fired Walt Disney for lack of creativity, he might have given up then and there. He also was forced to declare bankruptcy several times. Many of us wouldn't have blamed him for quitting after these multiple failures. But he continued to persevere and built Disneyland and Disney World—the most famous theme parks in the world.

Rita Levi-Montalcini was a Jewish biologist who went underground and survived World War II in Florence until Allied forces liberated the city. She won the Nobel Prize in Medicine in 1986. During the war she created a makeshift lab in her bedroom where she studied cell growth. Even though the primitive conditions were far from perfect, she wouldn't quit.

There are many stories of successful musicians who overcame criticism that easily could have dissuaded them from pursuing their dreams and instead steered them in a different direction. In refusing The Beatles a recording contract, Decca Records and Columbia Records said, "We don't like their sound. Groups of guitars are on their way out." After one performance, Elvis Presley was told by the manager of the Grand Ole Opry, "You ain't goin' nowhere, son. You ought to go back to drivin' a truck." Ludwig van Beethoven was told by his teacher that he handled the violin awkwardly and that he was "hopeless as a composer." Even so, he wrote five of his greatest symphonies while completely deaf. He could have easily given up when told that he didn't have the talent to compose music.

FIVE KEY POINTS
ABOUT PERSEVERANCE

1. Be prepared to work hard if you hope to succeed. Some say you'll need to put in ten thousand hours, or about ten years, of dedicated practice to achieve mastery.

2. Remember that perseverance without purpose is pointless.

3. Be willing to fail. In fact, try to fail. Push yourself beyond your current abilities.

4. Recognize that in all of history, science, and every imaginable pursuit, this simple formula has led to greatness: dreams and determination plus drive and effort lead to success.

5. The world will always need dreamers, but dreamers must also be doers. That's where determination and drive come in. In order to succeed you also need grit, or staying power. You need to be relentless in the pursuit of your dreams.

Consider how children learn to ride a bicycle. They fall down, get up, and fall down again, but they don't quit. Each time they ride a little better and regain excitement and motivation. As adults, we need to approach our dreams in the same way. Learning to ride a bike requires a dream of being able to pedal independently down the road. Like many dreams, it requires a great deal of determination and discipline to achieve.

Children are great role models for us because every time they get down the road a little farther, still upright and seated, they're delighted with themselves. They don't stop when they learn to ride with training wheels, either. We could all stand to follow their lead. So take some risks. Challenge yourself. Fall down. Get up again. That's what perseverance is, and it will strengthen your resilience.

NOTES

1. Vidya Chari, "Dr. Paul Stoltz Discusses How to Improve Our Reactions to Adversity," *Harker News*, Oct. 27, 2011, http://news.harker.org/dr-paul-stoltz-discusses-how-to-improve-our-reactions-to-adversity/ (accessed Nov. 2011).

2. Angela Duckworth, Christopher Peterson, Michael Matthews, and Dennis Kelly, "Grit: perseverance and passion for long term goals," *Journal of Personality and Social Psychology,* vol. 92 (2007): 1087-101.

3. Elizabeth J. Colerick, "Stamina in Later Life," *Social Science and Medicine,* vol. 21 (1985): 997-1006.

4. Craig Larson, "Learning to Get Back Up," *Afterhours Inspirational Stories,* http://www.inspirationalstories.com/2/205.html (accessed Sept. 2012).

5. Susan Olp, "Author Patsy Clairmont Makes Women Laugh," *Billings Gazette,* Apr. 9, 2011, http://billingsgazette.com/lifestyles/faith-and-values/religion/clairmont-a-woman-of-faith-shares-her-story-at-conference/article_71a21ae4-8f1f-54b6-8e02-98857a1bc47c.html (accessed Apr. 2011).

6. "Michael Phelps Biography," *A&E Networks,* http://www.biography.com/people/michael-phelps-345192 (accessed July 2013).

7. "Wilma Rudolph Biography," *A&E Networks,* http://www.biography.com/people/wilma-rudolph-9466552 (accessed Mar. 2011).

8. "Abraham Lincoln," *Our Presidents,* http://www.whitehouse.gov/about/presidents/abrahamlincoln (accessed July 2013).

9. "Seuss," *Seussville,* http://www.seussville.com/author/SeussBio.pdf (accessed July 2013).

10. "Winston Churchill Biography," *A&E Networks,* http://www.biography.com/people/winston-churchill-9248164?page=1 (accessed July 2013).

11. "Colonel Harland Sanders Biography," *A&E Networks,* http://www.biography.com/people/colonel-harland-sanders-12353545 (accessed 2013).

12. Erin Dunne, Carsten Wrosch and Gregory Miller, "Goal Disengagement, Functional Disability, and Depressive Symptoms In Old Age," *Health and Psychology,* vol. 30 (2011): 763-70.

13. Carsten Wrosch, Michael Scheier, Gregory Miller, Richard Schulz, and Charles Carver, "Adaptive Self-Regulation of Unattainable Goals: Goal Dis-

engagement, Goal Reengagement, and Subjective Well-Being," *Personality and Social Psychology Bulletin*, vol. 29 (2003): 494-508.

14. Gregory Miller and Carsten Wrosch, "You've Gotta Know When to Fold 'Em," *Psychological Science,* vol. 18 (2007): 773-77.

15. "Sean Swarner: First Cancer Survivor to Summit Everest," *Premiere Speakers,* http://premierespeakers.com/sean_swarner (accessed July 2013).

16. "Michael Dell Biography," *A&E Networks,* http://www.biography.com/people/michael-dell-9542199?page=2 (accessed Oct. 2013).

17. Carol S. Dweck, *Mindset: The New Psychology of Success* (New York: Ballantine Books, 2006).

18. Edna Ferber, *So Big* (New York: HarperCollins Publishers, 1984).

19. Emily Wilson, "Sotomayor – From the Bronx to the Bench," *Women's Media Center,* Feb. 21, 2013, http://www.womensmediacenter.com/feature/entry/sotomayorfrom-the-bronx-to-the-bench (accessed Oct. 2013).

20. Stephen R. Covey, *The 7 Habits of Highly Effective People: Powerful Lessons in Personal Change* (New York: Simon and Schuster, 1989).

21. Philippa Lally, Cornelia van Jaarsveld, Henry Potts and Jane Wardle, "How Are Habits Formed: Modeling Habit Formation In the Real World," *European Journal of Social Psychology*, vol. 16 (2009):674.

22. Matt Sloane, Jason Hanna, and Dana Ford, "Never, ever give up:" Diana Nyad completes historic Cuba-to-Florida swim," *CNN,* Sept. 3, 2013, http://www.cnn.com/2013/09/02/world/americas/diana-nyad-cuba-florida-swim/index.html (accessed Oct. 2013).

CHAPTER 3: EQUANIMITY

"You have power over your mind, not outside events. Realize this and you will find strength."

—Marcus Aurelius

IN THIS CHAPTER you will learn why equanimity is important as well as:

- Nine threats to equanimity
- Five ways to a balanced perspective on your life
- Five key points about equanimity

《《 》》

WHEN I WAS growing up, I had a friend whose mom reacted to everything in the same way. If she burned the casserole she would slap her forehead with her palm and scream, "Oh my God, this is terrible!" If someone died, same reaction. Every event was the worst thing that could happen and she lived her life ricocheting among events like she was traveling through a pinball machine. She was exhausting to be around. Not once did I see her pause, take a deep breath, and consider her response before exploding in a shower of expletives.

There's no question life can be difficult. Every day you and I have to deal with stressful demands, people, and a lot of circumstances beyond our control. Everything is constantly changing around us. Conflicts, crises, and occasional chaos are inevitable. Stress is here to stay. For many of us, this reality is unsettling. We'd like to have more control but we can't always control life events. The more resilient we are, however, the more likely it is we can control our response to what happens. As Robert Louis Stevenson, author of *Treasure Island*, said, "Life is not a matter of having good cards, but of playing a poor hand well."

Sometimes resilient people make it look easy. They just seem to know how to manage their stress. They appear balanced, poised, and in control of themselves when people around them are throwing up their hands and running in circles crying, "I'm doomed!"

Despite current adversities, resilient people recognize there's still hope in the midst of difficulty. The stock market, for example, has caused no end of consternation and anxiety. A resilient individual, however, will look at the history of the stock market, reflect on its volatility, and conclude that while it may be dropping now, it most likely will go up again.

Jacqueline Kennedy Onassis, when reviewing her remarkable life, said this: "I have been through a lot and have suffered a great deal. But I have had lots of happy moments, as well. Every moment one lives is different from the other. The good, the bad, hardship, the joy, the tragedy, love, and happiness are all interwoven into one single, indescribable whole that is called life. You cannot separate the good from the bad. And perhaps there is no need to do so, either."

Donald Trump was dealt a bad hand. When the real estate market declined in 1990, he was personally almost $900 million in debt. But he didn't break his stride. He learned from his mistakes, and became one of the most financially successful men in the world. "What separates the winners from the losers," he said, "is how a person reacts to each new twist of fate."

Life's difficulties come in different sizes and shapes. Some are relatively small and inconsequential, such as being stuck in traffic or getting a parking ticket. Others are more serious. Maybe your company is making cutbacks and you're afraid you could be next. Or maybe you've been diagnosed with a life-threatening illness or you've lost someone you love through death, separation, or divorce.

Kristina Anderson decided to enter the 2013 Miss Arizona USA Pageant after being diagnosed with ovarian cancer. After four rounds of chemotherapy that left her weak and exhausted, she said, "I have good days and bad days. I try to stay positive and just be at peace with myself because it is challenging to know what's in front of me." She wears scarves to cover her hair loss and chooses dresses that cover the permanent port above her heart. She went on to say, "We all face challenges, but don't let it get you down." [1]

Steven Callahan was crossing the Atlantic Ocean in his sailboat when he unexpectedly collided with a whale and his boat sank to the bottom of the ocean. He managed to get into his life raft, although it was leaking and threatened to take him to the bottom of the ocean, too. Worn out, starving, attacked by sharks, and dangerously dehydrated, he felt little hope of rescue as he drifted in the middle of the ocean at the mercy of the weather and well outside the shipping lanes. How did he respond? In his book, *Adrift: 76 Days Lost at Sea,* Callahan wrote that he believed he would survive because he compared his situation with those of other survivors and concluded he was fortunate. Seventy-six days later, he was rescued by fishermen.[2]

How would you have responded? We don't always know how we'd respond until the unthinkable happens, but we can practice our response and learn from others. Steven Callahan was able to stay levelheaded and not panic. He maintained an optimistic outlook and planned on surviving. He remained centered and calm and maintained a balanced perspective on his situation, which wasn't all good or all bad. In the years following his ordeal, his experience didn't prevent him from continuing to sail.

Think of the following scenarios that could happen in your life. Each will elicit a response. But what response? What would you do?

- You have a major presentation to give in three minutes to two hundred people, and you suddenly realize you left your briefcase with the flash drive and your hard copies at home.

- You're in your car and need to make a phone call that could change your life, but your cell phone has run out of power and your charger is at home.

- You're supposed to be at your child's graduation from college in a faraway city, but all flights are grounded due to bad weather and, assuming you can get there at all, you realize you're going to be quite late.

- You're right on time to interview for a job that you really want and need, but a quick glance at your reflection in the elevator reveals a smear of mustard on the front of your shirt.

- You're already late for an early-morning meeting with your boss when you finally find the only parking place for blocks, but another driver cuts in front of you and nabs it.

Did you respond to any of the above situations with fear, uncertainty, anxiety, frustration, dismay, or even anger? If you did, you aren't alone. Some people feel actual pain when they're stressed because they tense up their shoulders and neck and end up with headaches, jaw pain, or upset stomachs. Maybe you would have felt anger. It's not uncommon to have a short fuse when you feel stressed. Do you ever start arguments about things that aren't even related to what's bothering you? For instance, have you ever had a bad day at work and taken it out on the drivers in the next lane by honking your horn and yelling at them? Another common response is to be like my friend's mom and think only about the worst possible outcome. No matter what happened to her, she felt as if the end of the world was near.

Such feelings can lead to actions you might later regret. For instance, when someone takes your parking place, have you ever jumped out of your car to tell him or her a thing or two, or at least rolled down the window and shouted? People have been beaten up and even shot for that kind of response. Have you ever vented your emotions at an airline employee when your plane was grounded? Have you ever said, "This is the end. My life is ruined." Or maybe you've taken actions that affect your health such as overeating, drinking too much, exercising too little, or smoking. Even if you haven't smoked in years, a cigarette may seem like a perfect temporary solution.

A few weeks ago I was driving down the highway and approached a train crossing. The red lights began blinking and the arms came down slowly as a freight train hauling grain and oil accelerated down the track. Suddenly a man behind me pulled his car into the left-hand lane, charged the tracks, and rocketed between the barriers. The train whistle shrieked as the engineer gave an urgent warning to clear the tracks. The driver made it through with mere inches to spare. Two seconds later, he would have been mangled wreckage pushed down the track. What was so important to that driver that he chose to risk his life to cross the tracks?

Equanimity would have served him well! No matter what happens, we can choose to respond in healthy ways. To respond otherwise invites negative, if not tragic, outcomes. How you respond will make the difference between whether you stay healthy and balanced and succeed or veer off course and fail. Events may control you, but only if you let them. Stress doesn't just go away. Steven Callahan couldn't close his eyes and hope the sharks disappeared, and we can't wish away our difficult circumstances. But we can pay attention to how we respond to perceived stress and learn to cope.

How we deal with stress will make the difference between whether we succeed or fail, maintain or regain health or become ill, and sometimes whether we live or die. We are not powerless. Even Viktor Frankl, a prisoner in a World War II concentration camp who had no control over whether Nazis killed him, realized he wasn't powerless. He said, "Everything can be taken from a man or a woman but one thing: the last of the human freedoms—to choose one's attitude in any given set of circumstances, to choose one's own way." [3]

I have a friend and colleague who is working full time in a job that's increasingly stressful. She describes her supervisor as an unreasonable, unfair, and untrustworthy woman who steals credit from others to make herself look good. My friend goes to work because she needs health insurance for her family. Yet she dreads every day and is chronically depressed. She is seriously overweight, doesn't exercise, has high blood pressure, and takes antidepressants. Rarely does she sleep well. In short, she's at great risk for heart disease and diabetes. She needs to manage her stress and make changes that bring her life back into balance. Once she can do this, she'll be in a better position to make decisions that will improve her situation. Sometimes we have to "even out" our strong emotions before we can make good decisions on how to proceed in our lives.

IS YOUR LIFE BALANCED?

Resilient people understand that life is a mixture of good and bad. Some days go well. Others leave you discouraged and tired. It's unrealistic to think you'll be content all the time. No one is. But a quick review of the differences between a balanced life and an off-kilter one will help you see where you fit. Think about stressors in your life. How do you see yourself with respect to your response?

Balanced	Unbalanced
Cool, calm, and collected	Agitated and anxious
This too shall pass	It'll be like this forever
Have a sense of humor	Humorless
Takes things in stride	Easily knocked off-kilter
Balanced perspective	Skewed perspective
Flexible	Rigid
Looks forward and considers the possibilities	Looks backward and regrets the past

WHY IS EQUANIMITY IMPORTANT?

Difficulties in life are unavoidable. But the real issue isn't whether we can avoid them as much as what we do when they happen. The more resilient we are, the better we adapt positively and recover without becoming emotionally and physically ill.

In order for something to become stressful, we first have to recognize it's a problem for us. The same event may be stressful to me but not to you. For instance, about one in three people is anxious about flying. That means on any given flight some people will experience stress while others won't. Obviously, the problem isn't flying but rather the response passengers have to flying. There will be many different responses. The mind is a most powerful place. At the extreme ends are those who grip the armrest in terror and those who can't wait to buckle up and take off. Between them are a range of people on a continuum of stress.

Not all stress is bad. Positive stress, called "eustress," includes getting a new job, getting married, having a baby, and taking a vacation. Negative stress, often referred to as "distress," results in the stress response. A prolonged stress response can result in physical illness, depression, and absenteeism at work.

Each of us experiences stress every day. Often our stress falls into one of two categories: acute or chronic. Acute stress is immediate and intense. You know what it is if you've ever had a car accident or even a close call. Perhaps you were walking alone along a dark street and a stranger approached you. Remember how your heartbeat quickened and you became hyper alert? That's acute stress. If you've ever jumped out of an airplane or given a performance in front of many people, you may have experienced the same heightened sensations. This response is the result of a challenge or significant or scary event. By itself, a single acute episode of stress causes no long-lasting problems. Less than 10 percent of people may be afflicted with post-traumatic stress disorder from such an episode. A rare few may experience health problems, such as a heart attack.

Chronic stress, on the other hand, often comprises many stressors that accumulate and don't go away. Month after month, you're weighed down by difficulties. You awaken at night and slog through painful, exhausting days. Chronic stressors include unrewarding work, problems with coworkers or your boss, health concerns such as a chronic illness or lengthy treatment, relationship problems, loneliness and isolation, neighborhood crime, pollution, and the constant threat of war, economic ruin, and terrorism that bombard us all the time. Unremitting stress can lead to health problems including anxiety and depression, headaches, digestive problems, backaches, insomnia, heart disease, excessive use of alcohol or other drugs, and many other long-lasting problems.

HOW YOU RESPOND TO STRESS

When you experience stress, your brain goes to work, particularly three parts of it—the prefrontal cortex, amygdala, and hippocampus. Each of these three critical brain areas is densely packed with stress receptors that process all of the stress you perceive.

1. If there's a structure in the brain that supports a neurobiological basis for resilience, it's the prefrontal cortex. It receives and integrates all the information that enters the limbic system. The prefrontal cortex performs many extraordinary and complex functions such as deciding what you're going to eat for lunch and daydreaming about the meaning of life. It integrates experiences from your past and present, thoughts about your future, and helps

you make sense of who you are. The prefrontal cortex also helps you calm down and separate out what's truly threatening from what is not. It's the brain's executive command and control center and is responsible for your actions after you process information. Sometimes it's called the "gatekeeper of attention."

2. Deep inside the limbic system of the human brain is the amygdala, the brain's emotional switchboard that signals the rest of your brain and nervous system to respond. The amygdala is working day and night to detect danger. Once it senses a threat, it triggers the hypothalamic-pituitary-adrenal (HPA) axis to release the hormone cortisol, which is distributed throughout your body and prepares you to act, defend, and cope with a situation. Cortisol helps activate the famous "fight or flight" response. If a car comes careening around the corner just as you step off the curb, your amygdala sends an alarm that yells, "Get out of the way now!"

3. The hippocampus, which plays a critical role in forming new memories, is particularly susceptible to stress. There's evidence that chronic severe stress that results in high levels of cortisol in the bloodstream has two deleterious results. First, these levels slow the growth of new neurons. Second, they cause atrophy of dendrites in some cells in the hippocampus, which actually limits the ability to form new memories.

Integral to the prefrontal cortex is the Autonomic Nervous System (ANS). Without conscious thought on our part, it automatically regulates our heart rate, breathing, and digestive processes. The ANS is essential to our resilience capacity for equanimity because it keeps us physiologically calm. If we fear harm or hear the words "You're fired" or "I want a divorce," the sympathetic branch of the ANS is automatically set in motion. This branch, called the Sympathetic Nervous System (SNS), stimulates our heart rate and breathing and we become alarmed. We may even experience panic, agitation, and anxiety. In order to calm down this system, we need to activate the Parasympathetic Nervous System (PNS) to bring us back to a state of calm reflection and relaxation.

If stress becomes chronic, this hyperactivity begins to physically change the brain and have damaging effects on mental health. Too much prolonged stress in your life will cause a decline in your ability to process additional sensory information as it arrives. You will be too distracted to realize you're putting yourself in danger on a busy street. Over time, this process can cause physiological changes in the brain that can reduce or even destroy its neuroplasticity.

Chemical changes in your brain under stress

When you become stressed, a complex chain of events occurs in your endocrine system. Your body releases norepinephrine, which stimulates the HPA axis, which in turn signals the pituitary gland and then the adrenal cortex. Cortisol is then released directly into the bloodstream. When too much cortisol is circulating, T-helper cells are suppressed, which is a problem. Such cells reduce immune protection and leave you very vulnerable to infection and disease.

When the stress response system stays "on," even when you're no longer in imminent danger, the body is flooded with excess hormones, blood pressure rises, and blood sugar levels become elevated. Not good.

Neurotransmitters and hormones involved in the stress response include norepinephrine, serotonin, dopamine, and cortisol. Norepinephrine directly increases heart rate, releases glucose for energy, increases the brain's oxygen supply, and increases blood flow to the skeletal muscles. You can quickly see how critical this neurotransmitter is to responding to immediate dangers.

Serotonin is known as the "well-being" chemical in your brain and regulates your mood, as well as sleep and appetite. People with lower levels of serotonin levels do not deal with stress as well. Exercise increases serotonin and this is why exercise is usually recommended when you're feeling stressed.

Dopamine regulates your pleasure/reward system. Dopamine needs to be balanced because too much can cause risky behaviors or cravings and lead to addictions and too little may cause depression. When dopamine is depleted, the result is memory loss, poor concentration, and inadequate blood flow to the brain. Some even suggest that depletion of dopamine creates an internal body environment perfect for Alzheimer's disease, Parkinson's disease, heart disease, cancer, and other autoimmune disorders.

Cortisol is an important hormone secreted by the adrenal glands right above your kidneys. It helps you metabolize glucose, regulates your blood pressure, releases insulin, and serves important roles in immune function and the inflammatory response. A quick burst at a time of stress is protective and good. But if you're unable to calm down your stress response and cortisol continues to remain at high levels, you might experience some of the following outcomes:

- Impaired cognitive performance
- Suppressed thyroid function
- Blood sugar imbalances
- Decreased bone density
- Decreased muscle tissue
- Higher blood pressure
- Lowered immunity
- Increased abdominal fat

The stress response described above can be shut down or slowed down with the release of another hormone called oxytocin. According to neuroscientists, whenever you feel safe, secure, and loved, your brain releases oxytocin, which is the antidote to cortisol and the urge to fight or flee. Once you're calm again, you can pause and reflect and choose how to respond to whatever situation you encounter next.

The above neurochemical process may be one way of explaining how, as you learn to build and strengthen equanimity, your ability to respond with resilience grows. If you can learn ways to increase your levels of oxytocin, for instance, you can better control your panic and anxiety.

Another important part of equanimity is learning to perceive events as not stressful or less stressful in the first place, thus preempting the whole cycle of an activated amygdala and release of cortisol, leading to a SNS response. In other words, if you can help others feel safe, secure, cherished, and loved before the stressful event, they'll be less likely to respond with a burst of cortisol followed by panic.

How does the prefrontal cortex manage to bypass the stress response? It seems the cerebral cortex can send neuronal fibers to the amygdala that carry GABA (gamma-aminobutyric acid), which effectively quashes the fear response in the amygdala. Thus an individual with more equanimity will be less reactive to perceived stress.

The late Alan Marlatt introduced S.O.B.E.R., an approach in recovery programs that applies an understanding of neurobiology to the building and strengthening of equanimity. He explained it as follows.

When faced with something that elicits the stress response, put the following behaviors into motion:

S   Stop and just pause, wherever you are. Take a few seconds, count to ten, and breathe to give yourself time to process information coming in.

O   Observe what is happening in your body and mind. Dr. Marlatt recommended the practice of mindfulness to pay attention to what's happening in your mind and body without reacting, running, or judging. Doing this breaks what might otherwise be an automatic and perhaps knee-jerk reaction.

B   Breathe and bring focus to the breath as an "anchor." Breathe deeply and calm your nervous system. The practice will return your heart and breathing rates to a calm state.

E   Expand awareness to your whole body and surroundings. Widen your perspective. In other words, detach yourself from a typical response and consider other possible things you can do, think, and feel. You can choose to respond differently. You can choose whatever response you want.

R   Respond mindfully rather than automatically or in old ways that don't relieve stress. Choose a response to which you have given conscious thought and respond from that place of thoughtfulness and wisdom.[4]

In summary, unrelieved stress feels terrible and has very negative consequences. It can lead to increases in cortisol and other stress hormones and in turn to chronic inflammation, which can negatively impact the skin as well as the cardiovascular, endocrine, and digestive systems. Such a negative cascade of biological response can leave the body susceptible to infections as well as diseases such as rheumatoid arthritis and cancer. The cascade also can lead to psychological problems related to anxiety, agitation, anger, attention deficit, learning difficulties, depression, sleep disturbances, and permanent memory loss.

Stress can lead to poor eating habits and seems to raise glucose levels in people with Type 2 diabetes. Stress leads to tension and migraine headaches, irritable bowel syndrome, and heartburn. It makes ulcers worse. Other symptoms include poor sleep, muscle tension, fatigue, teeth grinding, and the inability to concentrate. Stress also can lead to anxiety, loss of interest in life, social withdrawal, and loss of sex drive.

Stress-associated outcomes are serious, but you can learn to manage your response to perceived stress and diminish the probability of unhealthy outcomes. If you do, you will feel better, and there's even evidence to suggest that learning to handle difficulties in a more balanced way can actually improve your health.

To have equanimity is to have a balanced perspective and an even disposition in the face of unavoidable stress. As the English said in World War II, "Keep calm and carry on." Resilient people experience stress like everyone else, but they have learned to pause and think before acting. In this way, stress does not get the upper hand.

NINE THREATS TO LIVING A BALANCED LIFE

You have control over what you think and how you feel even though at times it may not seem like you do. If you lose your job, for instance, you may think you'll never get another one or you can see the loss as an opportunity to find an even better job. You can choose to feel defeated and hopeless or you can choose to feel challenged and optimistic. It's up to you. But whatever response you choose will have a profound impact on whether you achieve your life goals.

People who are able to maintain a balanced view will not get mired down with unhealthy thoughts, feelings, or behaviors. If they do, the setback usually is temporary. These people also will manage their stress better, which will result in better emotional and physical health.

Following are nine common threats to a balanced and healthy interpretation of events in your life.

ONE: HAVING A DISTORTED PERSPECTIVE

Do you frequently blow things out of proportion? When something goes wrong, do you frequently feel your life is ruined? Do problems seem permanent to you? If you answered yes to any of these questions, you may have a distorted perspective. For instance, if you fail an exam or do poorly in a job interview, do you think the end of the world is near? If you could travel ahead in time even a few weeks, you would see this seemingly terrible event shrink into proper perspective. You would find that in the grand scheme of things such events lose their importance. In time they actually will be forgotten. If you find yourself going from one crisis to another, consider that you're making mountains out of molehills and that you have the ability to "de-catastrophize" things and live a much more peaceful life.

TWO: NOT TAKING THINGS IN STRIDE

During a steeplechase event, horses jump over fences. If all goes well, a horse will jump over every fence without breaking his stride or slowing down. In the same way, when we come up against setbacks and obstacles, we can learn to take them in stride. Or we can stumble, balk, look for an opening in the hedge, or find an excuse to quit. For instance, if you lose a sale, or if your business is on the brink of failure, or you forget an important appointment, you probably will be discouraged or upset. But if you let this defeat slow you down or stop you, you won't be able to achieve success.

THREE: FALLING PREY TO PESSIMISM

You know that optimists generally look to the future in a positive way and think about how they can make lemonade out of lemons, while pessimists are more likely to think about all the things that might go wrong. If you were to ask an optimist to describe pessimists, she'd likely say they're down on everything and eager to pour cold water on dreams. The pessimist, in contrast, is likely to say that optimists are not realistic about what might really happen.

Which way is better? Some people prefer optimistic thinking because it encourages visions of a positive outcome. Martin Seligman, who directs the University of Pennsylvania's Positive Psychology Center, explains that unrealistic optimism can prevent you from altering your course to swerve away from problems. An unrealistic optimist believes he or she is more likely to experience favorable outcomes than is actually the case.

Other people prefer a pessimistic approach because it helps protect them when things go wrong, which sometimes happens. A downside is that pessimists tend to see nothing but problems ahead. They also are more likely to believe that negative outcomes are their fault and that positive outcomes are a fluke that had nothing to do with them. Unfortunately, they also believe that such beliefs can't be altered, even by reality.

Is pessimism a threat to equanimity? It depends on what works for you. Several researchers led by Abigail Hazlett, a social psychologist at Northwestern University, reported that pessimists were more motivated to do better when thinking in negative ways while optimists did better when thinking in positive ways. Should we try to be one way or the other? According to this research, each approach has its place. It depends on what works best in balancing your expectations and preparing for possible outcomes.[5]

In general, most would say it's more important to maintain an optimistic outlook and that pessimists expect to fail. As Woody Allen once wrote, "I don't see the glass as half empty. I see it as half full—of poison." Pessimists are convinced that nothing will turn out well. They want to reach their goals, but when they think about the difficulties entailed, they decide failure is inevitable and don't bother.

Perhaps the best approach is realistic optimism, or a tendency to be cautiously hopeful of a favorable outcome. Realistic optimists do whatever they can to bring about desired results. But they don't indulge in magical thinking that everything will turn out OK, particularly if they don't have full knowledge of what needs to happen for a result to be desirable.

FOUR: INSISTING ON MY WAY OR THE HIGHWAY

Some people get a point of view into their heads and are unwilling or unable to consider alternative views or solutions to a problem. They not only cling tightly to their preconceptions but ferociously defend them to the exclusion of all other interpretations. This narrow-mindedness seriously limits their options and sabotages their ability to collaborate with others to come up with better solutions. In general, having strong opinions and a mind that changes very slowly are good traits that contribute to perseverance. But when people's thinking is rigid and immovable, they have a problem. When confronted with threats or difficulties, they're unable to adapt and can't move in any direction, making progress impossible and failure inevitable.

If you find yourself thinking you're right and everyone else is wrong, get outside yourself. Ask others for their advice and opinions. Consider their responses carefully and with an open mind. Dare to be wrong, and admit it to others when you are. Take advice when it's good and give credit where it's due. Your success rate will go up, and people's respect for you will grow.

FIVE: BORROWING TROUBLE

People who try to peer into the future and terrify themselves with potential pitfalls and setbacks are "borrowing trouble," as the old adage says. These people can't move forward with confidence or enthusiasm. So they stay where they are, wringing their hands, frozen in their tracks from the fear of everything that possibly could go wrong. Often they're wasting time and energy worrying about what could happen. As Mark Twain wrote, "I am an old man and have known a great many troubles, but most of them never happened." While it's not good to suppress the part of you that points out possible problems (it's trying to help), keep it in its place. Focus on the big picture and what you're trying to accomplish. Take heed of all the things that could go wrong, but plan well so they don't. You can get where you're going only if you keep your head up and persevere.

It turns out, we often dwell more on what might happen or did happen than what didn't. In his book *Stumbling on Happiness*[6] Daniel Gilbert, a Harvard University psychology professor, exemplifies the point using the scenario of a pigeon who poops on a person. Let's say you walk to work under a bridge every day and one day a pigeon poops on your head. You're more likely to think about the one time the pigeon's aim was accurate than the hundreds of times it may have missed you. We tend to do that in all of life.

SIX: TAKING YOURSELF TOO SERIOUSLY

Many people are unable to recognize the humorous aspects of their lives. They take themselves and their lives very seriously. Some things in life, of course, are not funny, but much of what happens is hilarious, if you look at it objectively. Humor and laughter have been proven to be good for mental and physical health. Laughing at yourself occasionally provides good release from stress and frustration. People who can't laugh at the absurdities in their own lives often are miserable, grumpy, thin-skinned, and uptight. They take everything to heart and get no relief.

SEVEN: LETTING REGRETS RUIN YOUR LIFE

Everyone has regrets from their past. Maybe they didn't finish school, stayed in a job they didn't like, made bad decisions about relationships, or missed lucrative financial opportunities. Regrets can lead to feelings of remorse, disappointment, and discouragement, and there's nothing wrong with feeling any of those emotions. It's problematic, however, when people stay stuck in their past and mentally replay their failures to the point their agony prevents them from enjoying the present or planning for the future. Sometimes they even mistakenly turn to alcohol or other drugs to lessen the pain.

EIGHT: FORGETTING TO COUNT YOUR BLESSINGS

People who focus on the negative parts of their life and don't count their blessings are not as healthy as those who do. Their negative view actually does them physical harm. Research shows that people who practice gratitude for the good things in life have more life satisfaction and get better sleep than those who focus on the bad. They also may have fewer illnesses, such as heart disease.

NINE: NOT PICKING YOUR BATTLES CAREFULLY

Some people argue about everything as if their lives depended on it. They defend every point and every issue, no matter how trivial. They give in to the passion of the moment with little thought to the future.

If they feel victimized, they seek revenge. If they've been treated rudely, they do their best to get even. They want an eye for every eye, and a tooth for every tooth.

Remember that some battles don't need to be fought at all. Sometimes losing a battle wins the war. Instead of spending your time and energy trying to win every disagreement, decide if the outcome is worth the effort. Be willing to put up with some injustice. Focus on those issues that are strategically important to you and forget the rest.

FIVE WAYS TO EQUANIMITY

How do people regain and maintain mental calmness and composure when adversity strikes or hardships go on for months or years at a time? How do they minimize the threats to their equanimity? How do they keep their emotional balance in a world that is constantly changing around them? There's no end to strategies aimed at minimizing the negative effects of stress and there's no universally effective technique. Each of us is different and our lives are different. Our responses to stress and adversity are different, too. What's important is that you find what works for you and use it daily.

If you're in the midst of trauma or are experiencing chronic unremitting stress—the kind that comes from relationship problems, caregiving, chronic illness, and a job that's wearing you down with demands and pressures—you can employ five basic strategies to achieve and strengthen your equanimity.

ONE: STRIVE FOR A BALANCED PERSPECTIVE

The Horseshoe Hills in Manhattan, Montana are a set of rounded hills, all about the same height, that cover thousands of acres. They border a vast wilderness area, so losing your bearings there can be deadly. Before the days of GPS, hunters and hikers frequently became lost in these hills because they couldn't climb to higher ground to look around and see where they were. There is no higher hill to give them any perspective or help them find a landmark. It's easy to panic and get into serious trouble.

If you've ever had a string of discouraging setbacks, it can seem like there's nothing in your future but more setbacks. Did you ever think, *What's the use? I'm never going to succeed!* If someone in your life doesn't call or write, have you ever thought, *He doesn't like me anymore* or *She's avoiding me because she thinks I'm a loser.* Maybe you even thought, *I'm going to be alone forever.* If so, you're like a hiker in the Horseshoe Hills, lacking perspective, unable to see the best way forward.

The following ten activities can help infuse your life with valuable perspective:

1. Take a trip, even a weekend away. You will return to your routines with a clearer mind and renewed energy.

2. Choose time to pause and let your thoughts carry you away. Ideally set aside thirty minutes twice a week. To get started, ask yourself, "What's going well?" or "What do I need to change in my life?" Let your mind take it from there.

3. Keep a journal of your problems and work through them in an orderly manner. Sometimes writing down your thoughts in the minutes before you go to bed does two things: First, you will sleep better knowing that you have started to address what's bothering you. Second, you will sleep on your problem, encouraging solutions to arrive soon thereafter.

4. Remember that most problems are not permanent. Say to yourself, This too shall pass. Be extra careful about making decisions that could be permanent when looking for a solution to a problem, especially one that's temporary. Take the time to think any potential solution all the way through before acting.

5. When faced with problems that are terrifying you, think to yourself, What's the worst thing that can really happen? Frequently, you'll realize things aren't as awful as you think.

6. Ask yourself, Is this problem that serious in the grand scheme of things? In other words, how important do you think it will be in a month? Six months? One year? Five years?

7. Hang out with different people. You'll gain fresh insights from new relationships that will change your perspective.

8. Take your focus off yourself for a while. You are not the center of the universe. Concentrate on those around you. Talk with

them about what they want to talk about and keep the conversation on their needs and interests.

9. Rearrange the furniture in your house or one room in your house. You'll see things differently and the shift will extend to other parts of your life as well.

10. Change your daily routine. Take a different route to work or eat at a different restaurant for lunch. The change may prove to be refreshing.

TWO: RENEW YOUR OPTIMISM

Optimistic people believe in successful outcomes, and this belief sustains hope. Even if their lives aren't going well in the moment, they are certain things will get better. They focus on what's going well rather than dwelling on what isn't going well. People who have a pessimistic outlook expect to fail.

Pete Rose was being interviewed about his hope of breaking Ty Cobb's all-time hits record. He was asked by one reporter, "You only need seventy-eight hits to break the record. How many at-bats do you think you'll need?"

Rose said, "Seventy-eight. Every time I step up to the plate, I expect to get a hit. If I don't expect to get a hit, I have no right to step in the batter's box in the first place."

It's well known that optimistic people live a longer life, experience less stress and anxiety, and have better health, better relationships, more successful careers, and increased creativity. They live lives to their fullest potential and are optimistic about their abilities. Practicing and strengthening optimism is worth the effort.

The following three ideas can help renew your optimism:

1. Martin Seligman, considered the father of positive psychology and the well-known author of *Learned Optimism* and *Flourish*, suggests the ABCD exercise. His approach to strengthen optimism is to stop thinking pessimistically. If you practice this exercise, it'll become easier for you over time to counter the pessimism in your life. The four steps Seligman suggests are:

a. Name the adversity or problem.

b. List your initial reaction to, or belief about, the problem.

c. Identify the consequences to this belief.

d. Dispute this belief. Given the problem, is it an accurate or even extreme belief?

For example, imagine that:

a. You overhear your supervisor saying that because of the economy, she will have to make some changes in the department.

b. Your initial reaction is fear and anger. You think you're about to get fired and then you start thinking how unfair that would be and you feel angry.

c. As a consequence, you start worrying about where you're going to get medical insurance, how you're going to pay the mortgage, and start telling coworkers how angry you are. You can't sleep and you start to drink more alcohol after your workday.

d. To think less pessimistically is to go back to what you overhead your supervisor saying. Can you conclude she is going to fire anyone, let alone you? Do you have any firm basis for your reaction?

2. Barbara Fredrickson,[7] another well-known researcher in optimism and the author of *Positivity*, says to "think in threes." Whenever you have a negative thought, think three positive ones. For instance, if you start thinking about the presentation that didn't go well, think about another presentation that went well, favorable comments from a friend, and how many friends at work support you. Fredrickson and Marcial Losada devised a positivity/negativity ratio referred to as the Losada Ratio and found people who flourish have more positivity than negativity in their lives.

3. Keep a journal at the end of the day in which you record three to four good and positive things that happened that day. Be sure to also write why each event happened. For instance, "My

presentation didn't go well, but afterward my coworker came up to me and said I had done a great job but that the group may not be ready for my ideas. 'Don't give up!' she said. 'You didn't do such a bad job, and you shouldn't let go of your ideas. Keep working at them and present them again.'"

THREE: ENLIVEN YOUR SENSE OF HUMOR

When you're feeling stressed about your life—your work, relationships, or perhaps your health—laughter is effective medicine. Research shows that every time you laugh, more oxygen reaches your organs, blood circulation increases, and stress eases and evaporates. Think about the last time you laughed at a joke, something someone said or did, or a funny movie. How much room was there for your stress and anxiety or even your depression while you were laughing? Laughter squeezes out stress. The two are incompatible.

What if you're going through severe adversity and truly can't think of a reason to even want to laugh? Life just hurts too much. Steven Sultanoff defined a type of humor that helps people be more resilient in "Integrating Humor into Psychotherapy," a chapter in *Play Therapy with Adults*. He called it "emotional chaos remembered in tranquility." Sultanoff talks about finding humor in events that are incongruous, absurd, and ridiculous. "Humor may be experienced," he wrote, "when the chaos of the past is viewed at a peaceful moment in the future." While the technique doesn't reduce the seriousness of a difficult event, it certainly lightens the load, helps individuals cope, and facilitates the healing process by offering perspective.[8]

Viktor Frankl kept his sense of humor in spite of everything he endured at the Auschwitz concentration camp in Poland during World War II. He shared a joke with a friend as they trudged off to their hard labor one morning. Both men were starving, freezing, and near death from exhaustion. Yet Frankl supposed that one day in the future they would be at a formal dinner party and, when the hostess served the soup course, they might forget themselves and ask her to please ladle from the bottom to get more peas. Frankl related this story many years later as an example of the importance of humor when living through dire circumstances.

Fourteen exercises to enliven your sense of humor

1. Smile when you're talking on the phone. You might be surprised at how cheerful and pleasant you sound and people will respond in kind.

2. Watch funny movies, commercials, or stand-up comedians. Check out lists of funny movies and ads at websites such as http://www.listal.com/list/100-funny-movies . They are sure to make you laugh.

3. Read comic strips every day and clip your favorites. Place them on your fridge, in your appointment book, on your desk, or on your computer screensaver.

4. Find simple opportunities to smile during the day. Smile at a clerk at the checkout counter, when you see someone having fun, or when you finish a job. Just smile.

5. Have you ever been embarrassed? Tell someone else what happened to you.

6. Every week check out the TV movie schedule or plays in your community and deliberately pick a comedy to watch.

7. Your family and friends probably talk to you about some of the stress they're experiencing and other difficulties. Start asking them to tell you about something funny that happened to them.

8. Hang around people who think *you* are funny. Many of us live and work with people who never laugh at our stories, which can squelch any attempt at humor and leave us feeling like a bore.

9. Hang out with people who laugh at themselves and life's absurdities as long as their laughter isn't caustic or sarcastic. Seek out people who like to laugh. You may need to limit time with people who are gloomy and depressing.

10. Play with a dog.

11. Sing a happy song, perhaps one you learned in childhood or one you've taught your own children.

12. Limit your complaining. If you aren't complaining, you leave more room for laughter.

13. Have you considered limiting your reading and viewing of the news? It tends to be negative and you might want to fill your mind with positive thoughts, too. At least balance your time between news and more cheerful reading and TV watching.

14. Read children's books.

FOUR: REDUCE YOUR STRESS

There are numerous and effective ways to manage the stress in your life. The techniques below will help you during a crisis. They also will help you manage on a daily basis when stress is unremitting, such as when you're living with a chronic illness, caregiving, experiencing relationship problems, or working in a stressful job.

If you need to reduce tension in your life or are experiencing serious distress, it's important you heed the early warnings of stress, including heartburn, headaches, and the inability to concentrate, before they become serious medical problems. If possible, find several times every day when you can let go and relax. There may be times you will need professional help. If none of the recommendations for reducing stress seem to help, talk to your healthcare provider for another point of view.

There are many effective stress management techniques available and hundreds of books and thousands of websites dedicated to managing stress. The following is an overview of some of the more widely used stress management techniques available.

Deep breathing

The stress response elicits shallow, quick breathing. Counteract that symptom by deliberate deep breathing to calm and balance yourself. Start by exhaling or sighing out your breath and inhaling so that your lower belly expands. Exhale and let your jaw relax, drop your shoulders, and keep your belly relaxed. Repeat this ten times and concentrate on your breathing. You can do this anywhere—sitting on an airplane, waiting for a meeting to begin, or going to sleep at night.

Progressive muscle relaxation

To benefit from this technique, you need to practice tensing a group of muscles as you breathe in, and relaxing them as you exhale. Doing this helps you become mentally calmer. Almost everyone who uses this method finds it very effective. You start with your feet and progress to your head, becoming more and more relaxed as you go.

Mindfulness

This here-and-now approach focuses on looking at your life as a child might, that is, without judging whether something is good or bad. It requires staying in the moment. One way to learn this technique is to practice focusing on only one thing, such as the song of a bird, water in a fountain, the ticking of a clock, or the rustle of leaves on trees. Or visually focus on the details of a flower or the clouds in the sky. Or pay close attention to how something is put together. When you're focused, stress is edged out and its power to take over your life withers.

FIVE: TAKE CARE OF YOURSELF

Finally, there are many practical and easy things you can do to take excellent care of yourself. Each will help you maintain your equanimity in the face of unremitting stress and strain and either regain or maintain optimum health.

Exercise reduces stress hormones, which means depression is less likely to affect your life if you stay active. Other benefits include increased concentration and energy, improved circulation, weight management, and better sleep. One of the easiest and most accessible exercises is walking. When you walk, your body produces feel-good hormones called endorphins and you focus on what you're doing rather than allowing stress and anxiety to crowd into your brain. Plus, if you walk outside, you will benefit from what Mother Nature offers, which could be sunshine, birdsong, trees, and a beautiful sky. Thirty minutes of brisk walking every day is a wonderful routine to establish. You will be rewarded in many ways for doing so.

Sleep is essential to coping with stress. When you don't get enough sleep, your immune system has to work harder and you'll be more susceptible to illness. Your judgment and decision-making abilities will suffer, and you will be more easily irritated over small things.

There are several ways diet can have a positive effect on stress. First, eating nutritious food strengthens an immune system that can be weakened by stress over time. Second, comfort foods like oatmeal and complex carbohydrates (whole grain breads and cereals) boost levels of serotonin in the brain and make you feel good. Some foods actually reduce the amount of the stress hormones cortisol and adrenaline. Vitamin C seems to have amazing properties. In one study, cortisol levels returned to normal faster among those who took Vitamin C, which can be found in oranges and other foods. In terms of stress reduction, tea is better than coffee.

If you have a pet, especially a dog, you know they give you unconditional love and are always eager to show affection. Research shows that if you pet a dog for a few minutes, your body releases hormones such as serotonin and oxytocin that lift your spirits. The added bonus is that hormones like cortisol and adrenaline are decreased.

FIVE KEY POINTS ABOUT EQUANIMITY

1. Difficulties in life are unavoidable but the real issue isn't whether you can avoid them as much as what you do when they happen. You have control over your response, that is, what you think and feel.

2. Next time you feel stress start to overwhelm you, pause and give yourself a time-out. Take a few deep breaths. Are you turning the situation into more of a crisis than it really is?

3. Get real and decide if your worries and fears are accurate. Is your situation truly dire and hopeless or is there some element of it that carries hope and positivity? You get to choose your next action. It might help to say, "Hope for the best, and plan for the worst."

4. Strive for and practice daily a balanced outlook that includes optimism, gratitude, and humor.

5. Learn tried-and-true stress management approaches that will help you stay calm, healthy, and hopeful. They include adequate sleep, good nutrition, exercise, and quality time spent with those who care about you.

A sense of equanimity will give you the perspective to respond to any event in your life with calm wisdom. It will lead to a comfortable sense of balance and composure even when you're under great pressure. Resilience is the capacity to respond and adapt positively to challenge and change. Equanimity will strengthen your ability to play your hand well even when you've been dealt less than perfect cards.

NOTES

1. Liz Fields, "Miss Arizona Hopeful Diagnosed With Rare Cancer," *Good Morning America*, Oct. 11, 2013, http://gma.yahoo.com/miss-arizona-hopeful-diagnosed-rare-cancer-005658393--abc-news-health.html (accessed Oct. 2013).

2. Steven Callahan, *Adrift: 76 Days Lost at Sea* (New York: Houghton Mifflin Company, 1999).

3. Frankl, 86.

4. G. Alan Marlatt, "Addiction and the Mind," http://www.dshs.wa.gov/pdf/oip/AddictionAndTheMindppt.pdf (accessed Oct. 2013).

5. Abigail Hazlett, Daniel Molden, and Aaron Sackett, "Hoping for the Best or Preparing for the Worst? Regulatory Focus and Preferences for Optimism and Pessimism in Predicting Personal Outcomes," *Social Cognition*, vol. 29 (2011): 74-96.

6. Daniel Gilbert, *Stumbling on Happiness* (New York: Random House, 2005).

7. Barbara Fredrickson and Marcial Losada, "Positive Affect and the Complex Dynamics of Human Flourishing," *American Psychologist*, vol. 60 (2005): 678-86.

8. Steven Sultanoff, "Integrating Humor into Psychotherapy," in *Play Therapy with Adults*, ed. Charles E. Schaefer (New York: John Wiley & Sons, Inc., 2003), 107-143.

CHAPTER 4:
SELF-RELIANCE

"The highest manifestation of life consists of this: that a being governs its own actions. A thing which is always subject to the direction of another is somewhat of a dead thing."

—Saint Thomas Aquinas

IN THIS CHAPTER you will learn how to build your self-reliance as well as:

- The differences between self-reliance and dependence on others
- Seven steps to more self-reliance
- Eight things you can do today to build your self-reliance
- Five key points about self-reliance

《 《 》 》

EACH OF YOU is the author of your own life script. It is basic to your nature to be self-directed and in control of your life. This is self-reliance, or the sure and certain understanding that you are capable and responsible for your own actions.

A strong self-reliance served Joanne Miller well. She was educated as a professional nurse but chose to be a stay-at-home mom. When her husband was tragically killed in a car accident, everything changed overnight. What did she do? Out of necessity, she had to get back on her feet quickly. She had always dreamed of returning to work as a pediatric nurse. Although she had been unemployed for fifteen years, she believed she'd find a way back into her field and viewed her experience as a mother of three, her powerful desire to help others, and her positive attitude as assets. She didn't just believe she had what it took to be an extraordinary pediatric nurse. She knew it. A clinic hired her, choosing her over several others with more experience and education. Two years later, she enrolled in a pediatric nurse practitioner program.

"My skills were a little rusty when I started two years ago," she said, "but I knew I could do the job."

Most everyone wants to be strong and independent. Being able to find your way through life's inevitable difficulties leads to success. Like Joanne, we like knowing we can figure things out for ourselves, make decisions that affect us, and thoroughly and carefully weigh what others tell us to do, feel, think, and believe before we act. When we're able to live in such a manner, we grow in self-confidence and maturity. This is self-reliance and it is essential to resilience.

Self-reliance is freedom from undue influence and control by others over your emotional, physical, spiritual, social, and economic needs. It's the hard-won knowledge that you're capable, competent, and resourceful and leads to an "I can do this" mindset and strong self-confidence.

Two Old Women is an Alaskan legend of self-reliance and courage told by Velma Wallis. During an especially brutal winter, a starving tribe was forced to abandon two old women in order to increase the tribe's probability of surviving. Left to freeze, starve, or be eaten by bears, the women, who had become totally dependent on others, were faced with two choices: figure out how to survive or die trying. When the tribe returned the next year, they found the two old women not only alive but thriving and able to provide food and other essentials for the entire tribe.[1] We all know people in our lives, including ourselves, who have been faced with this choice: figure it out or face the consequences. Thankfully, the consequences are rarely sudden death but they may include losing your home, health, or lifestyle. We each need to learn how to recognize, build, and strengthen our capabilities, rely on our own good judgment, and make sound decisions about our lives.

When we realize that responding to adversity comes from within, we begin to look to ourselves rather than others to deal with our problems.

This process never ends and continues to death. Even the very ill want to manage their own affairs as much as they are able. A lack of self-reliance, on the other hand, leads to conformity and dependence. Nothing is so damaging to the human spirit as taking away the ability to be self-reliant, that is, encouraging others to tell us what to do or allowing others to discourage us from choosing our own direction in life.

Self-reliant people can depend on themselves to find a way over, around, or through life's roadblocks and are likely to say, "I know I can do this." That powerful sentence carries an equally powerful impact in all areas of life, and people who can sincerely utter it make the best decisions for themselves. They are courageous and stay true to their values and life purpose. Self-reliant people also have learned to depend on their own experiences and strengths to thrive in the midst of change.

Self-reliance is a lot like self-efficacy, which is the belief you can do what needs to be done to reach a specific outcome such as losing weight or following through with an exercise program. Self-reliance, though, goes one step further. Those with self-efficacy believe they can overcome and achieve; those with self-reliance know they can.

Stacy Zoern, a 32-year-old University of Texas School of Law graduate, understands dependence, and she knew that she could do something to become more independent. She has spinal muscular atrophy and relies on others for just about everything. In her autobiography, *I Like to Run, Too*, she describes the obstacles she has faced her entire life. She can't dress herself, get out of bed, or go to the bathroom without help, let alone leave her home, run errands, and go out to a movie. She depends on her friends, family, and caregivers to take her everywhere.

And then she discovered a Hungarian company that manufactures a one-of-a-kind electric car called a Kenguru that can be operated from a wheelchair. She made plans to buy one for herself and also founded Community Cars Inc., which merged with Kenguru Services KFT. The new company makes the vehicles at its plant in Pflugerville, north of Zoern's hometown of Austin. Her vision is to improve the quality of life and self-reliance for many people who otherwise are dependent on others for just about everything. Zoern has learned that she can break down barriers and find her way to greater self-reliance.[2]

SELF-RELIANCE GROWS WITH PRACTICE

"A desire to be in charge of our own lives, a need for control, is born in each of us. It is essential to our mental health, and our success, that we take control."

—Robert F. Bennett

Self-reliance is built step-by-step through self-discipline and practice, which lead to mastery. It's borne of dedication and the desire to become better and better at what we love to do. Self-reliant people want to create their own destiny rather than wait for someone else to pave a way for them. In his book *Drive: The Surprising Truth about What Motivates Us*, Daniel Pink defines "mastery" as the compelling desire to improve at something that matters to us and "autonomy" as the desire to direct our own lives.[3] Mastery and autonomy are integral to self-reliance. Both require much hard work and effort and are essential to intrinsic motivation. Pink defines successful people as those "who aren't directly pursuing conventional notions of success. They're working hard and persisting through difficulties because of their internal desire to control their lives, learn about their world, and accomplish something that endures."

In her research over the past two decades Jean Twenge challenges the widely held belief that self-esteem and self-confidence are the keys to success.[4] She agrees with researcher June Tangney and others who say that self-control is much more powerful as a cause of personal success than self-esteem and both agree that there is no evidence that self-esteem by itself causes success.[5] "You need to believe that you can go out and do something," Twenge said, "but that's not the same as thinking that you're great." In other words, just believing that you're capable is not as powerful as *knowing* you are.

Captain Chesley B. "Sully" Sullenberger saved 155 people aboard the jetliner that he safely landed in the Hudson River on January 15, 2009 after a bird strike destroyed the jet engines at takeoff. He knew within seconds that morning that it was up to him alone to do what had to be done. He said, "It was the worst sickening, pit-of-your-stomach, falling-through-the-floor feeling I've ever felt in my life. I knew immediately it was very bad." He was confident, however, he'd be able to land the plane. Where did his confidence come from? He said, "One way of looking at this might be that for 42 years, I've been making small, regular deposits in this bank of experience: education and training. And on January 15 the balance was sufficient so that I could make a very large withdrawal." He said in an interview with Katie Couric, "I knew I had to solve this problem." She said, "But there was still a big 'if.'" And he coolly responded, "I was sure I could do it." [6]

HOW DO YOU BUILD SELF-RELIANCE?

We all must prepare for the inevitable difficulties of life. Most of the time they're going to come as a surprise, but we can prepare to meet every crisis by building self-reliance daily.

Many years ago when I was a struggling graduate student, I needed to drive across the country by myself from Montana to Texas. I had an old pickup truck and I was pulling a U-Haul trailer with my belongings, including a piano, up a steep two-lane highway with narrow shoulders. Near the top of Lincoln Pass in Montana, the trailer fishtailed wildly as the rear wheel on my truck blew out. I pulled the truck as far onto the shoulder as I could. My first thought was, *I need help. I hope someone stops.* No one did. I got out of the pickup and waved. Still, no one stopped. It was getting late, dark, and cold. Big snowflakes were falling. I had to do something. So I pulled out the instructions, jacked up the truck, changed the tire, and got back on the road. My story isn't dramatic and the ending is no more than mildly successful. But I learned a little about self-reliance that evening. That's how all of us begin to be self-reliant. We build confidence, strength, and resourcefulness over time.

In *The Survivors Club: The Secrets and Science that Could Save Your Life*, Ben Sherwood writes that we must be "armed and ready" because the day will come when we will face a crisis. We *can* be ready. He tells the story of a young man who was afloat in the Gulf of Mexico for seventeen hours and how, in order to survive, he had to "shut off the alarm switch in (his) head and channel fears into action." There was no room in the situation for panicking and self-pity.[7]

Aron Ralston was hiking in a remote Utah canyon in 2003 when he dislodged a boulder that pinned his arm against the canyon wall. No one could hear his cries for help and no one knew where he was. When he realized he was on his own, he made a series of decisions that led to his survival. He amputated his own arm with a dull knife, rappelled sixty-five feet down a sheer wall, and hiked several miles until he ran into other hikers able to radio for help. After his ordeal he wrote in his book, *127 Hours: Between a Rock and a Hard Place*, "At this point, I've got the confidence to know that I'll get through anything in my life given I have the motivation to do it ... I've got the capacity to do a lot more than I thought I could ... " 8 He found within himself the courage, resourcefulness, and determination to do what had to be done. He emerged from his ordeal with greater confidence than ever.

You can't get self-reliance from anyone else. You might ask for advice and support from others, hire a coach, and take self-help courses, but ultimately you must decide how you're going to deal with difficulties. Realizing this reality leads to confidence, the exact opposite of helplessness and dependence. Resilience will be out of reach if you aren't self-reliant.

SELF-RELIANCE DOES NOT MEAN GOING IT ALONE

Self-reliance isn't always about doing everything yourself. Ironically, you can't become self-reliant without help along the way. The help may be in the form of advice, information, analysis, assistance, education, and opinion. To be self-reliant means that you collect the information, analyze it for yourself, and make the decisions that affect you.

None of us is good at everything. Often there are skills and knowledge we don't have and we have to call on others to help us. If you have a plumbing problem and you're not a plumber, you're going to call for assistance. The same thing is true if you aren't a web designer, medical doctor, or mechanic. Being self-reliant doesn't mean you're completely self-sufficient and need no one else. It does mean that you know who, when, and how to find help when you need it.

Suppose your house is burning. If you're a self-reliant person, you don't put out the fire personally. But there are batteries in your smoke alarms and you have had fire drills with your family, so you evacuate and proceed to call 911. You are prepared, you have practiced, and you are confident because you know what to do in case of a fire. The same can be said about many areas in your life: have a goal, prepare, practice, achieve mastery, and feel confident about the outcome.

DIFFERENCES BETWEEN SELF-RELIANCE AND DEPENDENCE

When you doubt your own ability and look to others to approve and shape your opinions or even make decisions for you, you are leaning toward dependency rather than self-reliance. The danger is clear: you are transferring control of your own life to someone else.

When you become overly dependent on others, you're saying that someone other than yourself is more capable of gathering and analyzing information and arriving at a solution. You want others to take the lead and may even steer clear of situations where you'll have to accept responsibility for yourself. Over time, you may begin to feel helpless and increasingly rely on others. Eventually, you'll lose sight of your individuality. Fritz Perls, a twentieth-century psychiatrist who coined the term "Gestalt therapy," once said, "Our dependency makes slaves out of us, especially if this dependency is a dependency of our self-esteem. If you need encouragement, praise, pats on the back from everybody, then you make everybody your judge."

Most of us look to people we trust for support and guidance especially when we are making important life-changing decisions such as accepting a different job, relocating to a new city, getting married or divorced, or going through other life changes. Being self-reliant doesn't mean that you don't seek support and guidance. But it does mean that you'll make your own decisions and not wait for someone else to tell you what to do. Once you abdicate responsibility for yourself, you give power to others for your very happiness and then blame them when you're unhappy. Over time, and in extreme instances, your self-reliance will become so deeply eroded that you'll no longer believe you have the capability to do anything for yourself and you'll look to others for approval and decision-making in all matters.

The guide below will help you see whether you share more character-istics with those who are self-reliant or with those who tend to be dependent. As you look at these descriptors, think of Captain Sullen-berger and Aron Ralston. More importantly, take an inventory of your own life. Think of a time that changed your life, such as earning a college degree, getting a divorce, or joining the military. How would you describe your decision-making style?

Self-Reliant	Dependent and conformist
Resourceful	Look to someone else for ideas
Confident	Doubt your abilities
Trust in self	Believe others have a better plan
Independent thinker	Influenced by others
Courageous	Afraid to try anything new
Responsible	Irresponsible
Capable and competent	Helpless
Active coping	Passive coping
Decisive	Can't make decisions

HOW SELF-RELIANT ARE YOU?

It's very easy to fall into the comfortable rut of dependence on other people. It's tempting to let someone else take over responsibility for parts of your life that you don't want to manage yourself. The danger is that once you give away responsibility, you will begin to lose autonomy. And the longer you delay making a decision, the harder it is to regain self-reliance.

When this happens, you also may begin to lose confidence in yourself. When you encounter difficulties, you won't be able to assess your situation, reach a decision, and act on it. For instance, when faced with job loss, self-reliant people do not lose sight of their values and goals: they begin taking steps that will move them closer to reaching their goals. When all is said and done, self-reliant people are less likely to suffer regrets because they will have made decisions based on sound advice, accurate information, and self-understanding.

For a clearer picture of your self-reliance, check the items below with which you agree.

1. I have a history of making good and sound decisions. ❑

2. I know I can't blame someone else if I'm not happy with my life. ❑

3. I am a great problem solver. ❑

4. I am a confident and highly capable person. ❑

5. I can depend on myself to find a way through most situations. ❑

Checking most of the items above shows a strong self-reliance and confidence in yourself. You know what you are capable of doing. You probably have put a lot of time and effort into developing important skills in your life. While you've had as many setbacks as other people, you've turned them from potential roadblocks into mere detours on the way toward your goals. You're able to maintain your optimism about the future because you strongly believe that you know how to succeed even though you've had your share of failures.

Suze Orman, the famed personal finance expert, is a great example of self-reliance. Though highly successful by every definition, she had to learn self-reliance step-by-step. She tells the story of her father, who was badly burned in an on-the-job fire. Suze had to start working in the family business when she was thirteen years old and remembers her father saying, in spite of his physical pain and financial struggles, "An Orman never gives up." She worked hard and continues to make every minute count. She follows her interests, continues to take risks, and doesn't let critics get to her. Orman is self-confident and says, "Success comes when you know what you're doing and why you're doing it." These are the words of a very self-reliant woman.

ARE YOU AFRAID?

One of the most formidable barriers to self-reliance is fear. We can be afraid of failing, looking stupid, being rejected, being too old or too young, or not smart enough. We're all afraid at one time or another. We fear failing at our job, a competition, an exam, or maybe in our relationships. Fear results from a lack of confidence in our judgment and abilities. Once it begins to drive behavior, resilience becomes unattainable because fear can cripple us to the point we stop taking any risks. Some people play it safe their whole lives. But if we don't challenge ourselves, it's very difficult to learn and grow stronger from adversity. The antidote to fear is accepting challenges, facing them head-on, and not backing down.

Nelson Mandela was sentenced to twenty-seven years of hard labor on Robben Island, off the coast of Cape Town, due to his civil protest against the apartheid system in South Africa. Four years after his release he was elected the country's first black president. Throughout his imprisonment, Mandela refused to compromise his political position in exchange for a different sentence. "I learned that courage was not the absence of fear, but the triumph over it," he said. "The brave man is not he who does not feel afraid, but he who conquers that fear."

U.S. Supreme Court Justice Sonia Sotomayor has described how her knees trembled and her stomach churned when she presided over her first case on the U.S. Court of Appeals. She admitted, "Everything I've done, I've been afraid about doing, including being a Supreme Court Justice." Her solution has been to not give in but to find a way and work hard to prepare herself. She doesn't back down. She faces her fear of failing and takes steps to overcome what otherwise could be debilitating.

SEVEN STEPS TO SELF-RELIANCE

Self-reliance is built a little every day by the choices you make. Like other resilience skills, self-reliance takes practice and repetition. Steps toward self-reliance that will have the most lasting effects are those involving your thoughts, beliefs, and behaviors. Your aim is to make a deposit into your self-reliance bank every day. Acting on these steps is how you will find your way over, around, and through your fears.

The seventy-year-old Outward Bound program, the premier provider of experience-based outdoor leadership programs, has developed a great approach to building self-reliance by introducing challenging experiences. Its successful formula introduces a series of incremental problem-solving tasks that lead to a sense of competence. Results include confidence and independence in thought and decision-making.

Participants learn to accept responsibility and go beyond self-imposed limits. These are integral components of self-reliance. We can create our own Outward Bound experiences every day.

ONE: ACT LIKE A SELF-RELIANT PERSON

You know that your thoughts and beliefs can affect how you behave. It's also true that when you behave in a certain way, you'll begin to incorporate thoughts and beliefs about yourself. In other words, if you behave in a self-reliant way, you'll begin to believe and think that you're self-reliant. Meryl Streep, considered by many to be the greatest living actress today, has won three Academy Awards, including one for her portrayal of Margaret Thatcher, who was a very self-reliant woman. Yet at times Streep feels less than confident. In a media interview, she said she still doubts her abilities and says things to herself like, *I'm not a good actress* and *What am I doing? I'll never be able to pull this off.* How does she go on? "Fake it till you make it," she said. In other words, when she acts like a confident and self-reliant person, she becomes one.

William James, a nineteenth-century philosopher, was one of the first to claim that acting a certain way helps us feel that way, too. Since then, hundreds of studies have proved the assertion true. In James Laird's book *Feelings: The Perceptions of Self*, he writes that feelings are the consequence—not cause—of behavior.[9] So smile and you'll feel better. Walk and talk like a self-reliant person. Stand straight, walk purposefully, and speak with self-confidence. Helen Keller said, "Never bend your head. Always hold it high. Look the world right in the eye."

According to Amy Cuddy, a Harvard Business School researcher and social psychologist, nonverbal expressions of power, including posture, affect feelings, behaviors, and even hormone levels. For instance, she says that if you "fake" a body position more associated with success and confidence for even two minutes, your testosterone levels will increase, your cortisol (stress hormone) levels will decrease, and you'll be more inclined to take risks. Standing up straight, she found, and putting your hands on your hips leads to more confidence.[10]

In a nutshell, you can become self-reliant by thinking, behaving, and feeling your way to self-reliance. An expression often referred to as Hebb's Law states, "Neurons that fire together, wire together." Scientists used to believe that our brains were hardwired, which is another way of saying that when you learn something about life, the connections forged in your brain become fixed and permanent. You've probably heard the expression "He is 'fixed' in his ways" or "You can't teach an old dog new tricks." Well, it turns out that as you have new experiences, new connections form between brain cells. The more you revisit the new lessons learned, the stronger the connections become. So you can rewire your brain. Your brain is not hardwired from birth and can change. The phenomenon is called neuroplasticity.

In other words, when you make new mental associations, your malleable brain is literally able to create new paths in your nervous system as well. You can deliberately behave in a new way and create positive associations, or strong neuron pathways. You can develop in any direction you choose. For instance, if you can get in the habit of spending thirty minutes a day doing a specific activity that creates a new brain pattern, in a relatively short time, that pattern will be established. If you behave like a self-reliant person, your brain will make this new mental association, too.

TWO: LEARN SOMETHING NEW AND CHALLENGING

Doing things you didn't think you could do is guaranteed to build self-reliance. Once you begin to realize how you can depend on yourself in practical ways, you'll be able to depend on yourself in more complex ways, such as making major decisions for yourself. The short list below includes many activities that you might depend on someone else to do. If you learn at least one new skill a month, and continue practicing the more difficult skills, your self-reliance will grow. There are fun books full of lists of essential things to learn, including *The Experts' Guide to 100 Things Everyone Should Know How to Do* by Samantha Ettus; *An Incomplete Education: 3,684 Things You Should Have Learned but Probably Didn't* by Judy Jones; and *The New York Times Guide to Essential Knowledge*.

Practical easy-to-learn skills include:

- First Aid

- Car repairs

- Basic home repairs

- Basic cooking

- Financial management and budget-making

- Emergency preparedness, such as planning for power outages

Skills that will take longer to develop and may require training and additional practice include:

- Playing a musical instrument

- Speaking a foreign language

- Knowing basic geography of the world

- Using a computer or new computer software, games, and other applications

- Driving a car, piloting an airplane, or sailing a boat

- Swimming, scuba diving, horseback riding, canoeing, fly-fishing, skiing, bicycling, shooting, or skydiving

- Practicing self-defense

THREE: SURROUND YOURSELF WITH SUPPORTIVE PEOPLE

Keep people close to you who care about you. Thoughtfully prune those who don't have your best interests at heart. There may be people in your life who like that you are dependent on them in unhealthy ways, but having them in your life will cause you to lose your self-reliance and confidence and erode your ability to respond to adversity with resilience. You will instead be flattened.

Limit your time with unhealthy relationships as much as you realistically can. These include:

- A coworker who withholds information so you must depend on him for updates

- A friend who knows you need encouragement but laughs at you or belittles you when you make a mistake

- Anyone upon whom you are financially dependent and who controls your behavior by withholding money or threatening to do so

- Anyone who tells you you're weak, untalented, stupid, and have few useful skills

To increase your self-reliance, identify those in your life who don't support your self-reliance and instead work to keep you dependent. You probably know right now who these people are. Decide to meet new people. Do what you need to do to surround yourself with supportive, caring people who encourage and facilitate your self-reliance.

FOUR: KNOW WHAT YOU'RE GOOD AT

It's difficult to be self-reliant if you're not sure of the ways in which you can depend on yourself. Now is a good time to take an inventory of what you're capable of doing. Then you can consider what you'd like to learn to do next to add to your growing repertoire of skills, talents, strengths, and capabilities. Once you have a great idea of the things you're especially good at doing, develop them further. Concentrate on your strengths and don't worry so much about weaknesses.

Make a list of your strengths. Keep this list handy because when you have self-doubts, you can refer to it to remind yourself how capable and resourceful you actually are.

- Can you think of a situation in which you were forced to work out a solution all by yourself? Think of a time when you had no one to depend on and you had to figure something out yourself. How did you feel afterwards? Were you successful? How did it turn out? What did you learn?

- Make a list of activities you know you're good at doing.

- If you can't think of anything, has anyone ever told you that you were good at something?

- If you have a trusted friend, ask this person to list your strengths.

FIVE: LEARN TO MAKE GOOD DECISIONS

It's probably obvious that in order to be self-reliant, you need to be able to take in information, analyze it, and make decisions based on your interpretation of it. Self-reliant people want to get things right and will base decisions on a thorough analysis of information. They want to think for themselves. They don't need anyone else making decisions that will affect them. To achieve that level of confidence requires the following skills that you need to develop for yourself. You need to learn how to:

- Gather the right information.

- Judge the credibility and reliability of the information.

- Stay focused on the decision at hand and not be distracted by interesting but irrelevant information.

- Consider multiple positions and recommendations.

- Reach workable and acceptable conclusions.

- Trust yourself.

- Make a decision and act on it.

Remember the story about Captain Sullenberger who landed the plane in the Hudson River? He had incredible critical thinking skills that he'd practiced for several decades before he landed the plane. He followed all the steps—in three and a half minutes! He looked at his instruments and then talked to the first officer and the air traffic controller. He quickly assessed the information as credible and used it to make his decision. He was *very* focused and in fact described in interviews how narrow his vision became: "Land the plane safely." He briefly considered and discarded the air traffic controller's suggestions to land at the closest airport. Instead, he calmly said he'd be in the river. He told the air traffic controller exactly where they would be and prepared the crew for a water landing. He told Katie Couric, "I was sure." He trusted his decision. He landed the plane and saved everyone on board.

You can practice these skills today. Are you buying a car, furniture, a book? Are you choosing an insurance plan for your family or a destination for an upcoming holiday? Are you deciding to go back to school, retire, or change your career? The same set of skills will be useful to you. Practice going through this process each time you make a decision and the process quickly will become second nature to you. You will become much more self-reliant.

SIX: FACE YOUR FEARS

This exercise has almost instant results leading to self-reliance. Stepping outside your comfort zone is a tried-and-true method for strengthening self-reliance. Eleanor Roosevelt wrote, "We gain strength, and courage, and confidence by each experience in which we really stop to look fear in the face ... we must do that which we think we cannot."

Even if you aren't successful, you will feel more self-reliant for having tried. In order for this approach to work, you must choose something you really want to do but which you haven't done because fear held you back. Examples include:

- Enrolling in school
- Asking for a promotion
- Giving a speech or performance
- Taking a trip to a foreign country
- Competing in an athletic event
- Changing careers
- Applying and interviewing for a job
- Moving to a different city or country
- Selling your house and relocating

Living with autonomy and confidence is up to each of us. You might get support, advice, opinions, strong recommendations, and persuasive arguments from those around you. But when it comes right down to it, you alone need to make the decisions that affect your life.

Consider the alternative. When we abdicate responsibility for ourselves, we hand over the reins to someone else. Some people like to do this because they avoid making hard decisions. The danger is that when we give away responsibility for our lives we lose autonomy. The longer we live without autonomy, the harder it is to regain self-reliance. With practice, we can learn to be self-reliant and depend on ourselves and our capabilities and, ultimately, build confidence and resilience.

SEVEN: CELEBRATE

Nothing beats celebration for reinforcing and supporting newly learned skills in self-reliance. All of us need rewards for hard work. They are proven motivators. Promise yourself a reward and honor your promise to yourself no matter what. Make sure that the reward you've promised yourself is realistic and that you can give it to yourself. If not, you'll actually weaken your self-confidence. Make a list of rewards that are meaningful to you. Choose small rewards for small doable steps that you achieve on a daily basis. Using the list below, identify five ways you would like to reward yourself:

- At the end of every day, record the successes you experienced that day before you forget them. These might include things such as exercising, practicing a new skill, going to lunch with someone, meeting an important work deadline, studying for a test, or getting enough sleep. The list is endless. You know your own successes best.

- Reward yourself with something tangible every day. This might include a favorite treat after you exercise, a telephone call to a friend after you finish your studying, or a movie after you've paid the bills. Again, you need to create your own routine of rewards.

- Finally, you need to reward yourself for major accomplishments that have strengthened your self-reliance. What do you really love doing or would really love to give yourself? The sky is the limit and the reward needs to motivate you toward greater and greater self-reliance.

EIGHT THINGS YOU CAN DO TODAY TO BUILD YOUR SELF-RELIANCE

1. Choose one thing you've always wanted to do but didn't think you could.

2. Don't blame anyone else for things that went wrong in your life.

3. If you don't know how to do something, ask someone for help.

4. Decide for yourself what your priorities are and follow through.

5. Do one thing today you've been afraid to do—make a phone call, write a letter, or sign up for a class.

6. Walk and talk like a confident person.

7. If you have a decision that needs to be made, gather information before acting impulsively.

8. List times in your life when you figured out something on your own and keep the list as a reminder during times you feel helpless and dependent.

FIVE KEY POINTS ABOUT SELF-RELIANCE

1. Self-reliance is being prepared and confident in your abilities to make the best decision.

2. You are the captain of your own ship and responsible for your actions and the consequences of your actions.

3. Self-reliance is freedom from undue influence and control by others over your emotional, physical, spiritual, social, and economic needs.

4. Self-reliant people can say, "I'm going to make it. I'm going to find a way. I can do this."

5. Self-reliance is built with practice and results in self-confidence.

Most of you want to be in control of your own life. Knowing you have the capability to find your way through difficulties is a formidable force against obstacles that get in the way of success. With self-reliance comes self-confidence and self-esteem as well as a growing sense of your authentic self, which is the topic of the next chapter.

NOTES

1. Velma Wallis, *Two Old Women: An Alaska Legend of Betrayal, Courage and Survival* (New York: HarperCollins, 1994).

2. Carol Sowell, "Entrepreneur with SMA Starts Accessible Car Company," *Quest MDA's Research & Health Magazine*, Feb. 22, 2012, http://quest.mda.org/news/entrepreneur-sma-starts-accessible-car-company (accessed Oct. 2013).

3. Daniel H. Pink, *Drive: The Surprising Truth About What Motivates Us* (New York: Riverhead Books, 2009).

4. Elizabeth Weiss Green, "It's All About Me," *U.S. News and World Report,* vol. 142 (2007): 22.

5. June P. Tangney, Roy F. Baumeister, and Angie L. Boone, "High Self-control Predicts Good Adjustment, Less Pathology, Better Grades, and Interpersonal Success," *Journal of Personality*, vol. 72 (2004): 271-324.

6. "Flight 1549: A Routine Takeoff Turns Ugly," *CBS News 60 Minutes*, July 6, 2009, http://www.cbsnews.com/8301-18560_162-4783580.html (accessed May 2010).

7. Ben Sherwood, *The Survivors Club: The Secrets and Science that Could Save Your Life* (New York: Grand Central Publishing, 2009).

8. Aron Ralston, *127 Hours: Between a Rock and a Hard Place* (New York: Atria Books, 2004).

9. James Laird, *Feelings: The Perception of Self (Series in Affective Science)* (New York: Oxford University Press, 2007).

10. Dana R. Carney, Amy J. Cuddy and Andy J. Yap, "Power Posing: Brief Nonverbal Displays Affect Neuroendocrine Levels and Risk Tolerance," *Psychological Science*, vol. 21 (2010): 1363-68.

CHAPTER 5: AUTHENTICITY

"I know this now. Every man gives his life for what he believes. Every woman gives her life for what she believes. Sometimes people believe in little or nothing, and so they give their lives to little or nothing. One life is all we have and we live it as we believe in living it. And then it is gone. But to sacrifice what you are and live without belief, that's more terrible than dying."

—Joan of Arc

IN THIS CHAPTER you will learn:

- What it means to live an authentic life
- Three reasons why it's difficult to pursue an authentic life
- Seven approaches to a more authentic life
- Five key points about living an authentic life

《 《 》 》

STEVE JOBS WAS a bold nonconformist who lived his dream. He dared to be wrong. He dared to appear stupid to his colleagues, friends, and family. He could have settled for the status quo and still have led a very satisfying life, but he didn't. He found his own true north and went there. Although Steve Jobs died a wealthy man, leaving behind approximately eight billion dollars, making money was not his dream.

In a 1993 interview with the *Wall Street Journal*, he said, "Being the richest man in the cemetery doesn't matter to me. Going to bed at night saying we've done something wonderful ... that's what matters to me." [1]

Some people spend their whole life not knowing who they are or where they want to go, much less how to get there. They end up with a lifetime of regrets, wishing they'd done things differently. For thousands of years people have asked who they are and where they're going. The answers you can give to these questions are the foundation of your individuality; they are the key to every decision you make and every action you take. If you lie awake at night pondering these questions you know that you don't want to waste another minute trying to be someone you aren't or doing things that don't fit who you are.

An authentic life comes in many forms. Kristin Kimball, Harvard graduate, farmer, and author of *The Dirty Life*, "found" herself ten years ago when she had just turned thirty. A single woman and writer living in Manhattan, she traveled to Pennsylvania to interview a farmer about the local farm movement. It wasn't in her plans to abandon her glamorous career and leave behind everything she thought was important. Together, she and the farmer founded Essex Farm in 2004. Even her father felt sad that they were working so hard on something that he was sure would ultimately fail. But she didn't fail and, in the process, she discovered herself. She said, "You don't measure things like that with words like success or failure ... Satisfaction comes from trying hard things and then going on to the next hard thing, regardless of the outcome. What mattered was whether or not you were moving in a direction you thought was right." [2]

WHAT DOES IT MEAN TO LIVE AN AUTHENTIC LIFE?

"The privilege of a lifetime is to become who you really are."

—Carl Jung

Do you know of any people who took considerable risks to remain true to their beliefs and values? Perhaps they did something as simple as going against the advice of others. Perhaps their actions went against common wisdom and appeared foolish. Maybe one ditched a "great" job in order to start a business, or another decided late in a successful life to prepare for a new career. Maybe you know a mother of young children who joined the military, or someone who declined a job promotion because he wanted to spend more time at home. All these people made the difficult choice, but they also made the choice that was right for them. By living a life that's meaningful to you, one that you know in your heart is right, you'll strengthen your resilience.

Resilient people have the courage to do or say what they think is right no matter who disagrees with them. They live a life that fits them—not one they want others to admire. How many times have you conversed with someone who's outwardly successful but lacks that strategic fit between who they really are, what they do, and what they have become? Usually it takes only minutes of conversation before you become aware of the discrepancies.

Resilient people understand that they alone can choose their direction in life. No one else can. No one knows another's heart, not really. Frequently, people let life distract them from understanding, or even looking at, their own wants and needs. Resilient people pursue lives consistent with their deeply held beliefs and values. Before that kind of success is possible, though, they have to know those beliefs and values in detail.

AUTHENTICITY BRINGS OUT COURAGE, CREATIVITY, AND CONVICTION

The pursuit of individuality comes with costs. It's risky business. At times the pursuit can result in self-doubts and feelings of insecurity because you may envision a lifestyle and future no one else can imagine. You may have to take a stand to be true to yourself or risk punishment when you do what you know to be right. Individuality can be a very lonely place. Out of sincere concern, friends, family members, coworkers, and others may discourage you, try to talk you down. Some may even grow angry at you, reject you, and finally abandon you. But when you choose the life path that is uniquely yours, your resilience will grow because you'll be living authentically. Such a life is intrinsically and deeply rewarding. Once you begin experiencing an authentic life, you'll never turn back.

People who live authentically are willing to risk everything in order to remain true to their values and beliefs. Twenty-one-year-old Marine Sergeant Dakota Meyer saw his duty clearly on September 8, 2009. He was outside the village of Ganjgal in Kunar Province, Afghanistan. He heard on the radio that three U.S. Marines and a U.S. Navy corpsman were missing after being ambushed by a group of insurgents in the village. Despite orders to stay out of Ganjgal, he knew the right thing to do was to go in and get the missing men, which he did in a daring rescue mission. Despite shrapnel wounds to his arm, he made four trips to recover wounded soldiers and find the missing U.S. team members. Under heavy enemy fire, he made a fifth and last trip on foot to locate and recover the bodies of his team members. During the six-hour fight against Taliban insurgents, he saved thirty-six comrades. In an ABC interview he said, "I would do it a hundred times." 3

Andrée Peel, who lived to 105, was known as Agent Rose during World War II. She worked against the German occupation of France. As a member of the French Resistance, she saved the lives of more than one hundred airmen and aided more than twenty thousand people. Eventually she was captured, interrogated, and tortured. She was lined up to be shot by a firing squad, too, when the U.S. Army arrived. "It was a terrible time," she said, "but looking back I am so proud of what I did … It was a kind of fear that was not really fear. We had accepted we would die … I rarely thought of my personal safety. I just acted and did what I believed was the right thing." 4

Harriet Tubman was an abolitionist and Union spy during the American Civil War. She said, "I had reasoned this out in my mind, there was one of two things I had a right to—liberty or death; if I could not have one, I would have the other." She escaped slavery and went on to make more than thirteen missions to rescue more than seventy slaves using the network of activists known as the Underground Railroad. She was the first woman to lead an armed expedition in the war, the Combahee Ferry Raid, in which she liberated some seven hundred slaves in South Carolina.5

Aleksandr Solzhenitsyn was a Russian writer and a harsh and courageous critic of communist ideology. He wrote several books that exposed to the world the Soviet Union's forced labor camp system, which was responsible for the death of millions of people. He survived several Soviet gulags and, for the rest of his long life, remained committed to telling the world of Soviet atrocities. He wrote, "A genius doesn't adjust his treatment of a theme to a tyrant's taste." Solzhenitsyn was awarded the Nobel Prize in Literature in 1970 and subsequently was exiled from the Soviet Union.[6]

Georgia O'Keeffe, an American artist who painted unusually beautiful art of the American Southwest, said, "I've been absolutely terrified every moment of my life—and I've never let it keep me from doing a single thing I wanted to do. I found myself saying to myself … I can't live where I want to … I can't go where I want to … I can't do what I want to. I can't even say what I want to. I decided I was a very stupid fool not to at least paint as I wanted to … that seemed to be the only thing I could do that didn't concern anybody but myself." [7]

Maya Angelou was a poet, educator, and novelist who wrote more than thirty books by age eighty-five. She wrote of her early life and the brutal reality of racial discrimination in *I Know Why the Caged Bird Sings*. By the time she was seventeen, she was a single mother working at times as a waitress and cook. She was awarded the Presidential Medal of Arts in 2000 and the Lincoln Medal in 2008. She said, "There is no greater agony than having an untold story inside of you." [8]

Vincent Van Gogh, a Dutch Post-Impressionist painter who influenced much of twentieth-century art, was a prolific painter in his brief life and considered the greatest Dutch painter after Rembrandt. Van Gogh was known as a tormented artist suffering from anxiety and mental illness—he died at age thirty-seven of a self-inflicted gunshot wound—but in life he found release and freedom in his art. He wrote, "The fishermen know that the sea is dangerous and the storm terrible, but they have never found these dangers sufficient reason for remaining ashore." [9]

WHAT IS THE DIFFERENCE BETWEEN BEING TRUE TO YOURSELF AND FOOLING YOURSELF?

Resilient people have learned to make decisions and take actions that are deliberate and consistent with their values and beliefs. Others may not agree with these choices and may attempt to convince them another way is better. Nevertheless, resilient people know deep inside that the choices they make are the right ones for them. They hold their ground. They stop trying to live in ways that others find acceptable.

The quick guide below will help you see if you're living a life consistent with your basic values and beliefs.

True to Yourself	Deceiving Yourself
Honest with yourself	Hide the truth from yourself
Faithful to deeply held values and beliefs	Give way to external expectations
Bold and courageous	Timid and afraid
At peace with yourself	Anxious and overwhelmed
Stand your ground	Go with the flow
Be a nonconformist	Conform to others' ideas
Take responsibility for your own actions	Feel helpless, like a victim
Live your own dream	Chase someone else's dream

THREE REASONS WHY IT IS DIFFICULT TO PURSUE AN AUTHENTIC LIFE

At some time in your life, have you made any false starts, taken wrong directions, or veered off on a detour? Or maybe you are still trying to find direction. Living authentically requires soul searching and self-honesty. Nevertheless, once you're able to navigate by your own true north, much of your life, and the decisions you make, will begin to make sense and fall naturally into place. At first, though, you may find yourself holding back. Here are three common reasons for resisting change.

ONE: FEAR OF WHAT YOU WILL LOSE

Maybe you're so afraid of losing what you have that you're unable to let go and be yourself. Maybe you'll need to leave a job, change your lifestyle, downsize to a different house, or leave a relationship. You might need to relocate. Perhaps you have grown used to having the prestige and power of an important position, or you may be in the middle of a successful career that you only thought you wanted. You may have to give up money and security, or go back to school. Do you ever feel this way about your life? Many people have this fear.

In certain parts of the world, monkeys are a pest and, from time to time, need to be relocated. In order to do so, they first must be trapped. To do this, a jar is fastened securely to a tree and an orange is placed in it. Or sometimes, as the ancient parable is told, a coconut is hollowed out and filled with something sweet. In either case the opening created is just big enough for a hand to enter but not for a closed fist to exit. The monkey will place his hand in the jar and try to grab the orange. If he succeeds, he can't remove his hand with the orange in it. Unless he lets go, he'll be trapped. Generally, his greed overcomes his desire for freedom and he will remain stuck and so easy to catch and transport.[10]

TWO: PRESSURE TO CONFORM AND PLEASE OTHERS

"There is something in every one of you that waits and listens for the sound of the genuine in yourself. It is the only true guide you will ever have. And if you cannot hear it, you will all of your life spend your days on the ends of strings that somebody else pulls."

—Howard Thurman

If you're like many of us, you probably base many of your decisions on what others want you to do, think you should do, and convince you to do. But living someone else's dream for you doesn't work. Marilyn Monroe, who everyone considered an extraordinary success at the peak of her career, once said, "I'm a failure as a woman. My men expect so much of me because of the image they've made of me—and that I've made of myself—as a sex symbol. They expect bells to ring and whistles to whistle, but my anatomy is the same as any other woman's and I can't live up to it."

The world will mold and shape you if you let it. Advertising, TV, and the Internet dictate to us how we should live, what clothes to wear, how to talk, what to drive, and what size house to buy. The list is long. Your parents may have had expectations for you that still are part of the life decisions you make as an adult. Most of us tend to comply with what's expected of us because society rewards conformity. If you behave a certain way and do what you're supposed to do, you'll be promoted and accepted. If you don't, you might be overlooked and rejected. Unfortunately, we can lose our authentic selves along the way and sometimes it's difficult to find our way back.

Anne Lamott is a well-known novelist and nonfiction writer, political activist, public speaker, and writing teacher in the San Francisco Bay Area. She asks, "How do we gently stop being who we aren't? How do we relieve ourselves of the false fronts of people-pleasing and affectation, the obsessive need for power and security, the backpack of old pain, and the psychic Spanx (women's slimming undergarments) that keeps us smaller and contained?"

THREE: THE INCONVENIENCE OF CHANGE

Being who you are is a challenge. Often it takes work and many of us just don't want to put in the effort. There are so many reasons to put it off. John W. Gardner, Secretary of Health, Education, and Welfare under President Lyndon Johnson, resigned from the post because he couldn't support the war in Vietnam. He said, "Human beings have always employed an enormous variety of clever devices for running away from themselves."

He hit the nail on the head. We can all find so many reasons to ignore the inner voice that keeps nagging us to do something about our deep unhappiness, dissatisfaction, and restlessness. This voice will never go away, however. You may successfully ignore it, but it will be insistent. Sometimes the voice will be a mere whisper, but you will hear it. Sadly, many people ignore this call until it really is too late. Some even go to their grave without ever truly living.

Dietrich Bonhoeffer, a theologian and pastor in pre-World War II Germany, was opposed to the Nazi regime in power. A pacifist, he worried he'd be conscripted to fight for Germany and forced to swear allegiance to Hitler. So he moved to the United States and endeavored to fight Nazism from outside Germany. But he saw quickly that he'd made a mistake and returned to Germany. "If you board the wrong train," he said, "it is no use running along the corridor in the other direction." The consequences of his decision led to his arrest, imprisonment, and execution.[11]

At times we're so busy that we don't take the time to pay attention. Or we don't have the energy to devote to making even small changes that bring us closer to the truth of who we are. Ironically, we end up wasting time and nervous energy in denying our true needs with false starts, detours, and wrong directions. We fill our life with distractions and imitate what we think is a meaningful life, except that we feel empty. At the end of the day, we're still unfulfilled and ask, "What if this is as good as it gets?" So we run faster and faster, only to discover we've wasted years living a life that is a poor fit. But all is not lost. Starting now, each of us can begin to live an authentic life.

IT IS TIME TO PURSUE AN AUTHENTIC LIFE

"Any life, no matter how long and complex it may be, is made up of a single moment—the moment in which a man finds out, once and for all, who he is."

—Jorge Luis Borges

When do you begin living an authentic life? When you finally figure out that you *must* do something differently. The moment could come as a flash of insight. Sometimes circumstances seem to leave you no choice. Maybe you have to choose between your job demands and caring for a friend or family member who is ill. Coming to grips with such a decision brings your values and beliefs into sharp focus.

Sometimes, after years of unhappiness, feelings of emptiness, and lack of fulfillment, you finally may realize you can't ignore your pain any longer. You may deny your feelings, get dragged down with inertia, or procrastinate making any changes, but finally the time arrives when you must look deep inside and discover why you're miserable. Maybe you already know what you need to do but you've been avoiding the changes you'd have to make. Let's say you want to be a teacher, a clergyman, an engineer. Or you want to own a bicycle shop, move to Alaska, or spend more time with your children. When do you break the news to others? Are you prepared for the push back from others as well as yourself?

SEVEN APPROACHES TOWARD A MORE AUTHENTIC LIFE

"The unexamined life is not worth living."

—Socrates

Many of you may be feeling discouraged about your life, and some may even feel desperate. Maybe you don't have the courage, willingness, and know-how to swim against the tide. Henry David Thoreau wrote, "The mass of men lead lives of quiet desperation." Do you ever feel this way? Do you wonder if you're being swept along with the tide?

If the answer is yes, you need to do some serious soul-searching and get to know yourself better. Do you know your beliefs? Are you clear about your personal values? They will provide you with compelling direction.

Everyone makes choices in life—to take one job or another, to finish a college degree or not, to stay with or leave a spouse, to have children. By the end of your life you'll have made many decisions, big and small. In his poem "The Road Not Taken," Robert Frost describes coming to a fork in the road and having to choose one path:

> ... I shall be telling this with a sigh
> Somewhere ages and ages hence:
> Two roads diverged in a wood, and I—
> I took the one less traveled by,
> And that has made all the difference.

The approaches listed below will effectively help you come home to yourself. Reflection and insights don't usually happen overnight. They take time and require you to listen to yourself. Self-examination takes time and practice and requires you to pay attention to yourself and not let distractions divert you. You will need a notebook or journal because it's a good idea to write down your thoughts daily.

If you believe you may not be living an authentic life, it may be because you are not conscious of your life's meaning and purpose. Below are some suggestions for helping you discover thoughts, dreams, hopes, and yearnings, and bringing them to the surface of your mind. They can help you start leading a life that's more authentic today. You don't have all the time in the world.

ONE: DO SOME SOUL-SEARCHING

"Sometimes the best way to figure out who you are is to get to that place where you don't have to be anything else."

—Unknown

This is a good time to turn away from the influence of others for a while. The world is noisy and insistent and it's difficult to concentrate on anything else when it demands your attention. Continuous clamor from the outside can drive out introspection. So shut off the news and television. Check your email as needed but stop endlessly going from one Internet story to the next.

This discipline will help you quiet your mind in preparation for discovering what's critically important—your values and beliefs. You need to set aside time every day to quiet your mind. Start with ten minutes at a time and then work up to twenty minutes. You might start by asking yourself: What longings and dreams do I have? What seems to be missing in my life?

Some of you may resist writing in a daily journal for several reasons. You don't have time, or anything to say. Maybe you worry that someone might read it. But before you decide it's a waste of time, consider some of the benefits. By writing down your frustrations, fears, and anxieties, you will begin the process of having a conversation with yourself that will calm you and begin to allay the anxiety-producing demands in your head. You can write them down and get them in front of you where you can actually see them. When all of those concerns, some of them vague and undeveloped, crowd into your head, there is little room for anything else. Get them out of there. Deal with them.

Also, many people like to write down their problems, dilemmas, or confusion and then walk away from them. When they return later and read what they wrote, they realize they've already worked out a solution. Why not give a journal a chance?

TWO: KNOW WHAT YOU REALLY LOVE

"To know what you prefer instead of humbly saying Amen to what the world tells you you ought to prefer, is to keep your soul alive."

—Robert Louis Stevenson

Essential to soul searching is discovering and understanding what exactly is speaking to your soul. Here's a fun exercise: Peruse some favorite magazines. When a picture catches your attention, cut it out and put it aside. Go to a bookstore and write down the titles to which you're drawn. When you're going from story to story on the Internet, which ones grab your attention? This is one way of getting closer and closer to where your genuine interests lie and may provide a path to who you are—the person you may not be acknowledging.

You might even collect these images and titles and put them in a scrapbook. It won't take long before a story all about you begins to emerge. You'll likely discover long dormant desires and interests in your life that, with a little gentle encouragement, will help you reshape your life into what it's meant to be.

Learn to pay attention. As poet Anne Sexton writes, "Put your ear down next to your soul and listen hard." In the words of Saint Benedict, "Listen with the ear of the heart."

THREE: SPEND SOME TIME WITH PEOPLE YOU TRUST AND WHO MAY HAVE INSIGHT INTO YOUR LIFE

"Be who you are and say what you feel, because those who mind don't matter, and those who matter don't mind."

—Dr. Seuss

Often it helps to spend time with a friend, family member, group, or counselor. Choose someone you trust who will truly listen and set aside their judgment of what they think you should do. Let them ask you questions, then answer them as honestly as you can. Look for contradictions between how you're acting in your life, how you feel, and what you say is important to you.

What do contradictions look like? If you're pursuing a career that requires traveling or long hours at the office, and yet you claim your family is of great importance to you, there's a contradiction between what you say is important and how you behave.

Sometimes we're blind to the contradictions we reveal to others. For instance, you may love helping out at a day care center, singing in the choir, doing the bookkeeping for free for a local nonprofit, and hate your day job. A friend, coworker, or a family member may be the first to notice that you live for your hobbies and volunteer activities and that there's a mismatch between where you seem to come alive and where you are half-dead with boredom, stress, and fatigue.

FOUR: BE PERFECTLY CLEAR AND RELENTLESSLY HONEST WITH YOURSELF

"To thine own self be true, and it must follow, as the night the day, thou canst not be false to any man."

—Shakespeare, *Hamlet*

In your journal, write how you want to live and what you want to do with the precious one life you have. Over time your priorities may change but you will be surprised at how consistent some of them will be. How do you think yours have changed in the past five to ten years?

What events in your life have changed how you view your priorities? For instance, many people who have gone through a traumatic event, such as an accident or life-threatening illness, will say that what's important in life finally became clear to them. Many are even thankful for a near-death experience because of how it sharpened and defined the most precious boundaries of their lives. Pay attention to your innermost thoughts. Be your own best friend as you listen. Be completely honest with yourself. No one else is going to read what you write. Put your journal in a safe and secure place.

Ann Romney, wife of the 2012 Republican presidential nominee, was interviewed about her diagnosis of multiple sclerosis and her bout with breast cancer several years later. "You learn how to dig really deep," she said. "You say, *I'm going to get through this.* I think it has changed my heart. It has softened my heart. It has made me very concerned about others who are going through challenges and know that we'll all have a dark hour in our life. There are people who are suffering right now. They may be losing a parent, a child, or a spouse. Or they are being diagnosed with cancer ... I am grateful that my heart has been opened up and softened ... suddenly I couldn't even take care of myself. It's like a rug being pulled out from under you. And what are you left with? You really have to evaluate, *Who am I? Who am I, really?*" [12]

FIVE: START WHITTLING YOUR LIFE TO ITS VERY ESSENCE

> *"Every block of stone has a statue inside it and it is the task of the sculptor to discover it."*

> —Michelangelo

Michelangelo also said, "I saw the angel in the marble and carved until I set him free." That's what you must do: Let go of parts of your life that don't feel essential to you. Carve them away. Start slowly. You can change your mind. But stop being who you are not. Stop pouring out energy into something that is not very important to you. Say "no" when you find yourself going in the wrong direction.

Another exercise that can be revealing is to make note of pictures that are unlike you. For instance, when you see people sitting in an airplane, or someone scuba diving, or giving a speech, teaching a class of students, repairing a car, or performing surgery, you can say, "I know I am not drawn to that life. That is not an authentic reflection of my life."

These are expectations and images that you can whittle from yourself and say, "These are not me." As with all soul searching exercises, you will need to answer honestly for you and not who you think you should be or what you wish you could be. A picture of a surgeon may lead you to thoughts of, "She makes lots of money. She is respected and smart. I would like that for myself." But at the end of the day, do you deep inside want to be a surgeon or are you swayed by what you imagine the surgeon has?

Be yourself. Put your name in this short statement and post it on your door so you see it all the time as you come and go: "Be_____."

SIX: KNOW YOUR VALUES

"I think the world would be a lot better off if more people were to define themselves in terms of their own standards and values and not what other people said or thought about them."

—Hillary Clinton

Your values are the rules you live by, the concepts you feel are important for your own success. Did you know that the vast majority of people aren't consciously aware of their values? It's only after you give them some thought and understand which rules you find important that you start to truly play the game of life. Carl Jung, one of the fathers of psychotherapy, once said, "Your vision will become clear only when you look into your heart. Who looks outside, dreams. Who looks inside, awakens."

Can you list five of your personal values? If you can, then you're way ahead of most people. Even if you know some of your values, try a simple exercise to clarify them further.

1. Pick ten values from the list below, or write down some of your own. (Remember that a value completes the statement, "By seeking _____, my life will be satisfying and fulfilling.")

2. From this list, select the top five, then your top three.

3. Finally, choose your most important value. How closely do your actions in life reflect your top values? Could you live your values better? What are your five least important values?

Some sample values or success factors:

Achievement
Advancement
Adventure
Affection
Autonomy
Challenge
Cooperation

Creativity
Economic security
Fame
Family
Freedom
Friendship
Health
Inner harmony
Integrity in my relationships
Involvement
Loyalty
Order
Personal development
Pleasure
Power
Recognition
Responsibility
Safety
Self-respect
Spirituality/faith
Trust in my relationships
Wealth
Wisdom

SEVEN: FACE YOUR FEAR OF BEING YOURSELF

"One does not discover new lands without consenting to losing sight of the shore for a very long time."

—André Gide

The journey to find your authentic self can be very frightening and it's tempting to stay on shore, which you can do. Many of you try to keep one foot on shore, which, of course, you can't do. You have to finally make a choice.

Neil Simon, the American playwright, said:

Don't listen to those who say, 'It's not done that way.' Maybe it's not, but maybe you will. Don't listen to those who say, 'You're taking too big a chance.' Michelangelo would have painted the Sistine floor, and it would surely be rubbed out by today. Most importantly, don't listen when the little voice of fear inside of you rears its ugly head and says, 'They're all smarter than you out there. They're more talented, they're taller, blonder, prettier, luckier and have connections …' I firmly believe that if you follow a path that interests you, not to the exclusion of love, sensitivity, and cooperation with others, but with the strength of conviction that you can move others by your own efforts, and do not make success or failure the criterion by which you live, the chances are you'll be a person worthy of your own respect.

What exactly do you think will happen if you are true to yourself? Think about what or who is talking when you feel afraid to act on your own. Is it the voice of TV and Hollywood, a voice that has convinced you that you have to live a certain way? Is it someone close to you who has decided how you should live and who you must become? Is it a parental voice or chorus? Is it the voice of your children? Your supervisor? Is your fear justified? What is the worst that can happen? Is it really going to happen if you're true to yourself? Now, focus on one small step you might take toward being yourself. Be bold and take that step, and see if your fear is justified or if you've faced it down and are ready to take the next step.

FIVE KEY POINTS ABOUT LIVING AN AUTHENTIC LIFE

1. Be genuine and live true to your values, which means being the same person at home and at work.

2. Live today by whittling away that which isn't true for you and acknowledging that which is.

3. Accept that some people are not going to like you and don't compare yourself with others.

4. You don't have forever to be yourself. The clock will run out.

5. Live your own dream that fits you uniquely; don't live someone else's dream because it won't fit.

Resilient people have learned to navigate their lives by their true north and can say with certainty, "This is who I am and this is where I'm heading." They are comfortable in their own skin and recognize, accept, and celebrate their individuality. This self-knowledge removes uncertainty, which is a good thing because it allows us to get on with our lives: there is less second-guessing and fewer detours and wrong directions.

Living an authentic life opens up our daring and creative sides and finally releases us to pursue and live our dreams. It takes work. You have to do some soul searching to get acquainted with yourself, but when you find yourself, you find your answers. You can do it, and you will *never* regret taking the time to find your true north.

NOTES

1. G. Pascal Zachary and Ken Yamada, "From 1993: What's Next? Steve Jobs's Vision, So on Target at Apple, Now Is Falling Short," *The Wall Street Journal*, May 25, 1993, http://online.wsj.com/article/SB10001424052970203476804576614371332161748.html (accessed Dec. 2011).

2. Kristin Kimball, *The Dirty Life: A Memoir of Farming, Food, and Love* (New York: Scribner, 2011).

3. David Nakamura, "Marine Sgt. Dakota Meyer receives Medal of Honor," *The Washington Post*, Sept. 15, 2011, http://www.washingtonpost.com/blogs/checkpoint-washington/post/marine-cpl-dakota-meyer-receives-medal-of-honor/2011/09/15/glQACqAKVK_blog.html (accessed Sept. 2013).

4. "Andrée Peel," *The Telegraph*, http://www.telegraph.co.uk/news/7407992/Andre-Peel.html (accessed July 2013).

5. "The Life of Harriet Tubman," *New York History Net*, http://www.nyhistory.com/harriettubman/life.htm (accessed Nov. 2011).

6. "Aleksandr Solzhenitsyn (1918-2008)," *Pegasos*, http://www.kirjasto.sci.fi/alesol.htm (accessed July 2013).

7. "About Georgia O'Keeffe," *Georgia O'Keeffe Museum*, http://www.okeeffemuseum.org/about-georgia-okeeffe.html (accessed June 2013).

8. "Global Renaissance Woman," *Maya Angelou*, http://www.mayaangelou.com/biography (accessed May 2013).

9. "Vincent van Gogh Biography," *A&E Networks*, http://www.biography.com/people/vincent-van-gogh-9515695?page=1 (accessed May 2013).

10. Nathan S. Collier, "The Monkey's Fist: An Ancient Parable for Modern Times," *NSC Blog*, http://www.nscblog.com/personal-growth/the-monkeys-fist-an-ancient-parable-for-modern-times (accessed July 2013).

11. Eric Metaxas, *Bonhoeffer: Pastor, Martyr, Prophet, Spy* (Nashville, TN: Thomas Nelson, 2010).

12. "Ann Romney Biography," *A&E Networks*, http://www.biography.com/people/ann-romney-20950331 (accessed July 2013).

FOUR PILLARS OF
A RESILIENT LIFE

CHAPTER 6: TAKING CARE OF YOUR HEALTH

"When you have your health, you have everything. When you do not have your health, nothing else matters at all."

—Augusten Burroughs

IN THIS CHAPTER you will learn:

- Why self-care is essential to survival

- How self-care builds resilience

- Six common reasons why it's difficult to care for yourself

- Forty-four things you can do that will lead to a long and resilient life

《 《 》 》

I F YOU'VE EVER flown commercially, you've heard the safety speech that flight attendants give before takeoff. It says that in the event of a loss of cabin pressure you should put on your own oxygen mask before you try to help anybody else, especially children. Why? If you become unconscious while trying to help them put on their mask, you'll both be in trouble.

The same principle applies to life. If you don't take care of yourself, you will have less to share with anyone else. Let's be very clear here: taking care of yourself first is *not* acting selfishly. If you exhaust yourself trying to meet others' needs while ignoring your own, you finally will collapse under the load and be useless to everyone. And, if you practice good self-care, you will live a longer, happier, and healthier life.

People who have learned to take care of themselves:

- Have more enthusiasm for life
- Are healthier with fewer sick days
- Feel good about themselves
- Have enough energy and stamina for work and play

WHY SELF-CARE IS ESSENTIAL TO SURVIVAL

If you have a tendency to put others' needs ahead of your own, you probably feel guilty and selfish every time you do something for yourself. If you don't take care of yourself, though, you will not be able to live a full and meaningful life or learn and grow stronger from adversity. In fact, you will not survive. At the very least, you must care for yourself as well as you actually care for others. Have you ever warned a friend to get more sleep to avoid getting sick? Well, do *you* get enough sleep? Maybe when a friend is stressed, you've said, "Go out and take a walk to clear your head." But do you take a walk when your own head isn't clear? It may be that you know what to do, but you don't do it for yourself.

HOW SELF-CARE BUILDS RESILIENCE AND VICE VERSA

Taking care of yourself builds resilience in three major ways:

1. It improves your overall health so that you have physical, emotional, spiritual, and intellectual energy and stamina to keep going, even when you're tired and discouraged.

2. It helps you develop the self-discipline necessary to bounce back and keep moving forward despite roadblocks.

3. It builds in you a "can do" attitude that is hard to beat and that leads to self-confidence.

It's also true that the stronger your resilience, the more motivated you'll be to take care of yourself and the more capability you'll have for doing so. Why? Resilient people live purposeful lives and have a compelling reason to get up every morning. They desire a high level of wellness in order to fulfill their goals in life. For them, it makes sense to maintain a healthy weight, exercise, get enough rest, wear their seatbelts, manage their stress, and not smoke. They want to be productive and fully live.

Bottom line: if you want to lose weight, stop smoking, stick to an exercise regimen, or manage your stress levels, then build and strengthen your resilience. You will find motivation to take care of yourself even when it's really hard to do.

WHAT TAKING CARE OF YOURSELF IS NOT

Taking care of yourself takes effort and self-discipline and is not the same as indulging or pampering yourself. Indeed indulgence can be the opposite of self-care. It's not difficult to find a TV ad or program that persuades you to love yourself by doing whatever feels good at the moment. You may mistake such indulgence for self-care. It isn't. Eating unhealthy food, engaging in casual or unsafe sex, drinking alcohol to the point of drunkenness, or going on a shopping spree you can't afford is not taking care of yourself. While most occasional indulgences will not cause long-term problems, regularly giving in to the desire for instant gratification eventually will take a toll on your life.

Self-care, on the other hand, means choosing behaviors that promote best possible health. Self-care requires self-discipline. You won't be ready for life if your mind is stressed, your muscles are flabby, or if you're always tired, really overweight, or headed down the road to addiction.

Let's look at how caring for yourself differs from neglecting yourself.

Self-care	Self-neglect
I am aware of my own needs.	I am out of touch with my own needs.
I am creative.	I have run out of ideas.
I am good to myself every day, without being self-indulgent.	I neglect myself and therefore cause harm to myself in some way every day.
I am refreshed, full of energy, and am able to give of myself.	I am exhausted, empty, and have nothing left to give.
I have strong spiritual beliefs, and they feed my soul.	I have few, if any, spiritual beliefs.
My direction and destination are clear.	I am pulled here and there and really get nowhere.
I say "yes" because I want to say "yes."	I say "yes" when I really want to say "no."

DO YOU TAKE GOOD CARE OF YOURSELF?

Do you think about your health? Do you ever take your health for granted? If you're like many of us, you probably don't give much thought to getting up in the morning and going about your daily activities unless you can't. Jean-Dominique Bauby, author of *The Diving Bell and the Butterfly*, described his last normal day and how he took his health for granted as he went about his usual activities. Then he had a massive stroke and longed to merely speak a word, taste food, and scratch an itch, none of which he could do.

Can you answer these questions: Do you want to be healthy? Are you willing to take the necessary actions to achieve optimal health? We know from the World Health Organization that "health is a state of complete physical, mental, and social well-being and not merely the absence of disease or infirmity." When you're healthy, you have energy, enthusiasm, and vitality. Many of us know what we need to do to have good health, but for some reason we don't follow through. Pause and imagine you have the best health you can achieve. What would you have to do to achieve it? Lose weight? Exercise? Manage your stress? Get some sleep? You know what you need to do.

Learning to be healthy now, whatever age you are, means you will live better right now and likely experience fewer years of illness and/or disability at the very end of your life. James Fries, professor emeritus of medicine at Stanford University School of Medicine, suggests that if we can postpone the average age that disability and illness usually occur, then illness is compressed between the time it actually begins to occur and the time of death. Instead of a lengthy gradual decline during which you become less independent, you "live long and die fast." Fries called this the "compression of morbidity." [1] In other words, you will live longer in good health and spend a relatively shorter time in illness at the end of your life. This is yet another compelling reason to strengthen your health today.

If anyone achieved this goal, it was Jack LaLanne, who died in 2011 at the age of ninety-six. Often referred to as the "first fitness superhero," he was a proponent of exercise and good nutrition decades before they became popular. LaLanne demonstrated his total health with feats of strength. At age seventy, handcuffed and shackled, he towed seventy people in seventy rowboats in Long Beach Harbor, a distance of one mile. He proceeded to work out every day until the day before his death.[2]

The brief twelve-item checklist below is a good starting place for you to learn how well you're taking care of yourself. Check all of the areas that you know you do on a regular basis.

1. I get at least seven to eight hours of sleep every night. ❑

2. I rarely give in to my worries. ❑

3. I am not drinking too much alcohol (fewer than one drink a day if a woman and fewer than two drinks a day if a man). ❑

4. I eat nutritiously, including at least six to nine fruits and vegetables every day. ❑

5. I exercise at least thirty minutes five days a week. ❑

6. I do not use any tobacco products. ❑

7. I feed my faith and spirit through study, prayer, meditation, and/or attending services. ❑

8. I always wear my seatbelt. ❑

9. I rarely, if ever, eat junk food (candy, chips, pizza, cookies, and the like). ❑

10. When I feel down or blue, I take action to feel better. ❑

11. I watch fewer than two hours of television a day. ❑

12. I drink water rather than sugary drinks for my usual beverage. ❑

YOU KNOW WHAT YOU NEED TO DO

There is now a great deal of information on what you need to do to live a long and healthy life. Sometimes the information is contradictory, such as the warnings about drinking coffee followed years later by the advantages of drinking caffeine. But some information has been supported by decades of research. A recent Centers for Disease Control survey of seventeen thousand people identified four behaviors that lead to a longer life. You probably have heard these before but they are worth repeating: (1) Don't smoke; (2) Exercise regularly; (3) Eat a healthy diet; and (4) Avoid excessive alcohol use. People whose lifestyle includes these behaviors are 63 percent less likely to die at an early age and their risk of cancer and heart disease is about two-thirds lower.[3]

Don't smoke

If you're a smoker, quit now. Doing so will add years to your life. Sir Richard Doll, professor emeritus at the University of Oxford, started a study in 1951 in which he followed 34,439 medical doctors for fifty years until he himself was in his nineties. He found that those who smoked but quit by age thirty added a decade to their life span. Those who quit at age forty, fifty, or sixty increased their life expectancy by nine, six, or three years, respectively.[4]

Exercise regularly

If you don't exercise, get moving. Exercise and a healthy, long life are directly related. The evidence is overwhelming with dozens of studies weighing in on the importance between exercise and health. About two-and-a-half hours of moderate exercise every week is recommended and is strongly associated with a reduced risk for heart disease, diabetes, some forms of cancer, stroke, dementia, infection, and depression.

Steven Blair of the Arnold School of Public Health at the University of South Carolina says that exercise improves quality of life as well.[5] His research states that as little as thirty minutes of physical activity a day is enough to decrease mortality rates by 50 percent. A group of researchers at the University of Exeter in Great Britain combined data from nineteen previous studies and found that exercise acutely reduced cigarette craving. The reason may be because exercise improves mood and so the need to feel better by smoking is reduced.[6]

Eat a healthy and nutritious diet

You probably are aware when your diet is terrible. You feel sluggish, your skin and hair are dull, and you crave sugar or salt. The evidence for the positive effects of a healthy diet is compelling. The Nurses' Health Study has followed 121,700 registered nurses since 1976 and now reports that a Mediterranean-type diet reduces risk of heart disease and stroke.[7] What is a Mediterranean diet? Fruits, fresh vegetables, whole grains, olive oil, and fish. The American College of Cardiology analyzed the outcomes of fifty studies that included about 535,000 people. It found a Mediterranean diet was associated with lower blood pressure, blood sugar, and triglycerides.[8]

Dan Buettner studied people around the world who live into their nineties and hundreds and remain active and involved. In *The Blue Zones* he describes dietary habits that lead to a long and healthy life. Those who live long eat four to six vegetable servings daily, limit their intake of red meat, consume beans and nuts, and don't overeat.[9] In Okinawa, one of the Blue Zones, they say *Hara hachi bu* before each meal, which means, "Eat until you are 80 percent full." [10]

Avoid excessive alcohol use

Is alcohol healthy or are you risking your health when you drink it? The reality is complicated and each of us needs to consider several factors in arriving at the best answer for us. Researchers looked at 222 studies that included ninety-two thousand light drinkers (up to one drink a day) and sixty thousand nondrinkers. As little as one drink a day increased their risk of certain cancers, including breast, throat, mouth, and esophagus.[11]

On the other hand, alcohol appears to be good for heart health. In a large review of eighty-four studies, researchers found that the lowest risk of heart disease mortality was among those who consumed one to two drinks a day. For stroke, the lowest risk of death was less than one drink per day. Overall, there was lower risk for light drinkers than nondrinkers.[12]

If you are at higher risk for heart disease, then drinking no more than two drinks if you are a man—and one or fewer if you are a woman—is the healthy way to go. If you have a family or personal history of cancer and believe that you may be at risk yourself, then it's best to drink fewer than the above guidelines. The combination of alcohol and tobacco increases the risk for head and neck cancers, which is another reason to quit if you smoke.

Other effects of excessive alcohol consumption include high blood pressure, cirrhosis of the liver, and weight gain because alcohol stimulates appetite. And for those with alcohol dependency, no alcohol at all is the only way to go.

We know what we need to do to have a healthier life that leads to energy, stamina, and enthusiasm. Why are we unable to do it?

SIX COMMON REASONS WHY IT'S DIFFICULT TO CARE FOR YOURSELF AND STEPS TO OVERCOME EACH BARRIER

One: I believe I have no control over my own life

Try Googling "I have no control over my life" and see what you get. I found more than nine hundred million hits to this statement. One person wrote, "I am dissatisfied with my life. I want so much more out of life but can't get it, or don't know how to get it. If I had control over my life, I'd have so much more. I feel like everything I get in my life is always my plan G choice. Not even my plan B choice." When we believe that we have no control over our lives, we're saying, "I don't have a choice. Someone or something else is calling all the shots." With rare exceptions, however, you do have choices. It's entirely up to you whether you sit down and scarf down a pint of ice cream, slouch on the couch and watch hours of mindless television, go out and get drunk with your friends, or get up and go for a fast walk in the fresh air.

Getting control over your life

Below are four easy steps for getting control over your life.

1. Write down three self-care goals you'd like to accomplish, each on a separate sheet of paper. Maybe you want to lose a few pounds, eat more vegetables every day, exercise regularly, or just have some time to yourself. Write them as clearly and specifically as you can. For example: "I will lose fifteen pounds by June 1." "I will eat (at least) five veggies a day every single day for just this week." "I will exercise thirty minutes a day five days a week for one month, starting today." "From now on, I will take an hour every day just for me." Set your own goals. Be sure they're determined, realistic, and achievable. Be sure they're written in a specific way so you can measure your progress over a specific period of time.

2. Now write down as many ideas as you can for achieving these goals. Again, write these as positive, direct, "can do" statements. For instance, if you want to lose weight, you might say that you'll start exercising more, find an exercise buddy, join a gym, eat fewer

calories, learn a new sport or hobby to get yourself out of the house, walk the stairs at work, or park farther from the store. You get the idea. Write as many as occur to you, and do it without criticizing or censoring any of your ideas.

3.   After you have written up your ideas for each goal, identify specific steps you will take tomorrow to head toward this goal. For instance, you might decide to leave for work five minutes early and park a block from work. You might pack a lunch that includes nutritious, low-calorie food, or make a grocery list that includes fresh vegetables and fruits and limits sugary drinks and snacks.

4.   Make note of those things you will do less. For instance, if your goal is to lose fifteen pounds, you might need to spend one hour less watching television or eliminate the bowl of ice cream you eat every night before you go to bed.

Two: I feel guilty if I focus on my own needs first

Do you ever feel you're doing something wrong, and perhaps even being selfish, when you take care of yourself? Maybe you believe that the most important and valued activities are those related to work, that is, anything that requires performance, labor, completing tasks, duties, and meeting goals. To go a step further, you may even feel lazy and nonproductive whenever you're not working. Maybe taking care of yourself even feels lazy to you. Or maybe friends and family want you to do something with or for them. You want to please them, but you have to sacrifice time you'd hoped to have for your own needs in order to fulfill theirs. These experiences will leave you feeling ill and guilty.

If you don't take care of yourself, of course, your paid and/or unpaid work as well as your health and relationships will suffer. Burnout is frequently defined as what happens when you don't take care of yourself for an extended period of time. Think about the serious consequences of letting yourself down, and stop thinking about how you're letting everyone else down. (I'll bet you're not, by the way.) Too much stress, poor nutrition, lack of sleep, physical inactivity, and addictive behaviors such as smoking and excessive alcohol consumption eventually will leave you unable to work. Learn to let go of the guilt and take care of yourself. But how?

Letting go of guilt

You may need to redefine self-care. Rather than seeing self-care as self-indulgent or self-centered behavior, recognize that self-care is essential, meaning you can't live without it. If you don't take care of yourself, remember you eventually will pay the consequences when you get an illness from which you may not recover easily. Or at all. You only get one chance at living this life.

You may find out that others aren't as affected by your taking time for yourself as you think. It may be that no one is really let down because you've decided to go to the gym three times a week, or not answer your emails within an hour, or read a good book instead of cleaning out the fridge or making sure the windows sparkle. Even when we still feel guilty, taking action and behaving in a self-loving and self-accepting way will change our overall outlook for the better.

Three: I want to take care of myself but I can't find enough time

Of all of the excuses for not taking care of yourself, this one may be the most common for avoiding healthy habits such as exercising, relaxing, getting enough sleep, preparing a nutritious meal, or even taking the few extra seconds to put on a seatbelt.

What can you do to motivate yourself to take the time to do the right things for yourself? Here are some ways to push past this barrier:

- Find someone to hold you accountable. It might be a coworker, spouse, partner, or your child who helps or reminds you to exercise, wear your seatbelt, or stop smoking and eating junk food.

- Spend time with people who make healthy choices for themselves. Research shows such behavior is contagious. For instance, according to Nicholas Christakis and James Fowler, authors of Connected: The Surprising Power of Our Social Networks and How They Shape Our Lives, respondents said they were less likely to exercise if their friends didn't exercise.

- The average American spends 4.6 hours every day in front of the television, according to the Nielsen rating agency. Take back some of that time to do something good for yourself.

- You may never be able to find time but you can make time for yourself. You have to become the priority on your own "to do" list every day. It's up to you to figure out how.

Four: I am discouraged before I even start

Many of us have made resolutions to change our lives and have failed repeatedly to achieve our goals. It may seem to you like you'll never succeed. You lose five pounds and gain ten back. You start an exercise program and, within a week, find excuses to do something else. This is where your resilience kicks in. Remember these four things:

1. Your self-care goals are worth the time and effort. You don't want to be unhealthy, tired, and depressed. You desire a full, healthy, vibrant, and rewarding life and your efforts to achieve this are worth it.

2. Sometimes you have to put your head down and just keep plugging along, no matter how discouraged, tired, and frustrated you become. Diligence and determination are the only way to progress toward your goals.

3. You can achieve your goals by taking one step at a time. By now everyone knows the expression, "A journey of a thousand miles begins with a single step." But it's nonetheless a true and powerful statement. If you're trying to lose fifteen pounds, you have to cut out the junk food for the next hour, and then the next. One step at a time.

4. Finally, celebrate your successes every day. Don't be too hard on yourself, but don't be a pushover, either. Reward yourself for genuine progress with rest, visits with friends, a good movie, an engaging book, a walk in nature, a cup of tea, or a promised trip to somewhere you've never been or to a favorite place on a weekend.

Five: I don't see the point; why make the effort?

For many people, life has become a long, dreary journey with little purpose and few highs or lows. For those whose life has become aimless, the allure of instant gratification through food, alcohol and other drugs, and passive entertainment is understandable.

How do you get past these temptations? Learn more about yourself. People with a purpose have a reason to get up in the morning and find their way through just about any challenge life throws them, including losing weight, stopping smoking, and sticking to an exercise program.

Six: I have no self discipline

An eighty-year study followed 1,528 eleven-year-olds to see what characteristics would lead to a longer life. Howard S. Friedman and Leslie R. Martin found in their study that the key traits to longevity are prudence and persistence. People who took great care and effort and paid scrupulous attention to getting things done the right way also did more things to protect their health. They exercised, ate well, and wore their seatbelts, all of which led to healthy choices and a longer life. They also chose healthier relationships and better friendships. While their work was not stress free, they enjoyed and were challenged by it.[13]

Researchers who looked at twenty different studies found that being persistent, organized, and disciplined were significantly related to living a long and healthy life.[14] Exerting self-discipline reaps many rewards in life and, since it's a skill and not a trait, anyone can work at achieving it.

FORTY-FOUR THINGS YOU CAN DO THAT WILL LEAD TO A LONG AND RESILIENT LIFE

EMOTIONAL

"Most folks are about as happy as they make up their minds to be."

—Abraham Lincoln

Twelve ways to improve your emotional outlook and reduce your stress

1. Learn daily behaviors to reduce your stress such as listening to music, talking with a friend, or spending time with your pet.

2. Create comforting rituals in your daily life. For some the morning ritual of a cup of coffee or tea to start the day is essential. Routines relieve tension, strengthen our ability to cope, and create order in lives that otherwise might be chaotic.

3. Accept that stress is part of life for most people but that you can manage it through proven stress management techniques such as meditation and breathing exercises.

4. Manage your time better and prioritize what needs to be done.

5. Express your needs and feelings to someone you trust so you don't feel alone with your worries.

6. Accept that multitasking is not productive. Focusing on one activity at a time promotes relaxation and protects you against anxiety and depression.

7. Acknowledge and celebrate daily accomplishments with small but positive rewards.

8. Spend part of every day outdoors surrounded by nature. Listen to birds, breathe fresh air, bask in sunshine, and enjoy the trees, clouds, and changing seasons.

9. Take time at least weekly to be with friends with whom you can laugh and talk.

10. Find ways to enjoy your life and get out of your house. There are many ways to engage life, including gardening, volunteering, walking your pet, or playing a sport.

11. Set limits and learn to say "no" to requests that add too much needless anxiety to your life.

12. Listen to music for thirty minutes, especially music that's calming and has a slow tempo. Research shows that listening to thirty

minutes of tranquil music is able to produce as much relaxation as ten milligrams of Valium.

INTELLECTUAL

"Intellectual growth should commence at birth and cease only at death."

—Albert Einstein

Ten practices to strengthen your intellect

1. Do mentally stimulating activities such as reading, learning something new, memorizing a poem, singing or playing a musical instrument, trying out a new sport, or reading the newspaper every day.

2. Keep a daily journal and keep track of your thoughts about current events, people with whom you talked that day, and what you learned, felt, and experienced.

3. Write letters to friends and aim to write a letter to someone once a week.

4. Maintain a to-do list in the morning and check off your accomplishments.

5. Do something creative such as writing, art, crafts, gardening, rearranging the furniture in a room, or whatever you like as long as it requires a new perspective.

6. Jot down the worries or tasks you're anxious about completing before you sleep and vow to tackle them tomorrow. You'll sleep better.

7. Take a class in something that interests you, such as a foreign language, drawing, mechanics, raising livestock, flying an airplane, and so forth.

8. Visit a museum, attend a new gallery opening in your community, or travel someplace you've never been, even locally.

9. Attend or present at seminars, conferences, and workshops in order to learn something new or to share your knowledge and skills and spend time with people who have similar interests.

10. Read a nonfiction book once a month. Choose from biographies, history, how-to books, politics, current events, and other categories.

SPIRITUAL

"We must be ready to allow ourselves to be interrupted by God."

—Dietrich Bonhoeffer

There is growing evidence from research that people who are more involved in religious and spiritual beliefs and practices live longer and stay healthier. For instance, in a six-year study of almost four thousand adults, those who attended a religious service at least once a week were 46 percent less likely to die during the six years of the study. These people also had less depression and anxiety, exhibited signs of better health, said they felt healthier, and were more socially connected.[15]

Twelve activities to strengthen your spiritual life

1. Attend religious services at least weekly with others who believe as you do.

2. Meditate or pray frequently.

3. Mindfully connect your daily activities with your spiritual beliefs and values.

4. Practice daily forgiveness and forgive insults and injustices others have caused in your life.

5. Apologize to others you've hurt or betrayed in some way.

6. Express gratitude for everything you have and for the people in your life.

7. Love others unconditionally.

8. Talk with someone you trust about life's meaning and your purpose in the world.

9. Write your life story and consider what you want your legacy to be.

10. Join a small prayer group or meet with friends to talk about matters of spiritual importance to you.

11. Go on a spiritual retreat to get away from your normal work routine and to re-evaluate your life, find serenity, rest, relax, reflect, and return to your routines with a more balanced, healthier perspective.

12. You also can go on a brief at-home retreat by unplugging from your computer and phone, meditating, practicing aromatherapy, or soaking in a bathtub.

PHYSICAL

"Those who think they have not time for bodily exercise will sooner or later have to find time for illness."

—Edward Stanley

Ten activities to improve your physical health

1. If you haven't had a physical check-up within the past five years, be sure to schedule one soon. If you're due for diagnostic or screening tests, get them.

2. Exercise thirty minutes a day, five days a week. Choose a variety of activities that you like to do, which can include walking, cycling, fitness classes, hiking, weight lifting and so forth. Recognize your achievements, too. If your clothes fit better, you have more energy, or you're sleeping better at night, congratulate yourself.

3. Seek out friends who have good exercise habits and spend time with them. Physical fitness can be contagious.

4. Be sure you're getting enough sleep. You can take the *Psychology Today* Sleep Hygiene Test at

http://psychologytoday.tests.psychtests.com/take_test.php?idReg
Test=1329 or another reputable self-test.

5. Eat a healthy diet. Good nutrition is an excellent way to prevent
    and control many health problems, including heart disease, some
    types of cancer, Type 2 diabetes, and high blood pressure. Old
    guidelines recommended at least five fruits and vegetables daily,
    but that amount may not be enough. The new recommendation
    is seven to thirteen cups of produce daily.

6. Drink alcohol in moderation only (two drinks a day for men and
    one for women). While some alcohol use may cut Alzheimer's
    risk and improve heart health, drinking also has been linked to a
    higher cancer risk, especially in women. Very recent advice
    suggests abstaining at least two days a week to protect health.

7. Drink water to balance fluids in your body, control calories,
    prevent constipation, and keep your skin looking healthy. Recent
    research reveals that when you're dehydrated, your cortisol levels
    increase. Cortisol is a hormone released in response to physical
    or psychological stress.

8. Completely avoid all tobacco products, including secondhand
    smoke. Smoking increases mental decline, risk of autoimmune
    disease, impotence, age-related macular degeneration, acid reflux,
    breast cancer, emphysema, lung cancer, and many other problems.

9. Always wear your seatbelt; even if you are just driving to the
    corner grocery store for ice cream.

10. Hug a friend or family member, pet your dog, cat, or horse, and
    snuggle with your spouse. This simple action will lower your blood
    pressure, reduce stress hormones, and help you think more clearly.

Resilient people know that in order to respond to adversity with
strength and flexibility and to live full, productive, and committed lives,
they must take excellent care of themselves. If they don't, they will not
survive. No one else can do this for them. Self-care is not selfish. In fact,
it's just the opposite. If you don't take care of yourself first, you'll be of
no use to anyone.

NOTES

1. James S. Fries, Bonnie Bruce, and Eliza Chakravarty, "Compression of Morbidity 1980-2011: A Focused Review of Paradigms and Progress," *Journal of Aging and Research,* vol. 261 (2011): 261702.

2. UPI, "Jack LaLanne fit as ever at 70," *Lodi News-Sentinel,* Nov. 19, 1984.

3. Earl S. Ford, Guixiang Zhao, James Tsai, and Chaoyang Li, "Low-risk Lifestyle Behaviors and All-cause Mortality: Findings from the National Health and Nutrition Examination Survey III Mortality Study," *American Journal of Public Health,* vol. 101 (2011): 1922-29.

4. Sir Richard Doll, Richard Peto, Jillian Boreham, and Isabelle Sutherland, "Mortality in Relation to Smoking: 50 Years' Observations on Male British Doctors," *British Medical Journal,* vol. 328 (2004): 1519-28.

5. Steven N. Blair, Robert E.Sallis, Adrian Hutber, and Edward Archer, "Exercise Therapy: The Public Health Message," *Scandinavian Journal of Medicine and Science in Sports,* vol. 22 (2012): e24-28.

6. Marcela Haasova, et al., "The Acute Effects of Physical Activity on Cigarette Cravings: Systematic Review and Meta-analysis with Individual Participant Data (IPD)," *Addiction,* vol. 108 (2013): 26-37.

7. Teresa T. Fung, et al., "Mediterranean Diet and Incidence of and Mortality from Coronary Heart Disease and Stroke in Women," *Circulation,* vol. 119 (2009): 1093-100.

8. Christina-Maria Kastorini, et al., "The Effect of Mediterranean Diet on Metabolic Syndrome and Its Components," *Journal of the American College of Cardiology,* vol. 57 (2011): 1299-1313.

9. Buettner, 243.

10. Buettner, 83.

11. Vincenzo Bagnardi, "Light Alcohol Drinking and Cancer: A Meta Analysis," *Annals of Oncology,* vol. 24 (2012): 301-308.

12. Paul E. Ronksley, Susan E. Brien, Barbara J. Turner, Kenneth J. Mukamal, and William A.Ghali, "Association of Alcohol Consumption with Selected Cardiovascular Disease Outcomes: A Systematic Review and Meta-analysis," *British Medical Journal,* vol. 22 (2011): 342.

13. Howard S. Friedman and Leslie R. Martin, *The Longevity Project: Surprising Discoveries for Health and Long Life from the Landmark Eight-Decade Study* (New York: Hudson Street Press, 2011).

14. Margaret L. Kern and Howard S. Friedman, "Do Conscientious Individuals Live Longer? A Quantitative Review," *Health Psychology,* vol. 27 (2008): 505-12.

15. Harold G. Koenig, "Does Religious Attendance Prolong Survival? A Six-year Follow-up Study of 3,968 Older Adults," *The Journals of Gerontology Series A,* vol. 54 (1999): M370-76.

CHAPTER 7: GIVING AND SEEKING SUPPORT FROM OTHERS

"We few, we happy few, we band of brothers;
For he today that sheds his blood with me
Shall be my brother ... "

—William Shakespeare, *Henry V*

IN THIS CHAPTER you will learn:

- About the value and benefits of true friendships

- How friendship contributes to resilience

- About giving of yourself to others

《 《 》 》

OUR JOURNEY THROUGH life is more meaningful and rewarding when we travel with friends. Those we care about and who care about us are a treasure of incalculable value because they love and accept us, including our strengths and imperfections. Their acceptance and support help us to live resiliently. It's good to know how important it is to build a community of those who will go the distance with you and how you can nurture and strengthen these important relationships in your life.

People who have close relationships have a more positive self-image. They have better health, including lower risk of death due to illness, a stronger immune system, and fewer alcohol, drug, and addiction problems. They also have less depression and anxiety.

"It is a luxury to be understood," wrote Ralph Waldo Emerson, speaking of his closest friends, with whom he shared his hopes, dreams, and innermost thoughts. It's widely known and accepted, among scientists and philosophers alike, that friendship is important to our well-being.

Close and intimate friends support and encourage us to live meaningful lives, pursue our dreams, be ourselves, and to keep going even when we want to quit. In short, they help us recognize, build, and strengthen our desire and ability to live resiliently.

Can we be resilient without friends? Yes, but life wouldn't be nearly as rich or meaningful. As author and philosopher C.S. Lewis said, "Friendship has no survival value but it gives value to survival."

DO YOU MAKE ACQUAINTANCES OR FORM FRIENDSHIPS?

"A friend is not a fellow who is taken in by sham; a friend is one who knows our faults and doesn't give a damn."

—Author unknown

Think for a moment about the quality of your relationships with others. There's a qualitative difference between friends and acquaintances. An acquaintance is someone you know well enough to invite to lunch or coffee. You may have work or other interests in common and you're comfortable spending time together occasionally. But an acquaintance is not someone you'll trust with secrets or with whom you'll talk about issues of deep importance. You probably don't know much about an acquaintance's life, and you may not disclose much of your life to him or her. Over time an acquaintance can turn into a friend.

In contrast, a friend is someone you know well and care about on a deeper level. You know the likes and dislikes of your friends. You have seen them at their worst and still love them. You feel safe with them because you know they care about you, will listen to you if you need to talk, and be there if you get into trouble.

Likewise, you are there for them if they get into trouble. Friends are happy for you. Most of the time, you look forward to spending time with your friends and cherish your time together. Friends don't desert you. If you were to die today, your friends would gather at your graveside and grieve. Do you have people like this in your life? Strive for true friendships.

HOW FRIENDSHIPS IMPROVE YOUR HEALTH

Good friends will help you achieve health and happiness and celebrate every success with you. There is growing evidence that friendships carry health benefits, including strengthening immunity, reducing the likelihood of depression, and living a longer life. Having friends will add more years to your life than stopping smoking. Also, having friends helps you lose weight. Several well-designed research studies show that those who have supportive friends join them in their weight loss programs take off more weight and are better at keeping it off than those who go it alone.[1]

The benefits of friendship aren't limited to face-to-face contact. Mike and Albert Lee, who developed MyFitnessPal, a calorie-tracking app, analyzed data from a sample of five hundred thousand users. They tracked users' weights against how many friends they had on the service. The more friends they had, the more weight they lost. To break down the study results even further, those who gave others access to their calorie counts lost 50 percent more weight than the others, and those with at least ten friends lost an average of 20.5 pounds.[2]

As to longevity, an Australian study found that people with many friends were, over a ten-year period, 22 percent less likely to die than those with fewer friends.[3] Alameda County, California studies that spanned nine years found that men and women with little support from others were 1.9 to 3.0 times more likely to die from a variety of diseases, including cancer and heart disease.[4] The effect of support from friends and other social contacts may be as strong as the effects of obesity, cigarette smoking, hypertension, and exercise.[5]

A collaborative study at Brigham Young University and the University of North Carolina at Chapel Hill combined data from 148 studies on health outcomes and social relationships. The number of subjects from all studies totaled around three hundred thousand people. The study found that those with poor social connections had a 50 percent higher likelihood of death over a 7.5-year period than people with more friends. Regardless of age or sex, these were the results.[6]

How does friendship work, exactly? By what physiological mechanism? Researchers are beginning to believe that having friends and other social ties may help our bodies heal themselves or ward off illness in the first place.

For instance, people in stressful situations will show an increase in blood pressure and heart rate. We've all experienced such a physical reaction. But when we have someone with us who is a close friend or family member, blood pressure and heart rate don't increase as much. Sheldon Cohen at Carnegie Mellon University conducted a fascinating experiment on the effect that the number of social connections in people's lives has on their contracting a cold. He deliberately exposed hundreds of study participants to the cold virus and found that those with more social connections were less likely to get sick.[7]

Friendships help you have less stress in your life, too. People who have a strong support system don't feel alone; the burden of their problems is shared by others. They have a greater sense of belonging that lessens feelings of isolation and loneliness. They give each other encouragement, support, and even suggestions for success. It's always good to have support when going through traumatic events such as serious illness, divorce, job loss, or the death of someone close to you.

Happiness among friends is contagious. It spreads like a virus to your friends and then back to you. In fact, researchers say your chance of being happy increases by 15 percent for every happy friend you have, 10 percent for every happy friend of a friend, and even 6 percent for the happy friends of the friends of friends! Recent research indicates that people who are surrounded by happy people are more likely to become happy in the future. If a friend who lives within a mile of you becomes happy, the probability is greater that you also will be happy.[8]

Friendship strengthens your immune system. When we have friends in our life, they prevent our living isolated and lonely lives and offer us hope, encouragement, and remind us of our purpose when we've lost our way. This connection leads to an increase in hope and optimism when we work through adversity, and an increase in hope is associated with improved immune system functioning. That means fewer colds and, if you do get one, faster recovery.

HOW MANY FRIENDS CAN YOU KEEP, AND HOW MANY DO YOU NEED?

Anthropologist Robin Dunbar has offered an answer to this interesting question from his research.[9] He says our ability to handle complex social connections, which include our closest friends and family, coworkers, acquaintances, and old friends, is limited and argues that we can only maintain relationships with about one hundred and fifty people at any given time. These are the people in your life with whom you have established trust and a give-and-take relationship.

He further divides the one hundred and fifty people into what he calls "Circles of Acquaintanceship." The inner core includes about five people with whom you are intimate; the next layers include fifteen, then fifty, and up to one hundred and fifty people. The number of people in each circle increases as the level of emotional intimacy decreases.

WHAT'S LOVE GOT TO DO WITH IT?

"Only a life lived for others is worth living."

—Albert Einstein

Many people think of love in the context of romance or their children. There is perhaps a more noble definition in John 15:13:

Greater love than this no man hath, that a man lay down his life for his friends.

(Douay-Rheims Bible 1899 American Edition)

It would seem that according to this definition, love is sacrifice. True friendship requires sacrifice, perhaps in the form of love that is given without criticism and expects nothing in return. You give your friends love because you accept them the way they are and, in turn, they accept you. No matter how terrible you might be from time to time, a true friend will still love you. Whatever mess you get into, your true friends will stand fast. Your true friends will forgive you and not bear grudges. To love unconditionally is to freely invest your time and emotions in the happiness of another.

If a friend should give up his life for a friend, he gives up all that he has. Most of us will never be asked to give everything, but true friendship occasionally asks us to sacrifice. Perhaps a friend wants to do something other than what you had in mind. You might give a friend credit for something you did because he or she needs a boost, or you might give your share of scarce resources to a friend who needs them more than you do. Our sacrifice may be time and money, large or small. Our resilience—in other words, our capacity to live a full and rewarding life—will increase and strengthen because of a friendship like this.

RATE YOURSELF ON THE FRIENDSHIPS IN YOUR LIFE

Very few people want to be alone, and yet many find themselves wondering why they are without close friends. Check the items below that are true for you. This exercise will help you begin to understand how strong your friendships are right now and where you might begin to make some changes.

1. I have a friend I can call at 4 a.m. if I am sad and feeling lonely. ☐

2. When I'm feeling like everything is hopeless, I know someone who will offer me encouragement. ☐

3. I have a friend who gives me honest and impartial advice when I ask for it. ☐

4. There is at least one person I can name who would give me concrete help if were down and out (for instance, money, use of a car, or a job). ☐

5. I am a good listener. ☐

6. I am loyal; I never tear a friend down behind his or her back. ☐

7. I spend time every day giving something back to my friend(s). ☐

8. My friend(s) have always been there for me, no matter what. ☐

9. I live by the Golden Rule: "Love your neighbor as yourself," or "Do as you would be done by." ☐

WHAT DO YOU OFFER YOUR FRIENDS?

"At the end of your life, you will never regret not having passed one more test, not winning one more verdict, or not closing one more deal. You will regret time not spent with a husband, a friend, a child, or a parent."

—Barbara Bush

If you want a friend, you must first be one. I'm sure you've heard these wise words. A good friend is priceless, and the time and effort you take to nurture your friendships are worth it. Sometimes it helps to review what friends do for each other.

Friends provide emotional support. They offer empathy, concern, love, trust, acceptance, and understanding. They feel valued in each other's presence because to give a friend emotional support is to acknowledge that friend matters to you. How can you support another person? If your friend is anxious, depressed, sad, angry, ill, or just out of sorts, spend time together. Just the two of you. Don't force any conversation. Just listen, and listen some more, but unless you're asked for advice, don't give any.

Emotional support often includes patting someone on the back and hugging, or maybe holding someone's hand. Also, don't minimize or dismiss someone's fears and give false assurance. If you do, you will lose your friend's trust. Your caring and supportive presence is the most important emotional support you can give. Euripides said, "Friends show their love in times of trouble."

The seven commonly accepted tenets of friendship are:

1. Strive to be genuine, compassionate, forgiving, kind, and loving.

2. Trust others and be trustworthy.

3. Never break a confidence, unless a life is threatened.

4. Honor your friends and be respectful.

5. Have your friend's back.

6. Be there for your friends; drop what you're doing and help.

7. Never take your friends for granted.

Friends give tangible support when needed. One way of offering such support is taking on responsibility for someone else—providing financial help, services such as child care, a safe place to stay, a car to drive to a job interview, or a ride to a medical appointment. Support can mean buying groceries, cleaning a friend's house if he or she is ill, or giving a friend clothing. It can mean helping each other at work, developing a business plan together, or offering constructive feedback on a design or project.

Friends help solve problems and provide informational support. Sometimes we need help making decisions like, *Should I change jobs? Should I go back to school?* or *Should I buy a house?* A friend will listen to us and then give advice and suggestions to help us reach the best decision. Sometimes we need a friend to help us gather information so that we can make the most informed decisions. For instance, if your friend has been diagnosed with a serious illness, it may be too demanding and stressful for him or her to gather information and make a good treatment decision. In this case, your help in assembling the most important facts will relieve your friend of much stress.

Each of us has abilities and strengths that our friends don't have. Friends' strengths complement each other, and so they offer help that only they can give.

Friends also help create a sense of belonging. Our friends are our companions with whom we share common interests, including hobbies, work, or other social activities. These shared interests and activities lead to a sense of comfort and assurance that we are not alone in this world. Having a sense of belonging can actually relieve our depression because we feel that we fit into the world. "Being on the outside" is like being excluded from a campfire circle: it's cold and lonely and can be downright scary.

RECIPROCITY: A PRACTICE OF RESILIENT PEOPLE

Resilient people want to give back to others and find ways to help them. This is called altruism. The more we're able to give to others, the stronger our own resilience becomes. Generosity also has a way of strengthening the bond of friendship. You will get more happiness and satisfaction by helping others than by receiving help. How can you best give? Does giving always mean offering tangible support like money or gifts?

Generosity of spirit manifests when you speak words of enthusiasm, support, and kindness to a friend who is struggling. One of the best ways for you to strengthen and build your own resilience is to help someone else strengthen theirs. When you help someone clarify a purposeful life and not give up on their goals, you also strengthen your own resilience. And as your resilience grows, you will in turn inspire others.

When we become too preoccupied with ourselves, though, it's easy to be anxious and depressed because we focus on our problems and everything that's wrong in our lives. A study at the University of Massachusetts Medical School found that giving help, rather than receiving it, led to improved mental health on the part of the giver.

Researcher Carolyn Schwartz said, "The act of giving to someone else may have mental health benefits because the very nature of focusing outside the self counters the self-focused nature of anxiety or depression." [10]

When we reach out to help others, our personal stress is diminished, which results in the positive emotional and physical outcomes described by Allan Luks as "helper's high." He describes this phenomenon as a release of endorphins, or "feel good" hormones, that leads to a sense of joy followed by a feeling of serenity. [11]

Although the study is now several decades old, it often is used to show the power of altruism. James House studied twenty-seven hundred residents of Tecumseh, Michigan and found that those who volunteered for community organizations were 2.5 times less likely to die from any cause than those who didn't volunteer. [12]

Stephanie Brown at the University of Michigan followed 423 elderly couples for five years. Those who provided no help to others, whether practical or emotional, were more than twice as likely to die than their more altruistic peers. Of particular interest was her finding that 25 percent of the respondents had done nothing to help anyone else during an entire year. They hadn't offered to pick up mail, water plants, feed pets, go to the grocery store, make a phone call, and so forth. [13]

What activities lead to a "helper's high?" You probably already have some ideas but the list below may help you identify some additional possibilities.

- Visiting someone in a nursing home
- Tutoring schoolchildren
- Volunteering at hospitals or homeless shelters
- Donating to charities

Look for opportunities where you can be generous with your ideas and skills. Can you help someone fix the taillight on a car? Can you teach someone how to make Julia Child's Boeuf Bourguignon? Fix a computer? Lend a sympathetic ear or give good legal advice? I remember a very generous act when my mother was ill and hospitalized. We were at her bedside almost around the clock. It was early January and the temperatures outside were subzero. My car's battery had started being cranky when I started it up at 2:00 a.m. in the hospital parking lot. One day, my nephew Mike bought a new battery and installed it. So when I went out that night, my car roared to life. I will never forget his generosity and kindness.

Remember also that every day offers opportunities to perform random acts of kindness: Hold the door or elevator door open for someone. Let another car in your lane when traffic is congested. Write a note of thanks to a coworker. Make a phone call expressing appreciation to a neighbor or friend.

One caveat: In chapter six you read about taking care of yourself. Altruism does not mean you exhaust yourself helping others as you seek a "helper's high." As with anything else in life, overdoing will tire you out and the benefits of your generosity will rapidly diminish. Moderation and balance are key.

FALSE FRIENDSHIP

"An insincere and evil friend is more to be feared than a wild beast; a wild beast may wound your body, but an evil friend will wound your mind."

—Buddha

Not everyone who calls himself your friend is your friend. Read the descriptions below, and as you read, think about your friends. Do you have any friends who fall into any of the eight categories? If you do, you might want to rethink your friendship with these people or even find a way to drop them from your list of so-called friends. Remember, of course, that they may be true friends with someone else. They just aren't a good fit for you and may even cause you harm.

1. Toxic friends. These people frequently treat you badly. Maybe they let you down, are grumpy all the time, or discourage you from trying new things. You rarely laugh together. You don't feel good about yourself when you're with these people.

2. Frenemies. These folks are really your enemy, but they wear a "friend" disguise. Maybe you were once friends and you had some good times together, but they have since become competitive or

actively seek to make you fail. They may call you their friend, but they put you down in front of others or are unpredictable and untrustworthy.

3. Emotional vampires. As the label suggests, emotional vampires suck all the energy out of you. They are negative, and you just feel drained after you've spent time with them. An example is a drama queen who always has to be the center of attention. Her life is always harder or more complicated than yours and therefore more worthy of attention. Drama queens use guilt to draw you into their dramas.

4. Parasites. Have you ever met people who lean on you for everything? They're parasites. Eventually, their level of dependence will exhaust you, make you ill, and eventually cause you to collapse under their incessant demands. Parasites will take everything you have emotionally, financially, and physically. They know no bounds and only think of themselves. Once you're used up, they move on to the next "host."

5. Killjoys. These people deliberately spoil your fun or shoot you down. Maybe you're dancing or singing and enjoying yourself; a killjoy will let you know that you're acting silly. A killjoy will make sure that your "good idea" is full of holes and won't work. These people are also known as "party poopers" and "wet blankets," and they take pleasure in spoiling the enjoyment of others.

6. Fair-weather friends. As long as everything is going well, fair-weather friends will be at your side. But as soon as the going gets tough in your life, these people become scarce and don't have room for you in their schedules. From time to time, we all need a friend who is a rock—solid, dependable, immovable. But fair-weather friends will abandon you just when you need them most. Oprah Winfrey said, "Lots of people want to ride with you in the limo, but what you want is someone who will take the bus with you when the limo breaks down."

7. Control freaks. This type of person wants to control your life: which friends you spend time with, what food you eat, what you do for fun, and so forth. They are manipulative and take advantage of your goodwill to get you to do things you don't really want to do. These people use their anger to get what they want until you

finally go along just to get along. You may lose sight of yourself in the process.

8. Just plain dangerous people. These so-called friends are intent on involving you in unsafe or even dangerous activities. They might encourage you to do unhealthy things, such as drink too much alcohol, commit crimes, or do other things that are both dangerous and illegal, such as use cocaine or heroin and drive your car while under the influence. These are not people to hang out with. They may try to make you feel like a coward for not participating, but resist with all your might!

CLUES THAT POINT TO "UNTRUE" FRIENDS

The following clues will help you figure out if some of the people you hang out with are your true friends. Let's say you just had lunch with a particular person. How do you feel afterward?

- I am tense when I think about having lunch with this person again.

- I wasn't able to relax during lunch and now I'm tired and feeling stressed.

- I couldn't be myself, and the muscles in my face feel strained. I have a headache.

- This person took and took from me and gave nothing back. I'm worn out.

- The conversation focused entirely on this person, who never even asked me what was going on with me. I feel insignificant.

- I left feeling bad about myself.

If even one of these clues fits your experience, you might want to think about spending time with other friends instead.

FIFTEEN IDEAS FOR MEETING NEW FRIENDS

It's always good to keep a friend, and making new ones is one of life's joys. Some of these tips you will already know. Others might be new to you. They're all worth a try.

1. Call, write, or connect online with a friend who has lost touch with you or vice versa. Do this today. In fact, make a list of friends you have lost touch with and plan to set aside thirty minutes or an hour each week to write or call them. Follow through.

2. Join an organization. Choose one with people who have interests similar to yours. Choose a professional organization with annual conferences. Then plan to attend and meet people.

3. Join a religious group and actively participate in worship and fellowship. You can share your deeply held beliefs with others in such places, which are wonderful for meeting like-minded people.

4. Participate in online social networking sites such as Facebook, MySpace, LinkedIn, Twitter, Bebo, and Orkut. While the warnings about putting too much personal information on any social networking site are valid, you will find that social networking online is a really great way to stay in touch with large numbers of people and re-establish contact with old friends. You can select the type of relationship and the degree of closeness that you desire and shape your experience accordingly.

5. Volunteer for a cause in which you believe. You will meet many like-minded people who may soon become friends. For instance, volunteers are always needed for political campaigns. You will be doubly rewarded by making friends and doing something for others.

6. Join a group of people who play together. Groups that pursue leisure activities include garage bands and church choirs; basketball, softball, and volleyball teams; runner's clubs, book clubs, cooking clubs, or dinner and dancing groups. You might even start a group in your special area of interest.

7. Ask someone you'd like to know better to meet you for coffee or lunch. Repeat once a month or even once every two months. That schedule may sound doable, but you'll be surprised how easily your busy life will get in the way.

8. Schedule time to meet with every close friend. We are all very busy, which is sometimes why our friendships suffer and fade away. Before you know it, months have passed and you haven't even talked with your friends. Schedule a time once every two weeks, or once a month, whatever works for you, and get together. Write a date into your schedule, and keep the date.

9. Join online communities. Online games such as Call of Duty, FarmVille, and Halo engage people and encourage social interaction. They include the fun and competition of strategizing and teamwork and provide a sense of success and rewards for winning.

10. Join an online support group. You will meet many people who are potentially friends. Conversation and support are available all the time: while online activities are not face-to-face, the interactions are real.

11. Participate in a local self-help group to meet other people facing the same life situations you're encountering. These groups meet weekly or monthly to fight depression and addictions, provide support for caregivers or members recovering from a major illness, or for another specific reason. Many people you meet in such groups could become lifelong friends.

12. Follow up with someone new and interesting. If you've been to a party or work meeting and met someone new that you'd like to know better, call or email or stop by that person's desk. Suggest going out for a drink or coffee or lunch.

13. Care for friends who are ill or housebound. Don't forget them just because they aren't out and about. Many people who are ill are lonely, afraid, and feel isolated. Send cards regularly. Visit in person if they're up to having company. Take them a meal, or flowers, or some books and magazines they might like.

14. Make a point of remembering your friends with cards and gifts. Send a card or note for no special reason. Keep track of your

friends' birthdays, hobbies, favorite authors, and other special things about them on your computer, iPad, or notebook. We all feel treasured when someone remembers us.

15. Buy and read a copy of Dale Carnegie's classic book, *How to Win Friends and Influence People*. It's timeless and chock-full of the best advice on making and keeping friendships.

Resilient people know a true friend is a treasure. A friend is there for you no matter what. This sense of belonging and acceptance gives us confidence and assurance that we have someone to help us up when we fall and who will not desert us when we're not very lovable. In turn, resilient people give back the same unconditional love and support to their friends. Friendship strengthens our ability to respond to life's difficulties and to do so with resilience.

MOVIE LIST: STORIES OF HEARTWARMING FRIENDSHIPS

The Boy In the Striped Pajamas (2008)
The Bucket List (2007)
Driving Miss Daisy (1989)
Finding Nemo (2003)
Forrest Gump (1994)
Fried Green Tomatoes (1991)
Good Will Hunting (1997)
Harry Potter and the Sorcerer's Stone (2001)
The Kite Runner (2007)
Letters from Iwo Jima (2006)
The Lord of the Rings:
  The Fellowship of the Ring (2001)
  The Two Towers (2002)
  The Return of the King (2003)
Monsters, Inc. (2001)
Napoleon Dynamite (2004)
Never Let Me Go (2010)
The Notebook (2004)
Saving Private Ryan (1998)
Stand by Me (1986)

Thelma and Louise (1991)
Toy Story (1995)

NOTES

1. Adam Gilden Tsai and Thomas A. Wadden, "Systematic Review: An Evaluation of Major Commercial Weight Loss Programs in the United States," *Annals of Internal Medicine*, vol. 14 (2005): 56-66.

2. Owen Thomas, "Apps to Share Your Pride at the Gym," *The New York Times*, Feb. 9, 2011, http://www.nytimes.com/2011/02/10/technology/personaltech/10basics.html (accessed Aug. 2012).

3. Lynne C. Giles, Gary F. Glonek, Mary A. Luszcz, and Gary R. Andrews, "Effect of Social Networks on 10 Year Survival in Very Old Australians: The Australian Longitudinal Study of Aging," *Journal of Epidemiology and Community Health*, vol. 59 (2005): 574-79.

4. Lisa A. Berkman, "The Role of Social Relations in Health Promotion," *Psychosomatic Medicine*, vol. 57 (1995): 245-254.

5. Robert M. Sapolsky, *Why Zebras Don't Get Ulcers* (New York: Times Books, 2004).

6. James H. Fowler and Nicholas A. Christakis, "Dynamic Spread of Happiness in a Large Social Network: Longitudinal Analysis over 20 Years in the Framingham Heart Study," *British Medical Journal*, vol. 337 (2008): a2338.

7. Sheldon Cohen, William J. Doyle, Ronald Turner, Cuneyt M. Alper, and David P. Skoner, "Sociability and Susceptibility to the Common Cold," *Psychological Science*, vol. 14 (2003): 389-395.

8. Bert N. Uchino, "Social Support and Health: A Review of Physiological Processes Potentially Underlying Links to Disease Outcomes," *Journal of Behavioral Medicine*, vol. 29 (2006): 377-387.

9. Robin Dunbar, *How Many Friends Does One Person Need? Dunbar's Number and Other Evolutionary Quirks* (United Kingdom: Faber and Faber Limited, 2010).

10. Carolyn Schwartz, Janice Bell Meisenhelder, Yunsheng Ma, and George Reed, "Altruistic Social Interest Behaviors Are Associated with Better Mental Health," *Psychosomatic Medicine*, vol. 65 (2003): 778-785.

11. Allan Luks, "Helper's High: Volunteering Makes People Feel Good, Physically and Emotionally," *Psychology Today*, Oct. 1988.

12. James S. House, Cynthia Robbins, and Helen L. Metzner, "The Association of Social Relationships and Activities with Mortality: Prospective Evidence from the Tecumseh Community Health Study," *American Journal of Epidemiology*, vol. 116 (1982): 123-140.

13. Stephanie Brown, "Providing Social Support May Be More Beneficial Than Receiving It: Results from a Prospective Study of Mortality," *Psychological Science*, vol. 14 (2003): 320-27.

CHAPTER 8: BALANCING REST, RESPONSIBILITY, AND RECREATION

"Live a balanced life—learn some and think some and draw and paint and sing and dance and play and work every day some."

—Robert Fulgham

IN THIS CHAPTER you will learn:

- Four results of a life out of balance

- What we know about work and life balance

- Seven strategies leading to balance

- How to assess your balance now

- Five steps to regain balance

≪ ≪ ≫ ≫

SEVERAL PEOPLE WENT to a wise man to learn how to manage all life's demands and still have time for fun. The wise man said, "It's simple." He took out a large jar and placed several large rocks, two inches in diameter, up to the top of the jar and asked, "Is it full?" "Yes," they all said with conviction. He smiled kindly and proceeded to pour gravel into the jar until it too reached the top. "Now is it full?" he asked, a twinkle in his eye. They nodded, but more tentatively this time.

With a flourish the wise man poured sand into the jar and it filled in every space between the bits of gravel. "And now?" he said. They all raised their eyebrows and looked at each other and said, "It *looks* full." The wise man then poured a pitcher of water into the jar. The liquid soaked up the sand and truly filled the jar. Finally, he rubbed his hands together, crossed his arms, and regarded them. "So what was the point of all this?"

One man said, "No matter how busy your schedule already is, you can always squeeze something else in." The wise man laughed good-naturedly and said, "Good observation but incorrect." Then he said, "Unless you first place the big rocks into the jar, you are never going to get them in. What are the big rocks? The most important things in your life. Only you know what they are. The gravel is important to you and might include your car, phone, computer, and other things that make your life easier. The sand is everything else—the little stuff. What happens if you fill your life with the small stuff first? There's no room for the important things in your life."

When it comes to balancing our lives, it's a good idea to think about what we're balancing our lives around. The question that comes up in the "rocks in a jar" parable is, What exactly are the big things in your life?

In this chapter you'll learn more about how to achieve balance by identifying the big rocks—the things that truly mean something to you. How many times have you watched a news story after a natural disaster like a hurricane or tornado that has destroyed homes, jobs, and possessions? You often see survivors picking through wreckage for personal items such as pictures and other belongings that would mean little to anyone else. They say things like this, "My family survived and that's what matters." Then they look at the destruction around them and tearfully say, "We can always rebuild, but if I'd lost my family—" Their voices trail off. They recognize how blessed they are to have that which is most important to them. We each need to do the same. Before we can begin to think about balancing our lives and getting everything done that we think must be done, we must first know what's truly important to us.

People who have survived destruction of their homes have discovered, or learned anew, what the big rocks are. For each of us, they're different. But often you'll find that your big rocks are your family, friends, health, and dreams, along with finding ways to achieve your important goals. Once you know your big rocks, balance takes on a whole new meaning.

What is a life out of balance? Imagine you're riding a bicycle and pedaling hard. You know what it feels like when you lean too far to one side or take a corner too fast. You can feel yourself losing control and, before you know it, you're tumbling head over heels. Other times you slowly feel pulled to the side and suddenly the ground is coming right up at you. Has your life ever felt like that? Like it's careening out of control and headed for a crash?

Many of you are working longer hours with more responsibility. A Towers Watson study of more than 218 American companies in 2012 and 2013 revealed that 65 percent of employees worked longer hours than they did three years earlier and one in three is using less vacation time. The employers surveyed reported that 97 percent of their employees struggle with work/life balance and are affected by stress. The greatest sources of stress are workload and long hours (40 percent), technology or access to work outside of work hours (34 percent), and lack of work/life balance (28 percent).[1]

You may identify with the above report. Do you ever feel like the mythological Sisyphus, doomed to roll an immense boulder up a hill only to watch it roll back down, and repeat this futility forever? Demands in life sometimes seem to be too much. They seem endless, too. In contrast, when you're balanced, moving forward feels smooth and, at times, almost effortless. You won't feel that you're neglecting important parts of your life but rather that you're able to give equal measure to what's truly important to you. You will be more, not less, productive when you're balanced. You'll enjoy yourself and get things done. You'll be less stressed and anxious. You won't feel like you're being pulled in opposite directions. This is balance. It's achievable and it feels good.

Balance doesn't mean that you give equal time or effort to each part of your life, like a system of weights and measures suggests. More accurately, it refers to stability and maybe integration of all aspects of your life, including time and effort spent on friends and family, paid work, recreation and leisure activities, and rest. Balance is being able to give sufficient time and attention to meet your commitments to both your paid work and everything else in your life.

Indeed balance is unique for each of us and can't be determined with an exact formula that says you have to spend a certain percentage of your time doing this task or that one. A one-size-fits-all formula is impossible.

WHEN YOUR LIFE IS OUT OF BALANCE

You probably know how it feels when your life is out of balance. Everyone experiences imbalance differently, but it's not unusual to feel frazzled and worn out by competing demands. Just ordinary everyday responsibilities may seem huge and insurmountable.

"I feel like a crushed soda can on the side of the road," Miranda told me one morning. She had dark circles under her eyes and looked like she was about to cry. She is the sole support in a household of four—herself, her two teenage sons, and her 78-year-old father who is in early stages of Alzheimer's disease. "I'm completely worn out. I'm working fifty to sixty hours a week; I come home to a mess. My dad's trying to help and my kids, too, but I can't even breathe any more, let alone relax or have some 'me' time."

Miranda is about to have a meltdown. It's as if no one can understand she has run out of hours in the day. In the meantime, she cares less about everything, especially herself. Miranda is beyond being stressed out. She feels used up and empty. How long can she keep this up? More to the point, where can she ease up and bring her life more into balance?

Is there anything about Miranda's life that sounds familiar to you? According to the U.S. Bureau of Labor Statistics, most parents with children younger than eighteen work outside the home. It's not surprising that parents, especially those taking care of elderly family members, have trouble finding time to take care of their health, prepare nutritious meals, exercise, sleep, and pursue enjoyable hobbies.

But there are four serious results of a life that is out of balance. The first is obvious and you've probably experienced it: You are mentally, emotionally, and physically exhausted. Every cell in your body is tired.

You are so weary that you can't enjoy life at all. This depth of fatigue leaves you accident prone and irritable. And, ironically, if you've been exhausting yourself to get ahead, the unfortunate outcome is that you're less likely to work productively, which can lead to dangerous and perhaps costly mistakes. Exhaustion often also leads to depression and anxiety.

Second, you may feel full of regrets. You think you have plenty of time for everything you want to do but when you stop to reflect on your life you can see that time is slipping away. Have you ever missed important family events, parties, and milestones because you were working? Or do you feel you've missed out on professional opportunities because the demands from your personal life limit the time and attention you can give to your work? Other outcomes might include a sense of failure and self-doubt that you aren't ever good enough or doing enough. You might feel all alone in the world and that the weight of every responsibility rests squarely on your shoulders. Maybe you're reaching a point of, "Who cares? What difference does anything make anymore?"

A third result is illness. The relentless grind of obligations and often self-imposed deadlines take their toll on our physical health. Look in the mirror. Do you see the telltale signs of worry and bone deep exhaustion etched on your face, in the slump of your shoulders, and perhaps in your expanding midsection? More invisible, yet insidious, are the changes in your blood pressure and glucose metabolism that lead eventually to heart disease, diabetes, and stroke. Your immune system is likely compromised so that you catch colds and other illnesses easier. You may have frequent headaches, back pain, and muscle aches. It's not unusual in such a condition to experience a change in appetite so that you eat too much or too little.

Finally, when your life is out of whack and you're overwhelmed and feel helpless to turn things around, you may begin to withdraw from others and from getting your work done. You may prefer isolating yourself and even procrastinating or taking longer to get things done. In an effort to escape the discomfort, some people begin to use food, drugs, or alcohol to calm themselves down and dull the pain. Your behavior may seem out of character to coworkers if you've always been dependable and you begin going to work late, leaving early, or skipping work altogether. You might even take your deep frustrations out on your family and friends.

Common symptoms of imbalance are listed below and divided into three categories: physical (changes in your health), psychological (changes in your attitudes), and behavioral (changes in your behavior). Check any of the symptoms that you recognize in your life. Do you see a pattern? Do you see checkmarks in all three categories?

Physical symptoms

Fatigue ❑

Sleeping too much or too little ❑

Headaches ❑

Problems with digestion ❑

Weight loss or gain ❑

Grinding teeth ❑

Persistent colds and infections ❑

High blood pressure and cholesterol ❑

Stiff or tense muscles, especially in the neck and shoulders ❑

Heart disease ❑

Shortness of breath ❑

Shakiness or tremors ❑

Psychological symptoms

Irritability ❑

Loss of emotional control, such as crying ❑

Anger and resentment ❑

Frustration ❑

Inability to make decisions ❑

Poor concentration ❑

Depression and anxiety ❑

Feeling that you have to be everything to everyone ❑

Low morale and feeling that everything is futile ❑

Trouble remembering things ❑

Low self-concept ❑

Behavioral symptoms

High alcohol consumption ❑

Poor job performance ❑

Withdrawal from others ❑

Increased absenteeism ❑

More accidents ❑

Poor concentration ❑

Workaholism ❑

Procrastination ❑

Marital and family conflict ❑

Poor self-care ❑

Desire to leave your job ❑

WHAT WE KNOW ABOUT WORK AND LIFE BALANCE

The negative outcomes of a life that is out of balance have been well documented. We know that too much work and not enough balance can lead to the results listed above. We know imbalance results in feeling out of control and unrecognized for our efforts. We feel there are too many expectations from people at work and perhaps from our family. We also feel that the excitement has gone from life and work is no longer challenging or even important. In some cases, we may experience a sense of complete chaos.

It's especially exhausting and frustrating when we don't have enough time to relax, are expected to do too much given the amount of time we have, and don't have enough help, sleep, and support from others.

Increasingly, people are saying that while they would like a successful career, they also would like a life outside work. A healthy balance surpasses money, recognition, and even autonomy when choosing a job. In a 2013 study from *Accenture* that surveyed 4,100 people from thirty-three countries employed in medium-sized to large organizations, nearly two-thirds of men and women said they plan to have both a career and a life outside of work. In all, 52 percent said they had turned down a job because of the impact it would have on their lives outside work. The survey reported that about 75 percent of respondents said technology helped them achieve a balance because of increased flexibility.[2] This report is an important one for employers who will need to help their employees achieve balance which, in turn, will lead to stronger employee engagement and retention of top employees.

There are good reasons to encourage life balance. A study of 2,214 employees compared those who worked more than fifty-five hours per week to those working thirty-five to forty hours per week and found that fluid intelligence, which is associated with problem solving, short-term memory, and creativity, was significantly lower in the group that worked more than fifty-five hours.[3] In a 2011 study of 2,960 workers, women were at excess risk of depression and anxiety associated with long working hours.[4] Among 704 psychiatrists from sixty psychiatric departments in Japan, half reported emotional exhaustion as a result of work/life imbalance leading to burnout, although their condition was mitigated by social support.[5]

Work/life balance continues to be particularly difficult for women. The percentage of women in the workforce has increased from 43 percent in 1970 to almost 59 percent in 2010. Even so, they remain the primary caretakers of children, ill or disabled family members, or aging parents. Nearly two of three family caregivers are employed outside the home. Nurses frequently fall into the category of being female and working hospital shifts that can be very exhausting. There's increasing evidence of the deleterious effects of work/life imbalance among shift workers, especially nurses. In a recent study of more than a thousand nurses in seven hospitals, predictors of intention to leave their workplace were work or home life imbalance.[6-8] In work settings where shift workers were given more control over their hours, there was a decline in work/family and marital conflicts.[9]

BALANCE: FIRST THINGS FIRST

How do you achieve more balance? There are dozens of magazine articles and hundreds of blogs on the Internet that offer helpful and tactical tips for balancing your life. Often they include suggestions like turning off your computer and cell phone, scheduling time for yourself, telecommuting, and learning to say "no." They're all very helpful.

But before you deal with the details of your life, you must make sure that your life strategy is clear. Once you've nailed the strategy, the details tend to take care of themselves.

- The first and most important thing you can do is be absolutely clear about what gives your life meaning. Why are you here on this earth? Is it to make money? Is it to have the biggest house? Is it to love and be loved? This first step is essential. What are the big rocks in your life?

- Once you know what is most important, you must get your priorities straight. What is essential for the journey? Who do you want to spend time with and what do you want to do? Are you kidding yourself by saying things like, "I'll spend time with my family and friends just as soon as I finish this project or meet this deadline?" Or maybe you're waiting until you retire to pursue the things you want to do. There's a German proverb that says, "You can't direct the wind, but you can adjust your sails." Take responsibility for your own life. If you know what you want to do and what is non-negotiable in order for your life to be meaningful, it's up to you to make it happen.

- You need to be flexible. How you work out a balanced life for yourself will change, sometimes daily. Remind yourself that balance requires constant adjustment, which is normal and desirable. Remember that others, if you let them, are only too willing to map out your life for you. Carl Sandburg, famed

American writer and editor, once wrote, "Time is the coin of your life. It is the only coin you have, and only you can determine how it will be spent. Be careful lest you let other people spend it for you."

THE NEXT STEPS TOWARD BALANCE

When embarking on a new journey to make profound changes in your life, the road ahead can look intimidating, especially if you're tired and don't know if you have enough energy to even begin. That's why it's important to remember to start slowly and take one step at a time. But start. Take that step. It always gets easier. Many psychologists say with conviction that if you practice something for just one month, it will become a habit. The list below offers some useful suggestions.

Schedule time with your family or friends once this week

Plan something that you'll enjoy whether it's having lunch, participating in a recreational or sporting event, going to the movies, or having a small get-together in your home. You know what you'll enjoy doing.

Every time you build joy into your schedule, you have something to happily anticipate. When my youngest son played football in high school, I couldn't wait for the weekends when my husband and I would huddle in the bleachers, wrapped in woolen blankets and down parkas, to watch him play. It was a time we all shared and could talk about for weeks. We managed our schedules so we could be there for the kickoff.

Without a scheduled time, it's easy for hours to get absorbed by meaningless tasks and frittered away. Once lost, they're never regained. If you schedule time at the beginning of the week, you'll be more likely to keep your dates and arrange the rest of your schedule to include special events. It's very important not to cancel fun because of work.

Schedule time for exercise

Another thing you might try, if you haven't already, is scheduling time for mild exercise. Peter Katzmarzyk, a Louisiana State University lead researcher in a study on sedentary behavior, showed the dangers of sitting for long periods of time.[10] According to this study, sitting for more than three hours a day can shorten your life expectancy by two years, even if you're otherwise active. Watching television for more than two hours a day can make this outcome even worse by decreasing life expectancy by another 1.4 years.

Plan to take a walk every day while you're at work. Maybe you could go out at lunchtime and walk around the block, or even around your work area. But choose a time each day for five days and stick to that schedule. Plan to do this for five days and see how it goes.

Schedule rest

Maybe getting adequate rest is one area in your life that is out of balance. Do you ever toss and turn for hours and feel exhausted the next day? This week try establishing a healthy sleep routine: Begin to wind down about an hour before your normal bedtime. You might try a warm bath, a good book, aromatherapy, chamomile tea, or another hot, relaxing, soothing drink. Avoid caffeine and alcohol, however. Avoid watching television while in bed and keep the room cool. Try out this routine for five nights to see if it helps.

Eliminate defeating self-talk

Do you know how to reduce and eventually eliminate defeating self-talk? Do you find that depressing or anxious thoughts run in an endless loop in your mind? This week try experimenting with positive thoughts. You're probably aware when these negative thoughts start playing and you can put a stop to them. Try saying to yourself, "I can do this," "I can manage," "I am very capable," or other positive alternatives to the negative comments that maintain your anxiety. Pay attention to these thoughts each day for three days. In her book *Positivity*, Barbara Fredrickson suggests that whenever you have a negative thought, you should think of three positive things to cancel it out.[11]

Delete that which drains you

Have you ever spent time on email, the phone, or in person with someone who is taking you away from what is really important to you? They may be robbing you of time with your family, friends, work, or time spent on your own pursuits. Take note of how you spend your days. Pay attention today to how much time you spend in mindless activity or even in noxious behavior, such as listening or contributing to gossip and complaints.

Get some help and regain some energy

Can you outsource anything in your life? If at all possible, you can do many things online now—from buying stamps to shopping for clothes—that will save you time and energy. You can hire teenagers to mow your lawn and walk your dog. You always can find someone to clean your house and service your car. Think of the many ways you can open up time for yourself and simultaneously get many of your chores done. You also can order nutritious meals to be delivered, make all of your payments online and automatically each month, and even have your groceries delivered. At first all this may seem extravagant, but consider the time you spend doing things when you would rather be doing something with your family, friends, or pursuing a hobby. Consider these arrangements an investment in your health and well-being.

YOU CAN ALWAYS FIND FIVE MINUTES

In a busy and frenetic schedule, you can still find five minutes to turn off your cell phone, mute your computer, and rest. Listen to music, read something that isn't related to work, take a walk, or dream for a few minutes about an exotic vacation or cruise you're planning to take. Balance has a lot to do with making mental shifts that relax, regenerate, and fill you with brief moments of joy.

FIVE IDEAS THAT TAKE FIVE MINUTES

These five quick fixes that take less than five minutes will help reintroduce balance to your life.

1. Create order in your life. Make your bed, clean your desk.

2. Open the blinds and let in the sunlight.

3. Create an uplifting music playlist and listen to it for five minutes.

4. Try aromatherapy. Keep in your purse or drawer the fragrance of something energizing or soothing. Perhaps you'll choose a scent that evokes joyful memories. Take a whiff when you need to collect your thoughts and balance your emotions.

5. If stress is getting to you and you're feeling overwhelmed, breathe deeply and rotate your shoulders. Get your oxygen flowing and blood circulating.

Try any of the above for just five days and then respond to these statements:

Statement	Agree	Disagree
I found it very difficult to find the time.	❑	❑
I enjoyed myself.	❑	❑
I am going to keep doing this next week.	❑	❑
It took too much time away from work.	❑	❑

IS YOUR LIFE IN BALANCE RIGHT NOW?

Many of us are trying to balance our lives around work without necessarily changing anything about our work.

Read the short checklist below to find out if you're balancing your life around work rather than balancing work and life. This checklist does not offer a complete picture of your unique situation but it may give you some ideas about whether you're living a balanced life.

The Balanced Work/Life Checklist

		True	False
1.	I need to work more than forty hours a week to keep my job.	❏	❏
2.	I spend a lot of time at work because other parts of my life aren't too great right now.	❏	❏
3.	I feel I need to work even harder if I'm ever going to make enough money.	❏	❏
4.	I find it hard to say "no" to requests at work, even when saying "yes" leads to increased stress.	❏	❏
5.	If my supervisor or a colleague asks for a special favor, I almost always say "yes."	❏	❏
6.	I wake up and go to sleep thinking about work.	❏	❏
7.	If I don't work all those extra hours, I don't feel like I'm in control of my situation.	❏	❏
8.	I work this hard because no one else can do my job.	❏	❏
9.	I'm working hard for my family even though they wish I would work less and spend more time with them.	❏	❏
10.	I have a lifestyle and status to maintain and I can only do so by working this hard.	❏	❏
11.	I can't remember the last time I took a real vacation.	❏	❏
12.	I'm too busy to think about where I want to go in my life.	❏	❏
13.	I often feel like I'm running faster and faster but getting nowhere.	❏	❏
14.	I often find myself putting off life's pleasures until I finish the next project or meet another deadline.	❏	❏

Give yourself two points for every time you said "true." If you answered "true" more often than "false" (a score of at least sixteen), you probably are out of balance.

If you have a lot of checks in the "True" column, you might want to take a look at how you can bring balance back into your life. If you don't do something soon, chances are your life will become more unbalanced than it already is.

A BALANCED LIFE FEELS GREAT

Julie sought help from a lifestyle coach because she was feeling overwhelmed. She scored twenty points on the above checklist. Recently, the small business she worked for downsized and her job demands and responsibilities grew. As a single mom, Julie needed her job. But she also needed to learn how to juggle work and life before she burned out. She couldn't sleep, felt guilty, and couldn't find time to exercise. She also constantly worried that she could lose her job. What did she do?

She took back control of her life. First, she got honest with herself about her life's direction and purpose and what was really important.

She learned to be proactive and, at the beginning of each week, she scheduled time for her family and friends, exercise, and worship at her church. Unless there was an emergency, these scheduled events were non-negotiable.

Then she took a long hard look at how she spent an average workday and realized she was reading emails every time her computer signaled a new one had arrived. The distractions were robbing her of hours of productive time. She limited time spent with coworkers who wanted to gossip or complain about their personal lives or jobs. These conversations had often left her exhausted and feeling down. By avoiding them, she was able to leave work earlier, beat the rush, and spend more time with her teenage children.

Julie also took advantage of her company's on-site fitness center and the midday exercise gave her a much-needed energy boost. Every evening she promised herself at least thirty minutes to read something relaxing or listen to music that helped her sleep better. It wasn't long before she was feeling much better. She also was more engaged and productive at work.

What did Julie do that you can also do?

- Get honest with yourself about what is truly meaningful and non-negotiable in your life.

- Make a schedule at the beginning of the week that includes time for the people and activities that are most important to you. Stick to it.

- Plan your workday so you spend less time gossiping, procrastinating, and letting distractions such as email derail you.

- Find the time and place to exercise most days of the week.

- Relax in the evening and establish a healthy bedtime routine.

- Revitalize a much enjoyed hobby and schedule time for it every week.

FIVE STEPS TO REGAIN BALANCE

1. Make a list of things you have always wanted to do but haven't yet found the time to do. Start with eight to ten items that you can realistically achieve and, just to get started, aim for one that you can do this month.

2. Make a priority list at the beginning of each week that sets your goals and specific times for family, friends, hobbies, and other activities.

3. Do your best to keep your home clean as well as your office. Your life will more naturally feel balanced when you get rid of clutter and have a sense of organization.

4. Consider keeping a journal in which you can de-clutter your mind and focus on what brings meaning to your life. This practice will help bring balance and perspective back into your life.

5.   Do you have a "to do" list of things you feel you have to do? Try eliminating one unnecessary thing on it and you'll love how you'll feel. Shortening that list gives back control and lightens your burden.

Living a balanced life is a lifelong process. Sometimes things happen that throw everything off-balance. For instance, you might get sick or need surgery. You might win the lottery. You may have to put in extra hours at work for a special project or welcome a new baby into your family. Life can swing out of balance at times and that's to be expected. The trick is to bring it back into a more comfortable balance. If you can learn this skill, you'll be more satisfied, focused, productive, and successful in all aspects of your life.

Resilient people have a life strategy. They know what gives their life meaning, have learned to prioritize, are open and flexible, and take charge of their destiny. They navigate by their own true north and know it's up to them to plot their course. If you practice these skills, you'll live a life full of contentment, satisfaction, success, and few, if any, regrets.

NOTES

1. "Health, Wellbeing, and Productivity Survey 2012/2013," *Towers Watson*, http://www.towerswatson.com/en/Insights/IC-Types/Survey-Research-Results/2013/05/Health-wellbeing-and-productivity-survey-2012-2013-Infographic (accessed July 2013).

2. "Defining Success: 2013 Global Research Results," *Accenture*, http://www.accenture.com/SiteCollectionDocuments/PDF/Accenture-IWD-2013-Research-Deck-022013.pdf (accessed Sept. 2013).

3. Marianna Virtanen, et al., "Long Working Hours and Cognitive Function," *American Journal of Epidemiology*, vol. 169 (2009): 596-605.

4. Marianna Virtanen, et al., "Long Working Hours and Symptoms of Anxiety and Depression: A 5-Year Follow-up of the Whitehall II Study," *Psychological Medicine*, vol. 41 (2011): 2485-494.

5. Wakako Umene-Nakano, et al., "Nationwide Survey of Work Environment, Work-Life Balance and Burnout among Psychiatrists in Japan," *PLoS ONE*, http://www.researchgate.net/publication/235650567_Nationwide_Survey_of_Work_Environment_Work-Life_Balance_and_Burnout_among_Psychiatrists_in_Japan (accessed June 2013).

6. Ya-Wen Lee, et al., "Predicting Quality of Work Life on Nurses' Intention to Leave," *Journal of Nursing Scholarship*, vol. 45 (2013): 160-68.

7. Jennifer Zwink, et al., "Nurse Manager Perceptions of Role Satisfaction and Retention at an Academic Medical Center," *Journal of Nursing Administration*, vol. 43 (2013): 135-141.

8. Pamela Brown, et al., "Factors Influencing Intentions to Stay and Retention of Nurse Managers: A Systematic Review," *Journal of Nursing Management*, vol. 21 (2013): 459-472.

9. Karen Albertsen, et al., "Work-life Balance among Shift Workers: Results from an Intervention Study about Self-rostering," *International Archives of Occupational and Environmental Health*, Feb. 24, 2013.

10. Jason Koebler, "Study: Excessive Sitting Cuts Life Expectancy by Two Years," *U.S. News & World Report*, July 9, 2012, http://www.usnews.com/news/articles/2012/07/09/study-excessive-sitting-cuts-life-expectancy-by-two-years (accessed Feb. 2013).

11. Barbara Fredrickson, *Positivity* (New York: Random House, 2009).

CHAPTER 9: ENGAGING FULLY IN LIFE

"Life must be lived and curiosity kept alive. One must never, for whatever reason, turn his back on life."

—Eleanor Roosevelt

IN THIS CHAPTER you will learn about:

- The hazards of disengaging from life
- The joys of being alone from time to time
- Four reasons you may be tempted to retreat from life
- Thieves of happiness and contentment
- Fifty-two ways to live a fully engaged life

≪ ≪ ≫ ≫

WHEN THE FRENCH say "*joie de vivre*," they literally mean "joy of living." It's not to be confused, however, with frenetic activity or back-to-back social engagements. More accurately, *joie de vivre* is the state of being fully absorbed in the business of being alive. It's maintaining an active interest in the world, taking on a challenging project, staying connected, or putting yourself out there even if it means risking failure.

Do you remember Charles Dickens's story entitled *A Christmas Carol* featuring Ebenezer Scrooge? This avaricious and embittered character withdraws from society, family, and friends and lives a solitary life replete with wealth but bereft of human comfort and contact. He has no *joie de vivre*! When the Ghost of Christmas Yet to Come shows Scrooge the cheap tombstone and pitiful legacy that would be his if he continued his miserly ways, Scrooge begs the ghost for one last chance to re-embrace life. He repents just in time, becomes a model of generosity, and fully engages in life. He laughs, dances, and embraces everyone he meets.

The Grinch, a literary character given to us by Dr. Seuss, shares Scrooge's characteristics as a reclusive curmudgeon who lives on a mountain away from the townspeople. Although he plays mean pranks and steals their presents at Christmastime, the people remain undaunted and happy and continue to celebrate. Suddenly the Grinch, touched by their kindness, repents. The townspeople accept him and he is transformed into a kinder, generous person. Like Scrooge, he re-engages with life.

These stories remind us how good it feels to be connected and happy. Disengagement, however, leads to serious problems no matter your age or circumstances. If you've ever experienced a professional setback or been rejected by someone you love, you know how tempting it is to retreat from everyone around you. Or maybe you're afraid and weary from the effort of trying to succeed in life and feel like giving up.

WHAT WE KNOW ABOUT THE HAZARDS OF DISENGAGEMENT

The negative effects of disengagement and social isolation have been studied for fifty years. Isolation predicts death and illness. People who withdraw from life experience serious health risks, including psychiatric and physical illnesses. Disengaging compromises the efficiency of the immune system and may increase high blood pressure. Some researchers explain that the lonelier and less engaged you are, the less likely you are to use good problem-solving skills and active coping methods, such as exercising and talking things over with friends. Instead, you're more likely to rely on passive coping, such as sleeping, watching television, and drinking alcohol. The evidence leaves no room for doubt: disengagement, and the loneliness that frequently accompanies it, is life-threatening.

Aron Buchman writes that less frequent participation in social activities is linked with a more rapid decline in motor function. In other words, social engagement is critical for physical health. In a five-year study among older adults, those who participated infrequently declined faster and had a 40 percent increased risk of death.[1]

Steve Cole and others have linked social isolation to inflammation, which is the first response of the immune system. They also write that the important factor is not how many people you know but how many to whom you feel close over time.[2] People who discuss their problems with others reduce stress more effectively.[3,4]

Those who are more socially involved and not easily stressed may be less likely to develop dementias, including Alzheimer's disease. In a six-year longitudinal study, those who were calm and satisfied with their lives were 50 percent less likely to develop dementia in contrast to those who were isolated and prone to distress. Hui-Xin Wang, author of the study, wrote, "In the past, studies have shown that chronic distress can affect parts of the brain, such as the hippocampus, possibly leading to dementia, but our findings suggest that having a calm and outgoing personality in combination with a socially active lifestyle may decrease the risk of developing dementia even further." [5]

James House and his colleagues have studied the negative effects of disengagement and social isolation since the 1970s. He writes that smoking cigarettes and isolating behavior carry a comparable association with risk of death.[6] Staying engaged with others may be beneficial in part because of the positive influence others might have on encouraging healthy behaviors such as eating nutritiously, exercising, and not smoking.[7,8]

JOYS OF BEING ALONE FROM TIME TO TIME

"I want to be alone. I just want to be alone."

—Greta Garbo in *Grand Hotel*

You can choose to be alone and still remain connected and engaged in life. Do you ever need time to yourself? To different degrees, we all occasionally need some alone time. But time alone can be healthy: it's not the same as disengaging from life due to stress, loneliness, or awkwardness. Joseph Roux, the French surgeon, wrote, "Solitude vivifies; isolation kills." Removing yourself from the life flow to clear your mind, soak in peace and quiet, and think through problems can be energizing and clarifying. In fact, if you need time alone, and you don't get it, you will, ironically, disengage.

Seeking solitude is not a symptom of depression, loneliness, or sadness. Indeed solitude has many benefits. For one, it gives us freedom to be ourselves without external expectations to speak and behave in certain ways. When we're with others and have no opportunity to concentrate on our own thoughts, we can easily lose our own perspective

Solitude also allows us to focus without distraction. What a delicious opportunity to exercise our creativity and become even more productive. Also, it's in solitude that we come to understand our own needs and discern which people are good for us. How better to improve our relationships?

While carving out time for solitude isn't always easy, it is possible. Mute all alarms and bells that alert you to incoming mail and other messages. Better yet, turn off your cell phone, computer, and television. Schedule your alone time, too, and then limit interruptions by letting others know you want to be disturbed only if there's an emergency.

Seeking and enjoying solitude will increase your engagement in life. On the other hand, isolating yourself from human contact because you're avoiding people, unwilling to deal with your problems, or just retreating from life eventually will lead to loneliness, depression, and, in some cases, serious illness.

WHY YOU MAY BE TEMPTED TO RETREAT FROM LIFE

You give up

"But I quit. I give up … And being alone is the best way to be. When I'm by myself nobody else can say goodbye."

—Edie Brickell, "Circle"

Mandy's husband died on a Friday when she was sixty-four years old. On Tuesday, after his memorial service, she waved good-bye to friends and family from the porch, shooed her two grown daughters back to their families in distant states, closed and locked the front door, and turned her back on the world.

She continued to go to work and drove to Wal-Mart as needed, but otherwise she withdrew into her memories. At age sixty-five Mandy retired and severed ties with people at work. Her world became smaller. Friends coaxed her out for lunch once a month but she began to find excuses to decline their invitations. Her world became smaller still.

Does it ever seem like you're on the outside looking in? Frequently the feeling is due to a profound loneliness and a belief that you don't belong anywhere, that you have no purpose and no one needs you. Your very being is filled with pain. People who retire from their jobs and have no other activities to take the place of work, or parents whose children leave home for good, can connect with these feelings of meaninglessness. Many events in life can lead to giving up. It takes effort to keep living and recapture joy.

You experience a dark night of the soul

If you're like everyone else, you've thought about dying. Maybe you won't die today, but some day you will. Just contemplating your own end can make you uncomfortable or even terrified. The realization that death is unavoidable can send the most centered and well-adjusted person into a tailspin. When your death becomes the focus of your thoughts, you can't help wondering if your life has had any meaning and whether you're doing the right things, spending time with the right people, or making the right choices.

When facing their own mortality, some people withdraw into themselves as they grapple. In such times it's not unusual to feel emotionally and spiritually isolated or even disconnected. These experiences have been referred to as a dark night of the soul—a time when we feel that God is far away or even absent. Carl Jung wrote, "There is no coming to consciousness without pain. People will do anything, no matter how absurd, to avoid facing their own soul. One does not become enlightened by imagining figures of light, but by making the darkness conscious."

Most people are not overcome by such a dark night: they go on. Those with a strong religious faith find solace in their beliefs. For everyone, the experience of isolation has the potential to herald deep and constructive understandings that will draw us back into life and closer to God.

You don't want to leave your comfort zone

"We are plain quiet folk and have no use for adventures. Nasty disturbing uncomfortable things! Make you late for dinner! I can't think what anybody sees in them."

—Bilbo Baggins in *The Hobbit*

Todd is twenty-five years old and works as a mechanic. When not at work, he's at his apartment watching television, surfing the Web, and updating his Facebook page. Every night he plays FarmVille. He'd like to have a girlfriend but he's been turned down several times and doesn't want to go through another rejection. So Todd lives a virtual life. He even created an avatar that lives and engages in life for him. Over time, he's becoming more isolated and disengaged from others.

Being afraid to leave what's familiar and comfortable is a common reason people don't live full, vibrant lives. Motivational speaker and author Brian Tracy writes, "Move out of your comfort zone. You can only grow if you are willing to feel awkward and uncomfortable when you try something new." Remember the adage that the only difference between a rut and a grave is how deep it is. Not sure if you're living in a rut? Telltale signs include a lack of energy, a lack of motivation to do anything new, the loss of dreams about the future, and the absence of any enthusiasm about what could be right around the next bend in the road.

You are stressed and overworked

Kayla works full-time as a nurse at a local hospital. Her job has become increasingly stressful and she finds herself caring for more patients than ever. Administration keeps asking her to work extra shifts. While the money is good, she is completely worn out.

In the last five years Kayla gained twenty pounds because she uses junk food and alcohol to compensate for the stress. She rarely exercises. Kayla lives alone. She is finding it more and more easy to go home after work, close her door, and shut out the world. All she wants to do is retreat to a safe place and hide. But as she becomes more isolated, she also eats more and her alcohol consumption increases. The extra weight has put her at risk for diabetes and heart disease, and she is starting to fall asleep in front of the television every night while watching reruns of *Grey's Anatomy*.

Kayla is lonely and very worried about her future. She cut herself off from her friends and family to the point she's becoming a hermit. She has ceased to be engaged in life outside work, and, frankly, work isn't even satisfying anymore, either.

You know that life is stressful. If you're like millions of others, you're bombarded with demands from work and family. You probably worry about your finances, the economy, wars, natural disasters, your health, and a myriad of other events and conditions. Unfortunately, there are times all of us are so stressed that we "cocoon" ourselves away from anything that might cause distress. After a while, we find predictable ways to comfort ourselves or, more accurately, deaden our misery. Shutting down in front of the television, drinking too much, or sleeping all the time are not good long-term solutions.

The table below shows what outcomes you might expect as a result of disengaging from life. Do you recognize any in your life? Waning interest in the world is associated with loneliness, isolation, and depression, which can be deadly.

Disengagement	Outcome
Isolating yourself from others, or avoiding being around others.	Stop meeting new people; deprive yourself of a sense of belonging; feel lonely.
Rarely trying new things and preferring the safety of the familiar.	Lose interest in the world as your curiosity fades and dies.
Not feeling a part of the world around you.	Feel stressed, anxious, depressed, and as if life is pointless.
Using excess to compensate for stress and unhappiness: eating too much, drinking too much, watching too much television, or sleeping too much.	Suffer poor physical health and depression.
Losing interest in the work you used to love.	Become easily distracted and unable to focus to the point you're not completely present at work anymore.
Withdrawing from activities you once enjoyed.	Experience boredom and restlessness; lose the ability to have fun.

THIEVES OF HAPPINESS AND CONTENTMENT

Many people are not always aware of activities that either drain or energize them. When you get up in the morning, do you anticipate the day's activities with pleasure? Or do they leave you immediately stressed out, bored, or exhausted beyond explanation? In either case, have you ever thought about why?

Frequently you are worn out before you even start because you're not using your unique abilities and not being honest with yourself. Steve Jobs said:

> When I was seventeen, I read a quote that went something like: 'If you live each day as if it were your last, someday you'll most certainly

be right.' It made an impression on me, and since then, for the past thirty-three years, I have looked in the mirror every morning and asked myself: 'If today were the last day of my life, would I want to do what I am about to do today?' And whenever the answer has been 'No' for too many days in a row, I know I need to change something.*

We have a choice in the one life each of us has been given—to do draining work or engage in energizing activities. Try this: Draw a line down the middle of a sheet of paper, top to bottom. Label the left column "drainers" and the right column "energizers." At the end of each day for the next five days, write down the important activities you did, and whether they were drainers or energizers. Include approximately how much time you spent on these activities every day.

At the end of the week, look at your results: How much time did you spend doing draining work or energizing work? Your level of engagement in life will be low when you spend time in activities that drain you. When you are disengaged, you will:

- Find excuses to do little if anything

- Procrastinate

- Call in sick to work

While it's true that you have to do things every day that don't fill you with pleasure and enthusiasm, it's still very important that you don't spend the majority of your time doing things you truly dislike doing or that are a poor fit for you. If you do, the result will be withdrawal from life.

One thing that you can do today that will help you immediately is take one step forward. There are no rules about what you should do, or what your first step forward should be. The list below offers some useful suggestions, but you know what will work for you.

- Make a list of friends and family with whom you'd like to stay in touch. Start with four names. Today you're going to just make the list and spend a few moments thinking about each person on the list. How long have you known them? What are your memories of things you've done together? Did you laugh with these people?

- Make a list of things you enjoy doing that you no longer do but would like to resume. Aim for a list of three. It can include activities such as going out to dinner, a play, a ball game, or a movie with a friend. Other activities might include walking, golfing, bowling, or fishing.

- Make a plan to go to a religious service, or plan to volunteer at a local public service organization. Just choose one. For purposes of this exercise, you need only locate the address of a service or organization, call for a time schedule, choose a day to go, write the day on your calendar, and arrange your schedule so that you can carve out two to three hours for this activity. The goal is to get out and be with like-minded people.

- Imagine you could belong to any group in the world. What group would that be? Make a list of three groups that entice you, including professional organizations, book clubs, and running clubs. Find out where and how often the group meets, how to join, and other information, such as membership fees and other requirements. Do all the research this week for one of the identified organizations.

- If you're employed, look for a change in your job that will result in your doing more of what you love to do. Close your eyes. Think about what you enjoy doing so much that you can do it every day for the rest of your life. Think about what would make you go to work every day and say, "I can't believe I actually get paid for doing this!" Talk to your coach. Look on the Internet for variations on your job that would be more fun. Talk to your friends about what they see you enjoying. See what others are doing. If you find a position that encompasses your goals within your company, be bold and talk to your boss about the possibility of doing that kind of work.

FIFTY-TWO WAYS TO LIVE A FULLY ENGAGED LIFE

When your life gets stuck and you're unwilling to make changes, or you believe you're unable to make them, you can find yourself disengaging. These are times to think about what brings meaning to your life. Talk with someone you trust who can help you regain your perspective, or just take time out to think about where you are heading in your life.

Listed below are fifty-two things you can do to re-engage life. Read through the list and choose one or two things you can start doing today.

1. Don't let a day pass without spending time with those you love.

2. Spend one hour today doing something that gives you pleasure.

3. Just today, don't let fear dictate your every decision.

4. Remember the dreams you have for your life.

5. Leave the comfort and safety of the familiar today and be a little adventurous even if you do so from your favorite armchair.

6. Always remember that "this too shall pass."

7. Express your own personal style and don't be timid about it.

8. Remember that each morning is an opportunity to start over.

9. Forgive others and seek forgiveness.

10. Do one thing you've been avoiding: don't procrastinate.

11. Remind yourself of what is truly important.

12. Carve out twenty minutes today for reflection.

13. Remember that life is not a dress rehearsal and that today counts. Once gone, it is lost forever.

14. Give thanks for all that you've been given.

15. Be generous to others.

16. Play with and read to your children or grandchildren.

17. Listen to music, familiar and new, every day.

18. Write a note of encouragement and support to someone who's hurting.

19. Don't give up even though you may feel discouraged today. Success may be around the corner.

20. Go outside and breathe fresh air even if the weather is bad. Do it especially if the weather is bad.

21. Frame a picture of yourself as a child, put it in a place you can easily see, and remember how precious you are.

22. Take exquisite care of yourself today by eating well, resting, and getting a little exercise.

23. Appreciate what a wonderful and complex marvel you are.

24. Go out and change what should be changed. Have the courage of your convictions.

25. Establish and enjoy familiar daily routines.

26. Accept the challenge to try something you don't think you can do.

27. Visualize success. Start with the end in mind.

28. Remember what George Eliot said, "It is never too late to be what you might have been."

29. Be yourself at home, at work, and when out shopping.

30. Invite a friend out for coffee, a glass of wine, or a beer.

31. Listen with your whole being to another person. Turn off your phone and don't look anywhere but at the other person.

32. Stay open to new experiences even if you think you're not interested.

33. Everyone is passionate about something. Get back in touch with *your* passion.

34. Take a walk, listen to the birds, gaze at the clouds, and remind yourself how good it is to be alive.

35. Plan and dream as if you'll live forever, and live as if you'll die tomorrow.

36. Clean and organize your home and office. An orderly environment is a sure path to an orderly mind.

37. Realize you always control your response to whatever life throws your way.

38. Learn to be content in all of life's circumstances.

39. Do the best you can at all times whether you're at work, at home, or in pursuit of hobbies.

40. Live one day at a time. Don't be anxious. Don't worry.

41. Share yourself with someone else every day by writing a note or making a phone call. Always help someone in some small way.

42. Find something to laugh about today and someone to laugh with.

43. Eat well. Eat for pleasure and health. Share food and drink with others.

44. Thank God every day for the sunrise, wind, rain, and oxygen.

45. Practice moderation in all things, which means not overdoing alcohol consumption, food, sleep, worry, or any other area where you might tend toward excess.

46. Gaze at the stars one night or even at photographs of the heavens from the Hubble Space Telescope and recognize you are part of an extraordinary universe.

47. Don't compare yourself to others. Comparisons can paralyze you and lead to self-imposed exile.

48. Seek adventures with your children while they still want to have fun with you.

49. Learn something new even if you feel awkward and clumsy at first.

50. Remind yourself of your gifts, talents, and abilities that need to be shared with others.

51. Live without regrets. Ask for forgiveness. Move on.

52. Remind yourself that your life is significant.

To be engaged is to participate in life. Engagement is different for each of you. For instance, if you're an extroverted person, you know that involvement may mean activity, more social events, and the stimulation of novel experiences. If you are introverted, fully participating may mean maintaining an avid interest in activities that you prefer pursuing alone or more quietly. If you are engaged, it means you have chosen not to retreat from life.

Resilient people stay in the flow. They are driven by their purpose and passion and are determined to keep moving forward. They have learned to weather the ups and downs of life and to accept themselves. By making every effort to stay engaged, you will build and strengthen your resilience, which is no less than your capacity to adapt well and positively to all of life's inevitable changes and challenges.

CONCLUSION

Imagine you are setting out to sea in a sailboat with a crew of ten. Your boat is sleek, beautiful, modern, and stocked with enough fresh water and food for a two-week journey. You weigh anchor. Soon the land recedes and finally disappears. With great skill you tack the boat back and forth and trim the sails. The wind in the riggings is music to your ears.

But what if you have no overall plan and no direction in which to go? You may all be skilled sailors and run a tight ship, but eventually you'll run out of provisions and may find yourself, bewildered and lost, in the open sea. Perhaps you'll even run aground in rocky shoals and reefs.

On the other hand, what if you have an overall strategy to sail from San Francisco to Hawaii but you don't have the necessary day-to-day skills to actually sail the boat. Under those circumstances, you'll also never reach your destination.

As in successfully sailing a boat from one place to another, living a resilient life requires both strategy and tactics. The term "strategy" is defined as a perspective, an overall long-term plan, and a direction in which to head. It's the big picture. Tactics, on the other hand, are the ways in which the strategy will be executed. Tactics get the job done. They are the activities created and developed with the strategy in mind.

Without strategy to guide you, tactics will get you nowhere. Without good tactics, you won't achieve your strategy. Tactics and strategy, together, are essential for success.

The approach to recognizing, building, and strengthening resilience presented in this book offers both strategy and tactics. The strategy for resilience is to live a rich, rewarding, meaningful, and significant life. How do you achieve that goal? By employing the necessary and effective tactics that will keep you heading in the right direction. We're all born with the ability to dream of a life that is fulfilling and satisfying to us. And we can all learn the tactical skills that will help achieve our dreams.

Resilience is frequently defined as the ability to bounce back from adversity. That ability, however, is a tactic, not a long-term goal. Tactics are good. They're skills. They get the job done. But frequently what's missing from the conversation on resilience is an overall strategy, or blueprint, for learning and applying these skills. Indeed, many resilience interventions emphasize tactics to the exclusion of an overall strategy. As such, they teach many useful coping skills, including stress management, cognitive restructuring, and emotion regulation. All will help you feel and perform better, but if you focus just on them you'll be like the skilled sailor without a plan: you won't get anywhere.

Nowhere are we promised that our lives will be perpetually joyful and happy. At no time are we guaranteed a life without adversity and strife and challenges that threaten to overwhelm us. We can't inoculate ourselves against negative stress. But we can have an overall strategy and choose the best tactics for us—ones that will help us reach the goal of a resilient life.

This approach is proactive and preventive rather than reactive and geared to solving problems. You may have read about a public health story that goes like this: At the bottom of a waterfall is a unit of highly skilled EMTs, doctors, and nurses with the most advanced technical medical resources. They're poised to rescue people who tumble down the falls. As some people come careening over the water cascade, they can't be reached. Others are too far gone to recover. Still others are pulled out, only to fall back in farther downstream. Few are saved.

In the meantime, there are few resources upstream even though it's easier and less costly to prevent people from falling in, jumping in, or being pushed in than it is to retrieve them once they're hurt.

The resilience strategic approach is upstream. If we can help people develop an overall life strategy and teach the skills to achieve a resilient life, we can prevent much misdirection, many missteps, and disappointments downstream. We can facilitate lives that are fulfilling.

How can you achieve this for yourself? Start by doing the exercises in this book. Make sure especially to read Chapter One, about purpose, since it will help you begin to recognize and build your overall personal strategic blueprint for living a resilient life.

Once the principles in this book begin to guide you, much of your life will fall into place. For they are the keys to thriving, and sometimes just surviving, in a world where failure and disappointment are all too common.

When you have a strategy for your life, you have reason to persevere, live your values, take good care of yourself, and support others. You'll know how to maintain a balanced perspective, stay engaged, and, in even the most turbulent waters, keep on course.

NOTES

1. Aron S. Buchman, et al., "Association between Late Life Social Activity and Motor Decline in Older Adults," *Archives in Internal Medicine*, vol. 169 (2009): 1139-146.

2. Steve Cole, et al., "Social Regulation of Gene Expression in Human Leukocytes," *Genome Biology*, vol. 8 (2007): R189.

3. John T. Cacioppo, Louise C. Hawkley, Greg J. Norman, and Gary G. Bernston, "Social Isolation," *Annals of the New York Academy of Sciences*, vol. 1231 (2011): 17-22.

4. Louise C. Hawkley, Ronald A.Thisted, Christopher M. Masi and John T. Cacioppo, "Loneliness Predicts Increased Blood Pressure: 5-year Cross lagged Analyses in Middle-aged and Older Adults," *Psychology and Aging,* vol. 25 (2010): 132-141.

5. Hui-Xin Wang, et al., "Late Life Leisure Activities and Risk of Cognitive Decline," *The Journals of Gerontology* Series A, vol. 68 (2013): 205.

6. James S. House, "Social Isolation Kills, But How and Why?" *Psychosomatic Medicine*, vol. 63 (2001): 273-274.

7. Beverly H. Brummett, et al., "Characteristics of Socially Isolated Patients with Coronary Artery Disease Who Are at Elevated Risk for Mortality," *Psychosomatic Medicine*, vol. 63 (2001): 267-272.

8. Lisa F. Berkman, "The Role of Social Relations in Health Promotion," *Psychosomatic Medicine*, vol. 57 (1995): 245-254.

ACKNOWLEDGMENTS

I WISH TO ACKNOWLEDGE all of the encouragement and inspiration I received from my family and friends throughout the long process of writing this book. Ideas and the ability to express them, however inadequately, are gifts from God, to whom I give all thanks.

I am blessed to have my beloved mother, Dorothy Wagnild, who at 95 continues to be an unending source of love, support, and wisdom. She is truly the poster child for resilience and daily teaches me how to live resiliently. My dear sister Jeanette Collins has given of herself countless times to listen with the "ear of the heart" and gently guide me through rough spots.

My precious sons, Victor and Andrew, cheered me on, willingly giving me feedback and suggestions when asked. They were always ready to entertain and distract me with stories and the welcome relief of laughter. My husband, Paul Guinn, guided me more than once in the right direction and kept me on course. I am thankful for his unerring understanding of strategy.

My many friends and colleagues have been a continual source of ideas, energy, encouragement, and inspiration. My editor, Lorraine Ash, helped me shape and refine the manuscript until it was ready to print. This book would not have happened without her.

Finally, I extend my thanks and appreciation to the thousands of people from more than 130 countries around the world who have written personal letters, completed surveys, and shared their stories with me. They are living proof of resilience. It's because of them that we have a rich and detailed road map of how each of us can arrive at a stronger and more resilient life.

APPENDICES

APPENDIX A: HOW RESILIENT ARE YOU?

IF YOU'RE LIKE me, you've filled out a dozen or more surveys while surfing the Internet or flipping through a magazine in a doctor's office. I've tallied up points to find out how stressed I am, predict my life expectancy, and see how I rated as a good mother, friend, or spouse. Most surveys want to identify your level of risk and show you what's not going well in your life. You've seen them: How depressed are you? Why can't you lose weight? Why can't you sleep? What's wrong with your marriage? Why don't you get along with your boss?

The idea behind these surveys is that if you can identify what's wrong, you can fix the problem. In contrast, measuring resilience focuses on what's right. A resilience assessment measures strengths, not limitations. You'll immediately feel better when you realize how resilient you are. That knowledge is a strong and positive foundation upon which to build your life.

Plus, it's good to know if you're on the path to a satisfying and productive life. Evidence shows that the more resilient you are, the more rewarding and rich your life will be and the better able you'll be to handle stress and return to a normal life in the aftermath of adversity.

MEASURING RESILIENCE

Since the mid-1980s, I've been interested in understanding how people, particularly middle-aged and older adults, adapt positively during and after major losses and other difficult life events. I began my research on ischemic heart disease and stress among women when I was a doctoral student at the University of Texas at Austin and then an assistant professor at Incarnate Word College in San Antonio, Texas. At the University of Washington, Heather Young (then a graduate student) and I did two interview studies from which the Resilience Scale™ initially was developed. We put together twenty-five verbatim statements made by resilient people and assembled them into an easy-to-answer survey. The items in the Resilience Scale, below, are the exact strong and clear statements that resilient people made about how they adapt to life's difficulties and come through stronger than ever.

Several additional graduate students continued to work with me to further test the Resilience Scale over the course of several years. Since 1993 the scale has been completed by thousands of people of all ages and cultural backgrounds worldwide. When you complete the items in the Resilience Scale, you'll be able to celebrate your own strengths.

Are you resilient? Take five minutes and complete the Resilience Scale or go to www.resiliencescale.com . You'll get a measure of how resilient you are today.

THE RESILIENCE SCALE™

Think about your life. This might include your personal life and how you take care of yourself as well as your relationships, employment, and volunteer work. Read each statement and circle the number to the right of each statement that best indicates your feelings. Be sure to respond to all statements.

Circle the appropriate number (1-7) following each statement below	Strongly Disagree						Strongly Agree

1. When I make plans, I follow through with them.

1 2 3 4 5 6 7

2. I usually manage one way or another.

1 2 3 4 5 6 7

3. I am able to depend on myself more than anyone else.

1 2 3 4 5 6 7

4. Keeping interested in things is important to me.

1 2 3 4 5 6 7

5. I can be on my own if I have to.

1 2 3 4 5 6 7

6. I feel proud that I have accomplished things in life.

1 2 3 4 5 6 7

7. I usually take things in stride.

1 2 3 4 5 6 7

8. I am friends with myself.

1 2 3 4 5 6 7

9. I feel that I can handle many things at a time.

1 2 3 4 5 6 7

10. I am determined.

1 2 3 4 5 6 7

11. I seldom wonder what the point of it all is.

1 2 3 4 5 6 7

12. I take things one day at a time.

1 2 3 4 5 6 7

13. I can get through difficult times because I've experienced difficulty before.

1 2 3 4 5 6 7

14. I have self-discipline.

1 2 3 4 5 6 7

15. I keep interested in things.

1 2 3 4 5 6 7

16. I can usually find something to laugh about.

1 2 3 4 5 6 7

17. My belief in myself gets me through hard times.

1 2 3 4 5 6 7

Circle the appropriate number (1-7) following each statement below	Strongly Disagree						Strongly Agree
18. In an emergency, I'm someone people can generally rely on.	1	2	3	4	5	6	7
19. I can usually look at a situation in a number of ways.	1	2	3	4	5	6	7
20. Sometimes I make myself do things whether I want to or not.	1	2	3	4	5	6	7
21. My life has meaning.	1	2	3	4	5	6	7
22. I do not dwell on things that I can't do anything about.	1	2	3	4	5	6	7
23. When I'm in a difficult situation, I can usually find my way out of it.	1	2	3	4	5	6	7
24. I have enough energy to do what I have to do.	1	2	3	4	5	6	7
25. It's OK if there are people who don't like me.	1	2	3	4	5	6	7

SCORING

First, add up the numbers you circled. Another way to obtain this answer quickly and accurately is to go to my website www.resiliencescale.com—and take the Resilience Scale online where you will get an immediate score. The lowest score you can receive is twenty-five and the highest is 175.

There are five core characteristics of resilience described in the Introduction:

1. Purpose

2. Perseverance

3. Self-reliance

4. Equanimity

5. Authenticity

There are five survey items per core characteristic for a total of twenty-five items. So, for instance, there are five items that measure whether you have a strong sense of purpose, five items that measure your self-reliance, and so forth.

Below, in the interpretation chart, you can see how you compare to others who tallied scores similar to yours. Remember that your score is a snapshot of your resilience right now and that you can increase and strengthen your resilience with practice and repetition by using the exercises offered in this book.

Resilience Scale scores and interpretation

25-100

Your resilience level is very low but this doesn't mean you have zero resilience. Everyone is resilient to some degree.

Others who have scored between 25 and 100 have reported depression. Finding meaning is sometimes a problem for individuals who score 25-100. You may be lacking in energy. You may doubt your own abilities and see the glass as half empty. You may be overwhelmed. You may feel as if no one in the world can understand what your life is like and therefore feel isolated and alone. It can be very difficult to keep going at times like these.

You *can* strengthen your resilience and doing so will make a significant and positive change in your life.

101-115

Your resilience level is low but this doesn't mean you have zero resilience. Everyone is resilient to some degree.

Others who have scored between 101 and 115 have reported feeling somewhat depressed and anxious about their life. Meaning may be lacking in your life. You may feel dissatisfied in general and feel a need to make some changes. Some who score between 101 and 115 say they tend to be pessimistic. Maybe you have a lot going on in your life and you feel a little out of control.

You *can* strengthen your resilience and doing so will make a significant and positive change in your life.

116-130

Your resilience level is on the low end but this doesn't mean you have zero resilience. Everyone is resilient to some degree.

Other who have scored between 116 and 130 report some depression and anxiety in their lives. If you are like others, you are experiencing some problems in your life and are trying to resolve them. Some people have trouble letting go of things over which they have no control. Maybe you feel unappreciated. Life may not seem very fulfilling but there are times you can see the light at the end of the tunnel.

You *can* strengthen your resilience and doing so will make a significant and positive change in your life.

131-145

Your resilience level is moderate—neither high nor low. The good news is that you possess many characteristics of resilience and can build on those to keep strengthening your resilience.

Others who scored between 131 and 144 have reported that while they are satisfied in general, many aspects of their life are not satisfactory. But you may be thinking that you need to make some changes. You are probably able to keep moving forward though you may not do so with enthusiasm. You may feel tired and emotionally drained at the end of the day. Overall, you are probably experiencing ups and downs. You can see the good things in your life if you work at it but tend to dwell on the things that aren't going well. Your sense of humor may still be intact but you would like to laugh a little more and fret a little less.

You *can* strengthen your resilience and doing so will make a significant and positive change in your life.

146-160

Your resilience level is moderately high, which means that you are doing well but believe you could do better. You possess all of the characteristics of a solid resilient personality but would like to strengthen your resilience.

Others who scored between 146 and 160 find life meaningful in general and are rarely or only sometimes depressed. There may be many aspects of your life with which you are not satisfied such as your work, personal and/or professional relationships, leisure time activities, and physical health, for example. You recognize that there is room for improvement. Most of the time you have enough energy to get through the day and then some. You probably have a balanced life perspective in which you recognize that sometimes things go well and sometimes they don't. You enjoy your own company most of the time. You are dependable.

You would benefit from recognizing your strengths in resilience but also areas where you are not as strong. You know from taking the Resilience Scale where you probably scored lower.

161-175

Your resilience level is high, which means that you are doing very well in almost all aspects of resilience.

Others who scored between 161 and 175 report that they are rarely if ever depressed or anxious about their lives. When you score high in resilience, it usually means that you find life very purposeful and you are eager to get on with each new day. You tend to see life as an adventure and others describe you as optimistic and upbeat. You enjoy your own company and the company of others. Your life is balanced between work and play. Like everyone else, you sometimes have difficult and painful events, including illness, death of family and friends, unemployment, and so forth. But unlike less resilient people, you are able to regain your equilibrium and keep moving forward. You have weathered many storms before and you are confident that you will manage again. You are dependable. You are definitely resourceful. Others seek you out because you are able to look at situations in a number of ways and therefore have a healthy perspective on life. You are self-confident. Overall, you are satisfied with your life.

When your score on the Resilience Scale is consistently low, you do need to change something.

HOW OFTEN SHOULD YOU TAKE THE RESILIENCE SCALE?

There's always some degree of error and bias with any measurement, especially those that are self-reports, but the Resilience Scale is a stable measure. Over time, unless you are making a specific effort to change some aspect of your resilience, your score will remain fairly constant, especially if you strive to answer very honestly. For instance, the Resilience Scale statement that reads "When I make plans, I follow through with them" reflects behavior that may not change much over time unless you make an effort to do so. Maybe you have always had a tendency to be a quitter and so you gave yourself a 3.

The item that reads "I have a sense of purpose" also may not change. If you have always had a very purposeful and meaningful life, you might give yourself a 6 or 7 and this may not change much over time. Or maybe up until now you've felt that your life is aimless and you're drifting from one thing to another and so you gave yourself a 3 or 4. But once you begin to identify changes you'd like to make, and start to practice these changes, your Resilience Scale score will go up and up.

If you're not sure that the Resilience Scale score accurately reflects your resilience, it's also a good idea to take the scale several times over a few weeks and average your score. This practice will provide a more realistic resilience score for you. To make repeated test-taking easy, go to www.resiliencescale.com , complete the scale, and print your results. Keep track of five total Resilience Scale scores, add them up and divide by five or however many times you've taken the scale.

APPENDIX B: EARLY RESEARCH

ONE OF THE best ways to understand how to do something well is to learn from the experts who, in this case, are highly resilient people. I went straight to those who are true examples of resilience to learn what it means to live resiliently. My premise is that one of the best ways to build your resilience is to follow the example of resilient people.

Almost twenty-five years ago, I completed the first studies on resilience that serve as the foundation for the Resilience Core, the Four Pillars of Resilience, and the Resilience Scale. Together with several graduate students at Incarnate Word College in San Antonio, the University of Washington in Seattle, and Montana State University in Bozeman, I interviewed people who had experienced much adversity—severe illness, loss of loved ones, accidents, natural disasters, and other hardships—and went on to lead fully engaged, satisfying lives. In other words, they were ordinary people with extraordinary resilience.

In our interviews, we asked them to describe how and what they did to manage difficulties. We also asked them to describe what continued to cause them stress. In this way we learned about the effects of daily small stressors as well as major life events. Rather than focusing on problems and illnesses resulting from adversity, we wanted to know what steps these people took to adapt and resolve the difficulties. We also asked people to tell us what they do to sustain their optimistic outlook and stay fully involved in life.

The in-depth interviews were conducted with the following samples:

- Twenty-four community-dwelling middle-aged and older adults who had experienced a major loss and had adapted positively in the aftermath;

- Twenty-four caregivers of spouses with Alzheimer's disease who were under great personal strain;

- Forty-three low-income adults with chronic health conditions who lived in public housing; and

- Thirty-nine adults who lived in geographically isolated communities.

As we analyzed thousands of lines of interview narratives, we identified five themes common to most participants. I now call these characteristics the Resilience Core. These core characteristics were present in people who adapted positively despite change, challenge, and adversity, and demonstrated emotional and spiritual growth.

The five characteristics constituting resilience are:

1. Purpose

2. Perseverance

3. Self-reliance

4. Equanimity

5. Authenticity

The results were grounded in prior research and philosophical writings, including Elizabeth Colerick's work on stamina[1] and Michael Rutter's research on resilience.[2-3] There also was evidence of this adaptive capacity in philosophical writings describing endurance, individual fortitude, and survival.

The findings of the qualitative interview studies were intriguing because in the late 1980s, there were fewer studies that explored positive aspects of adaptation to adversity than there are today. Since the positive psychology movement, which started in the late 1990s, there has been a great increase in research that emphasizes positive factors associated with adaptation and a well-lived life. These include mindfulness, flow, optimism, flourishing, and happiness.

In the interests of studying the five core characteristics with larger samples, the Resilience Scale was developed and tested in the late 1980s and first published in 1993. From the very first survey study of 810 middle-aged and older adults, it was apparent that the twenty-five statement survey instrument with a seven-point Likert Scale was measuring individual emotional strength, flexibility, grit, and courage. It also was clear that the composite results correlated significantly, strongly, and negatively with depression but positively with life satisfaction, morale, hardiness, stress management, and healthy lifestyle behaviors.[4-8]

Since that time the Resilience Scale has been used worldwide with predictable results. Resilience is associated with self-esteem, active coping, forgiveness, health promotion, family health, psychological well-being, a sense of community, social support, a sense of coherence, purpose in life, self-transcendence, religiosity, optimism, high physical functioning, and spiritual well-being. It has been inversely related to stress, number of perceived stressful events, depression, anxiety, fibromyalgia impact, battle fatigue stress, compassion fatigue, and burnout.[9]

WHAT WE LEARNED

A disastrous childhood didn't doom people to a life of unhappiness and failure. Many of those we interviewed and surveyed had experienced difficult childhoods but their challenges didn't lead to a failed life as an adult. Their difficult beginnings in life included molestation, abuse, violence, alcoholism, poverty, or other deprivations, but they nevertheless learned to live satisfying lives filled with purpose. They were not victims of the circumstances of their childhood. For several decades this finding has been supported in longitudinal research studies, which have concluded that more than two-thirds of children raised in adverse circumstances learned to protect themselves, pull themselves together, and emerge as productive and healthy adults.

One consistent finding is that resilience and depression are incompatible. When resilience is high, depression is low and vice versa. Resilient people feel anxiety, distress, and anguish. They are not inured to pain. Nor are they inoculated against stress. They may even have greater empathy for others because they, too, have suffered much. The difference is that they aren't defeated forever. They come back and keep trying.

Greater resilience also is associated with the ability to forgive others and to have an overall sense of well-being, life satisfaction, and coherence. Furthermore, resilience is associated with higher self-esteem and optimism.

Resilient people have meaningful and rich relationships with others. They enjoy life and, rather than withdraw or retreat, stay involved. Resilient people are unlikely to look back at their lives and dwell on regrets because they are able to put events in perspective. They seek forgiveness and get on with their lives.

One woman in particular stands out. She had lost her three-year-old child in a tragic accident. Within months, both her parents died as well. When asked how she managed to keep going and build a fulfilling and meaningful life, she quickly said that she still had two other children and that caring for them gave her purpose and determination. For the sake of her surviving family, she got up every morning and rediscovered joy and laughter. Over time she learned she was able to survive despite pain and sorrow. The woman emerged from this trying period as a strong and capable person with greater compassion who was capable of doing much good for others.

Sometimes people confuse resilience and physical hardiness. While resilience is associated with better self-care, not all resilient people are in good health. Indeed many exceedingly resilient people are very ill, in frail health, or near death. Yet their resilience remains intact and they continue to live with meaning and maintain a balanced outlook.

Resilient people I've interviewed reported experiencing times in their lives when they've lost their balance and would not have described themselves as resilient. Yet they recognized their desire and ability to regain equilibrium and keep going.

I've learned ten practical ideas and suggestions to manage stress from the people I interviewed:

1. Don't blame others when things don't go as planned or hoped.

2. Accept that you can't control much of what happens around you, including traffic jams and bad weather, but that you can choose your response.

3. Take good care of yourself by getting enough exercise, eating nutritious meals and snacks, getting enough sleep, and learning how to manage stress.

4. Follow through on your plans and don't procrastinate.

5. Find things to laugh about every day and don't give in to negative emotions and thoughts.

6. Take things one day at a time and don't borrow trouble.

7. Don't feel a need to please everybody.

8. Give to others and know when to ask for help and support.

9. Learn to balance your need for rest, responsibility, and recreation and always include time for nature—walking, fishing, golfing, skiing, bicycling, camping, canoeing, and the like.

10. Don't retreat from life. Dive in and enjoy the challenge.

In the twenty years since the early interview research discussed above, studies of thousands of individuals using the original Resilience Scale, based on the five underlying characteristics, continue to support the definition of resilience described in the original research.

NOTES

1. Elizabeth J. Colerick, "Stamina in Later Life," *Social Science and Medicine*, vol. 21 (1985): 997-1006.

2. Michael Rutter, "Resilience in the Face of Adversity," *British Journal of Psychiatry*, vol. 147 (1985): 598-611.

3. Michael Rutter, "Psychosocial Resilience and Protective Mechanisms," *American Journal of Orthopsychiatry*, vol. 57 (1987): 316-331.

4. Gail Wagnild and Heather Young, "Resilience among Older Women," *Image: Journal of Nursing Scholarship*, vol. 22 (1990): 252-255.

5. Gail Wagnild and Heather Young, "Development and Psychometric Evaluation of the Resilience Scale," *Journal of Nursing Measurement*, vol. 1 (1993): 165-178.

6. Gail Wagnild, "Resilience and Successful Aging: Comparison among Low and High Income Older Adults," *Journal of Gerontological Nursing*, vol. 29 (2003): 42-49.

7. Gail Wagnild, "A Review of the Resilience Scale," *Journal of Nursing Measurement*, vol. 17 (2009): 105-113.

8. Gail Wagnild and Jeanette Collins, "Assessing Resilience," *Journal of Psychosocial Nursing and Mental Health Services*, vol. 47 (2009): 28-33.

9. Gail Wagnild, *The Resilience Scale User's Guide* (Worden, MT: The Resilience Center, 2009).

APPENDIX C: RESILIENCE FOR KIDS

HELPING CHILDREN reach for their dreams, respond resiliently to life's challenges, and recognize that they are unique and precious

《 《 》 》

THE RESILIENCE FOR Kids program grew out of a demand to develop and test high quality programs to build and strengthen resilience for youth ages 8 through 18. Through our research we have learned that we can teach children to recognize, build, and strengthen their resilience core and put it to work in their lives. Our results indicated that students were able to experience greater academic success, better prepared to deal with rejection, failure, and anxiety, and practiced healthier lifestyle behaviors following the intervention.

Our Resilience for Kids program helps students identify and develop their abilities and unique talents, work toward goals that are important to them, and learn good decision making skills. They discover different ways of keeping things in perspective and practicing optimism. They learn how they can depend on themselves and others can depend on them, leading to self-confidence. They learn to appreciate themselves as unique, irreplaceable, and precious.

WHY RESILIENCE FOR KIDS IS IMPORTANT

Children experience stress and adversity for many reasons. The years that some children spend in middle and high school can be very stressful as a result of academic expectations, new social situations, bullying, and in some cases, abusive families. These are years that can be filled with anxiety and uncertainty.

We can help children learn to face new situations, manage stress effectively, and meet challenges with confidence and skill. Even at a very young age, it's possible to help children recognize and build on their unique talents and gifts, a strategy that will serve them well into adulthood. We have concluded through our research that living resiliently can be learned.

RESILIENCE FOR KIDS PROGRAM

Our Resilience for Kids five-hour/five-session program is based on several years of research to develop, test, and evaluate resilience interventions for youth. From 2009 through 2012 we conducted a $375,000 study funded by the Health Resources and Services Administration (HRSA), an agency of the U.S. Department of Health and Human Services.

We created resilience building programs for students that include group exercises, self-reflection, teacher guided learning, community participation and support. Materials include teacher's manuals, student workbooks, and activities to help students recognize, build, and strengthen their resilience.

As a result, we have selected and refined the best approaches for teaching resilience and offer a brief and effective program that is ideal for schools, summer camps, and organizations anywhere in the world. Our approach is solid, research-based, and effective.

The student goals for the five-hour/five session resilience curriculum are to build and strengthen individual resilience by helping students first recognize how resilient they already are and then by supporting them as they learn the essential skills and knowledge to live a resilient life and respond with resilience to life's challenges.

Expected outcomes for students who actively participate in the five-hour/five-session resilience program include:

1. Beginning knowledge of core characteristics of resilience indicated by higher scores on the RS-10 or RS-14 from pre- to post-test

2. New resilience skills to use when responding to life's challenges evidenced by learned behaviors in exercises

3. Insights into own responses gained by journaling and discussion during the resilience sessions

Each student session requires approximately one hour. Completing all five sessions will take five hours.

YOUTH AGED 8-12

Program includes:

1. Five-session/five-hour research-based resilience curriculum, which includes exercises, self-reflection, activities, teacher script, and other teaching materials

2. Ten-item Resilience Scale (RS-10)

3. Resilience summary for each student

4. Teacher/counselor training (e.g., onsite one-day training, webinar training)

5. Two hours consultation via Skype

6. Data analysis and reporting if desired

YOUTH AGED 13-18

Program includes:

1. Five-session/five-hour research-based resilience curriculum, which includes exercises, self-reflection, activities, teacher script, and other teaching materials (link to outline)

2. Fourteen-item Resilience Scale (RS-14)

3. Resilience summary for each student

4. Teacher/counselor training (e.g., onsite one-day training, webinar training)

5. Two hours consultation via Skype

6. Data analysis and reporting if desired

TRUE RESILIENCE™ WORKSHOP FOR TEACHERS

We offer a one-day *True Resilience*™ workshop for teachers/counselors who will be responsible for delivering the resilience programs in order to help them:

1. Recognize, build, and strengthen their own resilience

2. Be prepared to teach and model the resilience core characteristics to their students

3. Participate in tailoring Resilience for Kids materials for their specific population/culture

Expected outcomes for counselors/teachers who use the adult resilience training materials include:

1. Beginning knowledge of core characteristics of resilience

2. New resilience skills to use when responding to life's challenges evidenced by learned behaviors and greater insight into personal responses to change, challenge, and adversity

3. Tailored Resilience for Kids exercises and examples that fit the needs of their specific students and culture

HOW DO WE MEASURE RESILIENCE IN YOUTH?

We offer two different surveys for measuring resilience in kids.

RS-10 (10-item Resilience Scale)

For those between the ages of 8 and 12, we recommend the RS-10. This is a ten-item Resilience Scale written at the 2nd grade reading level. As with our other resilience measures, it captures the resilience core characteristics (i.e., authenticity, purpose, perseverance, equanimity, and self-reliance). This is a new scale with limited reliability and validity data.

RS-14 (14-item Resilience scale)

For those between the ages of 13 and 18, we recommend the RS-14. This is a fourteen-item Resilience Scale written at the 6th grade reading level. It measures the five resilience core characteristics. This is a very popular, highly valid and reliable tool to measure resilience.

Please check out www.resiliencescale.com for more details on the Resilience for Kids program.

APPENDIX D: RESILIENCE FOR COLLEGE STUDENTS

HELPING STUDENTS discover their callings, respond resiliently to life's challenges, and live authentically as they prepare for productive and meaningful lives

《 《 》 》

WE DEVELOPED THE Resilience for College Students materials as a result of numerous requests from counseling and coaching departments within colleges and universities for products and services that would help traditional college students (ages 18-25) recognize, build, and strengthen their resilience.

WHY RESILIENCE FOR COLLEGE STUDENTS IS IMPORTANT

Attending college can be stressful for most students. A study from the American College Health Association reported that 75 percent of students are stressed, nearly all say they are anxious, and a quarter say they have been so depressed, sad, and hopeless in the past year that they can't function. Moderate to severe stress is associated with depression, anxiety, alcohol abuse, exhaustion, and in some instances, suicide.[1]

Common sources of stress for students include the following:

- Dealing with greater academic demands than encountered in high school

- Being on their own and making decisions about spending time and money

- Meeting new people and wanting to belong and be socially accepted

- Becoming more aware of sexuality

- Missing family and friends and feeling lonely

- Learning to say "no" and limiting or controlling the use of alcohol or other drugs and tobacco

We have learned that in order for college students to succeed, they need greater resilience, which comprises a sense of direction and purpose, recognition of authenticity based on a student's values and belief, perseverance to finish strong, self-reliance and confidence. They also need to maintain a balanced perspective and choose healthy and resilient responses to the many stressors they will encounter. Research-based approaches that help them build and strengthen their resilience will help students achieve success in school and throughout their lives.

RESILIENCE FOR COLLEGE STUDENTS RECOMMENDATIONS

We suggest the following approaches for college students. This information is available in more detail on www.resiliencescale.com .

1. Offer the RS or RS-14 to students to complete for instant feedback to learn how resilient students already are. Scores can be reported individually or in the aggregate. Either the RS or RS-14 is ideal for measuring resilience over time.

2. Provide the *True Resilience* workbook to students for self-paced learning by completing the exercises and brief assessments in the workbook that accompanies this book.

3. Provide access to *True Resilience Profiles*, which are detailed 9-page personal reports specific to college age students that explain their RS-14 scores and offer suggestions and recommendations for building and strengthening resilience while in college.

Other considerations for helping students recognize, build, and strengthen their resilience include the following:

- Because the first six to eight weeks of school are critical to success, the *True Resilience* book and workbook could be recommended to students as soon as they arrive on campus.

- The *True Resilience* book would be an excellent textbook for students enrolled in counseling, psychology, nursing, social work, and other professional programs of study.

- Resident hall advisors (RAs) could participate in resilience building exercises using the *True Resilience* book and accompanying workbook during their orientation program before students arrive on campus. They would learn how to be more resilient personally as well as learn to help students under their supervision learn to grow and strengthen their resilience as they begin their college studies.

NOTES

1.   Arthur Levine and Diane R. Dean, *Generation on a Tightrope: A Portrait of Today's College Student* (San Francisco, CA: Jossey-Bass, 2012).

APPENDIX E: RESILIENCE FOR ORGANIZATIONS

HELPING ORGANIZATIONS and the people in them thrive by recognizing, building, and strengthening resilience

« « » »

W E ARE DEVELOPING Resilience for Organizations materials as a result of frequent requests from Employee Assistance Programs (EAPs), Wellness Programs, coaches, psychologists, and other professionals from around the world who want to measure individual resilience as well as the resilience of their organizations. They also want to offer programs that go beyond traditional stress management, which tends to be a short term approach and situation specific, and instead teach, promote, and support resilience—a strategic approach that leads to long term change.

WHY RESILIENCE FOR ORGANIZATIONS IS IMPORTANT

Dissatisfaction with work and life has been on the rise for the past two decades. In 2008 about 49 percent of employees reported satisfaction with their work. By 2013, that percent had dropped to 45 percent. There are a variety of reasons, including lower incomes and take-home pay, but the truth is that only 51 percent even find their jobs interesting.[1] Many are sacrificing satisfaction and contentment for a steady paycheck and medical insurance. Some people are asking, "Is it possible to have job and financial security and enjoy a rich and rewarding life, too?"

A July 2013 Gallup report states that if organizations want to attract and retain valuable employees, they'll have to do more than reward them with nice perks such as on-site massages. Even satisfied employees who have good benefits aren't necessarily engaged with their work, which is essential for a high level of performance.[2] Organizations need employees who exercise discretionary effort, believe and know that they belong, and have a strong sense of shared purpose with the organization and their coworkers. Alarmingly, approximately 70 percent, or 70 million, of the 100 million full-time workers in the United States, are either not engaged or are actively disengaged.[3]

A growing body of evidence shows that people who do work they consider meaningful are more committed. They outperform others who don't find their work meaningful, tend to be more cooperative, and help others by sharing information as well as workload. Doing what's meaningful is important because it leads to satisfaction and fulfillment.

We have learned that promoting and supporting employee resilience can lead to a greater sense of purpose, but it also is associated with less anxiety, perceived stress, and depression. Greater resilience is positively related to physical and mental health, health promoting behaviors, and many other positive long term outcomes. Building and strengthening resilience goes beyond stress management—tactical and short term solutions to stress-producing situations—and instead teaches and supports behaviors that sustain long term life satisfaction and intrinsic motivation.

RESILIENCE FOR ORGANIZATIONS RECOMMENDATIONS

We suggest the following resilience products and services for organizations; more detail is available on www.resiliencescale.com .

1. Offer the RS or RS-14 for employees in your organization for instant feedback on their resilience.

2. Provide the *True Resilience* workbook for employees for self-paced learning.

3. Provide access to *True Resilience Profiles*, which are detailed 9-page personal reports that interpret the RS-14 score, offer suggestions and recommendations for building and strengthening resilience, and identify behaviors and thought patterns that can hinder the development of a strong resilience core.

4. In addition to building individual resilience, we recommend building and strengthening resilience at the organizational level. Even individuals who learn to strengthen their personal resilience can't thrive without an optimal work environment that supports and encourages resilient behaviors.

NOTES

1. "I Can't Get No … Job Satisfaction, That Is," *The Conference Board*, http://www.conference-board.org/publications/publicationdetail.cfm?publicationid=1727 (accessed July 2013).

2. Susan Sorenson, "Don't Pamper Employees—Engage Them," *Gallup Business Journal*, July 2, 2013, http://businessjournal.gallup.com/content/163316/don-pamper-employees-engage.aspx?utm_source=WWW&utm_medium=csm&utm_campaign=syndication&ref=image (accessed July 2013).

3. "State of the American Workplace: Employee Engagement Insights for U.S. Business Leaders," *Gallup*, http://www.gallup.com/strategicconsulting/163007/state-american-workplace.aspx (accessed July 2013).

ABOUT THE AUTHOR

GAIL WAGNILD, RN, Ph.D, is the founder and owner of the Resilience Center in Montana. Clinically trained as a psychiatric nurse and social worker, she has been conducting research and consulting in the area of resilience for more than thirty years. Dr. Wagnild was a faculty member in nursing schools, including Incarnate Word College in San Antonio, Texas; the University of Washington in Seattle; and Montana State University in Bozeman. She is the principal author of the widely used Resilience Scale and the *True Resilience* program, which helps people of all ages recognize, build, and strengthen their resilience. For the past ten years she has been a research and evaluation consultant.

Gail Wagnild sits in the doorway of the original barn on her 100-year-old family homestead with Oscar, her devoted English Shepherd, during the winter of 2014.

For more information, contact Dr. Wagnild through the Resilience Center website at www.resiliencecenter.com .

BIBLIOGRAPHY

"About Georgia O'Keeffe." Georgia O'Keeffe Museum. Accessed June, 2013. http://www.okeeffemuseum.org/about-georgia-okeeffe.html .

"Abraham Lincoln." Our Presidents. Accessed July, 2013. http://www.whitehouse.gov/about/presidents/abrahamlincoln .

Albertsen, Karen et al. "Work-life Balance among Shift Workers: Results from an Intervention Study about Self-rostering." *International Archives of Occupational and Environmental Health 87* (2014): 265-74.

"Aleksandr Solzhenitsyn (1918-2008)." Pegasos. Accessed July, 2013. http://www.kirjasto.sci.fi/alesol.htm .

"Andrée Peel." *The Telegraph.* Accessed July, 2013. http://www.telegraph.co.uk/news/7407992/Andre-Peel.html .

"Ann Romney Biography." A&E Networks. Accessed July, 2013. http://www.biography.com/people/ann-romney-20950331 .

Barnardi, Vincenzo. "Light Alcohol Drinking and Cancer: A Meta-Analysis." *Annals of Oncology 24* (2012): 301-308.

Bauby, Jean-Dominique. *The Diving Bell and the Butterfly.* New York: Alfred A. Knopf, 1997.

Berkman, Lisa F. "The Role of Social Relations in Health Promotion." Psychosomatic Medicine 57 (1995): 245-254.

Blair, Steven N. Robert E. Sallis, Adrian Hutber and Edward Archer. "Exercise Therapy: The Public Health Message." *Scandinavian Journal of Medicine and Science in Sports* 22 (2012): e24-28.

Boyle, Patricia et al. "Effect of Purpose in Life on the Relation between Alzheimer disease Pathologic Changes on Cognitive Function in Advanced Age." *Archives in General Psychiatry 69* (2012): 499-505.

Boyle, Susan. *The Woman I Was Born to Be.* New York: Atria Books, 2010.

Brown, Pamela et al. "Factors Influencing Intentions to Stay and Retention of Nurse Managers: A Systematic Review." *Journal of Nursing Management 21* (2013): 459-472.

Brown, Stephanie. "Providing Social Support May Be More Beneficial Than Receiving It: Results from a Prospective Study of Mortality." *Psychological Science 14* (2003): 320-27.

Brummett, Beverly H. et al. "Characteristics of Socially Isolated Patients with Coronary Artery Disease Who Are at Elevated Risk for Mortality." *Psychosomatic Medicine 63* (2001): 267-272.

Buchman, Aron S. et al. "Association between Late Life Social Activity and Motor Decline in Older Adults." *Archives in Internal Medicine 169* (2009): 1139-146.

Buettner, Dan. *The Blue Zones: Lessons for Living Longer from the People Who've Lived the Longest.* Washington, DC: National Geographic Society, 2008.

Butler, Robert. *The Longevity Prescription: the 8 Proven Keys to a Long, Healthy Life.* New York: Penguin Group, 2010.

Cacioppo, John T., Louise C. Hawkley, Greg J. Norman and Gary G. Bernston. "Social Isolation." *Annals of the New York Academy of Sciences 1231* (2011): 17-22.

Cain, Susan. "Introverted Leaders: Three Reasons Larry Page Will Succeed as Google CEO (As Long As He Avoids One Fatal Misstep)." Accessed October 8, 2013. http://www.thepowerofintroverts.com/2011/01/23/introverted-leaders-three-reasons-larry-page-will-succeed-as-google-ceo-as-long-as-he-avoids-one-fatal-misstep/ .

Callahan, Steven. *Adrift: 76 Days Lost at Sea.* New York: Houghton Mifflin Company, 1999.

Carney, Dana R., Amy J. Cuddy and Andy J. Yap. "Power Posing: Brief Nonverbal Displays Affect Neuroendocrine Levels and Risk Tolerance." *Psychological Science 21* (2010): 1363-68.

Carroll, Lewis Carroll. *Alice's Adventures in Wonderland.* Dover: Thrift Editions, 1993.

Chari, Vidya. "Dr. Paul Stoltz Discusses How to Improve Our Reactions to Adversity." Harker News. October 27, 2011. Accessed November, 2013. http://news.harker.org/dr-paul-stoltz-discusses-how-to-improve-our-reactions-to-adversity/ .

Cohen, Sheldon, William J. Doyle, Ronald Turner, Cuneyt M. Alper and David P. Skoner. "Sociability and Susceptibility to the Common cold." *Psychological Science 14* (2003): 389-395.

Cole, Steve et al. "Social Regulation of Gene Expression in Human Leukocytes." Genome Biology 8 (2007): R189.

Colerick, Elizabeth J. "Stamina in Later Life." *Social Science and Medicine 21* (1985): 997-1006.

Collier, Nathan S. "The Monkey's Fist: An Ancient Parable for Modern Times." NSC Blog. Accessed July, 2013. http://www.nscblog.com/personal-growth/the-monkeys-fist-an-ancient-parable-for-modern-times .

"Colonel Harland Sanders Biography." A&E Networks. Accessed July, 2013. http://www.biography.com/people/colonel-harland-sanders-12353545 .

Covey, Stephen R. *The 7 Habits of Highly Effective People: Powerful Lessons in Personal Change.* New York: Simon and Schuster, 1989.

"Defining Success: 2013 Global Research Results." Accenture. Accessed September 2013. http://www.accenture.com/SiteCollectionDocuments/PDF/Accenture-IWD-2013-Research-Deck-022013.pdf .

Doll, Sir Richard, Richard Peto, Jillian Boreham and Isabelle Sutherland. "Mortality in Relation to Smoking: 50 Years'

Observations on Male British Doctors." *British Medical Journal 328* (2004): 1519-28.

Duckworth, Angela, Christopher Peterson, Michael Matthews and Dennis Kelly. "Grit: Perseverance and Passion for Long Term Goals." *Journal of Personality and Social Psychology 92* (2007): 1087-101.

Dunbar, Robin. *How Many Friends Does One Person Need? Dunbar's Number and Other Evolutionary Quirks.* United Kingdom: Faber and Faber Limited, 2010.

Dunne, Erin, Carsten Wrosch and Gregory Miller. "Goal Disengagement, Functional Disability, and Depressive Symptoms in Old Age." *Health and Psychology 30* (2011): 763-70.

Dweck, Carol S. *Mindset: The New Psychology of Success.* New York: Ballantine Books, 2006.

Ferber, Edna. *So Big.* (New York: HarperCollins Publishers, 1984.

Fields, Liz. "Miss Arizona Hopeful Diagnosed With Rare Cancer. Good Morning America, October 11, 2013. Accessed October, 2013. http://gma.yahoo.com/miss-arizona-hopeful-diagnosed-rare-cancer-005658393--abc-news-health.html .

"Flight 1549: A Routine Takeoff Turns Ugly." CBS News 60 Minutes, July 6, 2009. Accessed May, 2010. http://www.cbsnews.com/8301-18560_162-4783580.html .

Ford, Earl S., Guixiang Zhao, James Tsai and Chaoyang Li "Low-risk Lifestyle Behaviors and All-cause Mortality: Findings from the National Health and Nutrition Examination Survey III Mortality Study." *American Journal of Public Health 101* (2011): 1922-29.

Fowler, James H. and Nicholas A. Christakis. "Dynamic Spread of Happiness in a Large Social Network: Longitudinal Analysis over 20 Years in the Framingham Heart Study." British Medical Journal 337 (2008): a2338.

Frankl, Viktor E. *Man's Search for Meaning.* New York: Washington Square Press, 1984.

Fredrickson, Barbara and Marcial Losada. "Positive Affect and the Complex Dynamics of Human Flourishing." *American Psychologist 60* (2005): 678-86.

Fredrickson, Barbara. *Positivity*. New York: Random House, 2009.

Friedman, Howard S. and Leslie R. Martin. *The Longevity Project: Surprising Discoveries for Health and Long Life from the Landmark Eight-Decade Study*. New York: Hudson Street Press, 2011.

Fries, James S. Fries, Bonnie Bruce and Eliza Chakravarty. "Compression of Morbidity 1980-2011: A Focused Review of Paradigms and Progress." *Journal of Aging and Research 261* (2011): 261702.

Fung, Teresa T. et al. "Mediterranean Diet and Incidence of and Mortality from Coronary Heart Disease and Stroke in Women." *Circulation 119* (2009): 1093-100.

Gantner, Rose K. *Workplace Wellness: Performance with a Purpose*. Moon Township, PA: Well Works Publishing, 2012.

Gilbert, Daniel. *Stumbling on Happiness*. New York: Random House, 2005.

Giles, Lynne C., Gary F. Glonek, Mary A. Luszcz and Gary R. Andrews. "Effect of Social Networks on 10 Year Survival in Very Old Australians: The Australian Longitudinal Study of Aging." *Journal of Epidemiology and Community Health 59* (2005): 574-79.

"Global Renaissance Woman." Maya Angelou. Accessed May, 2013. http://www.mayaangelou.com/biography .

Green, Elizabeth Weiss. "It's All About Me." *U.S. News and World Report 142* (2007): 22.

Haasova, Marcela et al. "The Acute Effects of Physical Activity on Cigarette Cravings: Systematic Review and Meta-analysis with Individual Participant Data (IPD)." *Addiction 108* (2013): 26-37.

Hawkley, Louise C., Ronald A. Thisted, Christopher M. Masi and John T. Cacioppo. "Loneliness Predicts Increased Blood Pressure: 5-year Crosslagged Analyses in Middle-aged and Older Adults." *Psychology and Aging 25* (2010): 132-141.

Hazlett, Abigail, Daniel Molden and Aaron Sackett. "Hoping for the Best or Preparing for the Worst? Regulatory Focus and Preferences for Optimism and Pessimism in Predicting Personal Outcomes." *Social Cognition 29* (2011): 74-96.

"Health, Wellbeing, and Productivity Survey 2012/2013." Towers Watson. Accessed July, 2013. http://www.towerswatson.com/en/Insights/IC-Types/Survey-Research-Results/2013/05/Health-wellbeing-and-productivity-survey-2012-2013-Infographic .

Helft, Miguel. "Mark Zuckerberg's Most Valuable Friend." *New York Times*, October 2, 2010. Accessed October 6, 2013. http://www.nytimes.com/2010/10/03/business/03face.html?_r=2 &pagewanted=print .

House, James S. "Social Isolation Kills, But How and Why?" *Psychosomatic Medicine 63* (2001): 273-274.

House, James S., Cynthia Robbins and Helen L. Metzner. "The Association of Social Relationships and Activities with Mortality: Prospective Evidence from the Tecumseh Community Health Study." *American Journal Epidemiology 116* (1982): 123-140.

"I Can't Get No...Job Satisfaction, That Is." The Conference Board. Accessed July, 2013. http://www.conference-board.org/publications/publicationdetail.cfm?publicationid=1727 .

"J.K. Rowling Biography." A&E Networks. Accessed October, 2013. http://www.biography.com/people/jk-rowling-40998 .

"Jack LaLanne fit as ever at 70." *Lodi News-Sentinel*, November 19, 1984.

Jobs, Steve. "Stanford University 2005 Commencement Address." *Stanford News.* Accessed July 1, 2013. http://news.stanford.edu/news/2005/june15/jobs-061505.html .

"Julia Child Biography." A&E Networks. Accessed October 8, 2013. http://www.biography.com/people/julia-child-9246767 .

Kastorini, Christina-Maria et al. "The Effect of Mediterranean Diet on Metabolic Syndrome and Its Components." *Journal of the American College of Cardiology 57* (2011):1299-1313.

Kern, Margaret L. and Howard S. Friedman. "Do Conscientious Individuals Live Longer? A Quantitative Review." *Health Psychology 27* (2008): 505-12.

Kimball, Kristin. *The Dirty Life: A Memoir of Farming, Food, and Love.* New York: Scribner, 2011.

Koebler, Jason. "Study: Excessive Sitting Cuts Life Expectancy by Two Years," *U.S. News & World Report*, July 9, 2012. Accessed February, 2013. http://www.usnews.com/news/articles/2012/07/09/study-excessive-sitting-cuts-life-expectancy-by-two-years .

Koenig, Harold G. "Does Religious Attendance Prolong Survival? A Six-year Follow-up Study of 3,968 Older Adults." *The Journals of Gerontology Series A 54* (1999): M370-76.

Laird, James. *Feelings: The Perception of Self (Series in Affective Science).* New York: Oxford University Press, 2007.

Lally, Philippa, Cornelia van Jaarsveld, Henry Potts and Jane Wardle. "How Are Habits Formed: Modeling Habit Formation in the Real World." *European Journal of Social Psychology 16* (2009): 674.

Lam, Frances. "Tama Matsuoka Wong, High-End Forager." *Bon Appetit.* March 28, 2013. Accessed March 28, 2013. http://www.bonappetit.com/people/article/tama-matsuoka-wong-high-end-forager-interviewed-by-francis-lam .

Larson, Craig. "Learning to Get Back Up." Afterhours Inspirational Stories. Accessed September, 2012. http://www.inspirationalstories.com/2/205.html .

Lee, Ya-Wen Lee et al. "Predicting Quality of Work Life on Nurses' Intention to Leave." *Journal of Nursing Scholarship 45* (2013): 160-68.

Luks, Allan. "Helper's High: Volunteering Makes People Feel Good, Physically and Emotionally." Psychology Today, October, 1988.

Marlatt, G. Alan. "Addiction and the Mind." Accessed October, 2013. http://www.dshs.wa.gov/pdf/oip/AddictionAndTheMindppt.pdf .

"MBTI® Basics." The Myers & Briggs Foundation. Accessed July 1, 2013. http://www.myersbriggs.org/my-mbti-personality-type/mbti-basics .

Metaxas, Eric. *Bonhoeffer: Pastor, Martyr, Prophet, Spy.* Nashville, TN: Thomas Nelson, 2010.

"Michael Dell Biography." A&E Network. Accessed October 2013). http://www.biography.com/people/michael-dell-9542199?page=2 .

"Michael Phelps Biography." A&E Networks. Accessed July, 2013. http://www.biography.com/people/michael-phelps-345192 .

Michaelis, Vicki. "Running down a dream: Leg amputee makes U.S. Track Team." *USA Today.* Accessed June, 2013. http://usatoday30.usatoday.com/sports/olympics/summer/track/2010-04-25-amputee-runner_N.htm .

Miller, Gregory and Carsten Wrosch. "You've Gotta Know When to Fold 'Em." *Psychological Science 18* (2007): 773-77.

Nakamura, David. "Marine Sgt. Dakota Meyer receives Medal of Honor." *The Washington Post,* September 15, 2011. Accessed September, 2013. http://www.washingtonpost.com/blogs/checkpointwashington/post/marine-cpl-dakota-meyer-receives-medal-of-honor/2011/09/15/glQACqAKVK_blog.html .

O'Connor, Clare. "How Sara Blakely of Spanx Turned $5,000 into $1 Billion." *Forbes.* Accessed March 14, 2012. http://www.forbes.com/global/2012/0326/billionaires-12-feature-united-states-spanx-sara-blakely-american-booty.html .

Olp, Susan. "Author Patsy Clairmont Makes Women Laugh." *Billings Gazette.* April 9, 2011. Accessed April, 2011. http://billingsgazette.com/lifestyles/faith-and-values/religion/clairmont-a-woman-of-faith-shares-her-story-at-conference/article_71a21ae4-8f1f-54b6-8e02-98857a1bc47c.html .

Pink, Daniel H. *Drive: The Surprising Truth about What Motivates Us.* New York: Riverhead Books, 2009.

Ralston, Aron. *127 Hours: Between a Rock and a Hard Place.* New York: Atria Books, 2004.

Ronksley, Paul E., Susan E. Brien, Barbara J. Turner, Kenneth J. Mukamal and William A. Ghali. "Association of Alcohol Consumption with Selected Cardiovascular Disease Outcomes: A Systematic Review and Meta-analysis." *British Medical Journal* 22 (2011): 342.

Rutter, Michael. "Psychosocial Resilience and Protective Mechanisms." *American Journal of Orthopsychiatry* 57 (1987): 316-331.

———. "Resilience in the Face of Adversity." British Journal of Psychiatry 147 (1985): 598-611.

Sapolsky, Robert M. *Why Zebras Don't Get Ulcers*. New York: Times Books, 2004.

Schwartz, Carolyn, Janice Bell Meisenhelder, Yunsheng Ma and George Reed. "Altruistic Social Interest Behaviors Are Associated with Better Mental Health." *Psychosomatic Medicine* 65 (2003): 778-785.

"Sean Swarner: First Cancer Survivor to Summit Everest." Premiere Speakers. Accessed July 2013. http://premierespeakers.com/sean_swarner .

"Seuss." Seussville. Accessed July, 2013. http://www.seussville.com/author/SeussBio.pdf .

Sherwood, Ben. *The Survivors Club: The Secrets and Science that Could Save Your Life*. New York: Grand Central Publishing, 2009.

Sloane, Matt, Jason Hanna and Dana Ford. "Never, ever give up:" Diana Nyad completes historic Cuba-to-Florida swim." CNN, September 3, 2013. Accessed October, 2013. http://www.cnn.com/2013/09/02/world/americas/diana-nyad-cuba-florida-swim/index.html .

Sorenson, Susan. "Don't Pamper Employees – Engage Them." *Gallup Business Journal*, July 2, 2013. Accessed July, 2013. http://businessjournal.gallup.com/content/163316/don-pamper-employeesengage.aspx?utm_source=WWW&utm_medium=csm&utm_campaign=syndication&ref=image .

Sowell, Carol. "Entrepreneur with SMA Starts Accessible Car Company." Quest MDA's Research & Health Magazine, February 22, 2012. Accessed October 2013. http://quest.mda.org/news/entrepreneur-sma-starts-accessible-car-company .

"State of the American Workplace: Employee Engagement Insights for U.S. Business Leaders." Gallup. Accessed July, 2013.

http://www.gallup.com/strategicconsulting/163007/state-american-workplace.aspx .

Sultanoff, Steven. "Integrating Humor into Psychotherapy." *Play Therapy with Adults*, edited by Charles E. Schaefer, 107-143. New York: John Wiley & Sons, Inc., 2003.

Tangney, June P. Roy F. Baumeister and Angie L. Boone. "High Self-control Predicts Good Adjustment, Less Pathology, Better Grades, and Interpersonal Success." *Journal of Personality 72* (2004): 271-324.

"The History of Little Free Library," *LittleFreeLibrary.org*™. Accessed October 8, 2013. http://littlefreelibrary.org/ourhistory .

"The Life of Harriet Tubman." New York History Net. Accessed November, 2011. http://www.nyhistory.com/harriettubman/life.htm .

Thomas, Owen. "Apps to Share Your Pride at the Gym." *The New York Times*, February 9, 2011. Accessed August, 2012. http://www.nytimes.com/2011/02/10/technology/personaltech/10basics.html .

Tsai, Adam Gilden and Thomas A. Wadden. "Systematic Review: An Evaluation of Major Commercial Weight Loss Programs in the United States" *Annals of Internal Medicine 14* (2005): 56-66.

"Two CIA Prisoners in China, 1952-73: Extraordinary Fidelity." Central Intelligence Agency Library. Accessed August, 2010. https://www.cia.gov/library/center-for-the-study-of-intelligence/csi-publications/csi-studies/studies/vol50no4/two-cia-prisoners-in-china-1952201373.html .

Uchino, Bert N. Uchino. "Social Support and Health: A Review of Physiological Processes Potentially Underlying Links to Disease Outcomes." *Journal of Behavioral Medicine 29* (2006): 377-387.

Umene-Nakano et al. "Nationwide Survey of Work Environment, Work-Life Balance and Burnout among Psychiatrists in Japan." PLOS ONE. Accessed June, 2013. http://www.researchgate.net/publication/235650567_Nationwide_Survey_of_Work_Environment_Work-ife_Balance_and_Burnout_among_Psychiatrists_in_Japan .

"Vincent van Gogh Biography." A&E Networks. Accessed May, 2013. http://www.biography.com/people/vincent-van-gogh-9515695?page=1 .

Virtanen, Marianna et al. "Long Working Hours and Cognitive Function." *American Journal of Epidemiology 169* (2009): 596-605.

————. "Long Working Hours and Symptoms of Anxiety and Depression: A 5-Year Follow-up of the Whitehall II Study." *Psychological Medicine 41* (2011): 2485-494.

Wagnild, Gail and Heather Young. "Development and Psychometric Evaluation of the Resilience Scale." *Journal of Nursing Measurement 1* (1993): 165-178.

————. "Resilience among Older Women." Image: *Journal of Nursing Scholarship 22* (1990): 252-255.

Wagnild, Gail and Jeanette Collins. "Assessing Resilience." *Journal of Psychosocial Nursing and Mental Health Services 47* (2009): 28-33.

Wagnild, Gail. "A Review of the Resilience Scale." *Journal of Nursing Measurement 17* (2009): 105-113.

————. "Resilience and Successful Aging: Comparison among Low and High Income Older Adults. *Journal of Gerontological Nursing 29* (2003): 42-49.

————. *The Resilience Scale User's Guide for the U.S. English Version of the Resilience Scale and the 14-Item Resilience Scale (RS-14).* Worden, MT: Resilience Center, 2009.

————. *The Resilience Scale User's Guide.* Worden, MT: Resilience Center, 2009.

Wallis, Velma. *Two Old women: An Alaska legend of Betrayal, Courage and Survival.* New York: HarperCollins, 1994.

Wang, Hui-Xin et al. "Late *Life Leisure Activities and Risk of Cognitive Decline.*" *The Journals of Gerontology Series A 68* (2013): 205.

"Wilma Rudolph Biography." A&E Networks. Accessed March, 2011. http://www.biography.com/people/wilma-rudolph-9466552 .

Wilson, Emily. "Sotomayor – From the Bronx to the Bench." Women's Media Center, February 21, 2013. Accessed October, 2013. http://www.womensmediacenter.com/feature/entry/sotomayorf rom-the-bronx-to-the-bench .

"Winston Churchill Biography." A&E Networks. Accessed July, 2013. http://www.biography.com/people/winston-churchill-9248164?page=1 .

"Workplace Survey." American Psychological Association. Accessed May, 2013. http://www.apa.org/news/press/releases/phwa/workplace-survey.pdf .

Wrosch, Carsten, Michael Scheier, Gregory Miller, Richard Schulz and Charles Carver. "Adaptive Self-Regulation of Unattainable Goals: Goal Disengagement, Goal Reengagement, and Subjective ell-Being." *Personality and Social Psychology Bulletin 29* (2003): 494-508.

Zachary, G. Pascal and Ken Yamada. "From 1993: What's Next? Steve Jobs's Vision, So on Target at Apple, Now Is Falling Short." *The Wall Street Journal*, May 25, 1993. Accessed December 2011. http://online.wsj.com/article/SB1000142405297020347680457661 4371332161748.html .

Zwink, Jennifer et al. "Nurse Manager Perceptions of Role Satisfaction and Retention at an Academic Medical Center." *Journal of Nursing Administration 43* (2013): 135-141.

INDEX

C

W

CPSIA information can be obtained
at www.ICGtesting.com
Printed in the USA
FSHW021714250821
84297FS